100 SCIENCE LESSONS

NEW EDITION

TERMS AND CONDITIONS

IMPORTANT - PERMITTED USE AND WARNINGS - READ CAREFULLY BEFORE USING

SCOTTISH PRIMARY 2

YEAR 1

Minimum specification:
- PC with a CD-ROM drive and 512 Mb RAM (recommended)
- Windows 98SE or above/Mac OS 10.1 to 10.6
- Recommended minimum processor speed: 1 GHz

For all technical support queries, please phone Scholastic Customer Services on 0845 603 9091.

Carole Creary
and Gay Wilson

Authors
Carole Creary
Gay Wilson

Series Editor
Peter Riley

Editors
Nicola Morgan
Tracy Kewley
Kate Pedlar

Project Editor
Margaret Eaton

Illustrators
Kirsty Wilson and Ann Kronheimer

Series Designers
Catherine Perera and Joy Monkhouse

Designer
Catherine Perera

CD-ROM developed in association with
Vivid Interactive

Published by Scholastic Ltd
Book End
Range Road
Witney
Oxfordshire OX29 0YD

www.scholastic.co.uk

Designed using Adobe InDesign.

Printed by Bell and Bain Ltd, Glasgow

7 8 9   2 3 4 5 6

Text © 2007 Carole Creary and Gay Wilson

© 2007 Scholastic Ltd

British Library Cataloguing-in-Publication Data
A catalogue record for this book is available from the British Library.

ISBN 978-0439-94503-5

ACKNOWLEDGEMENTS

All Flash activities developed by Vivid Interactive

Material from the National Curriculum © Crown copyright. Reproduced under the terms of the Click Use Licence.

Extracts from the QCA Scheme of Work © Qualifications and Curriculum Authority.

Extracts from the Primary School Curriculum for Ireland, www.ncca.ie, National Council for Curriculum and Assessment.

Every effort has been made to trace copyright holders for the works reproduced in this book, and the publishers apologise for any inadvertent omissions.

Post-It is a registered trademark of 3M.

MIX
Paper from responsible sources
FSC® C007785
www.fsc.org

SHEFFIELD HALLAM UNIVERSITY
WL
TP 500
CR
ADSETTS LEARNING CENTRE

This new edition of *100 Science Lessons* follows the QCA Science Scheme of Work and also meets many of the demands of the curricula for England, Wales, Scotland, Northern Ireland and Eire. The book is divided into six units – one unit to match each unit of the QCA scheme for Year 1.

The planning grid at the start of each unit shows the objectives and outcomes of each lesson, and gives a quick overview of the lesson content (starter, main activity, group activities and plenary). The QCA objectives for Year 1 provide the basis for the lesson objectives used throughout the book.

After the planning grid is a short section on Scientific Enquiry. It is based on a QCA activity and provides a context for children to develop certain enquiry skills and for you to assess them. The section ends by showing where the activity can be embedded within one of the lessons.

Each unit is divided into a number of key lessons, which closely support the QCA scheme and all units end with an assessment lesson which is based on those key lessons. In addition to the key lessons, a unit may also contain one or more enrichment lessons to provide greater depth or a broader perspective. They may follow on from a key lesson or form a whole section, near the end of the unit, before the assessment lesson. The lesson objectives are based on the statements of the national curricula for England, Wales, Scotland, Northern Ireland and Eire, which are provided, in grid format, on the CD-ROM.

Lesson plans

There are detailed and short lesson plans for the key and enrichment lessons. About 60 per cent of the lesson plans in this book are detailed lesson plans. The short lesson plans are closely related to them and cover similar topics and concepts. They contain the essential features of the detailed lesson plans, allowing you to plan for progression and assessment. The detailed lesson plans have the following structure:

OBJECTIVES

The objectives are stated in a way that helps to focus on each lesson plan. At least one objective is related to content knowledge and there may be one or more relating to Scientific Enquiry. When you have read through the lesson you may wish to add your own objectives. You can find out how these objectives relate to those of the various national curricula by looking at the relevant grids on the CD-ROM. You can also edit the planning grids to fit with your own objectives (for more information see 'How to use the CD-ROM' on page 6).

RESOURCES AND PREPARATION

The Resources section provides a list of everything you will need to deliver the lesson, including any photocopiables presented in this book. The Preparation section describes anything that needs to be done in advance of the lesson, such as collecting environmental data.

As part of the preparation of all practical work, you should consult your school's policies on practical work and select activities for which you are confident to take responsibility. The ASE publication *Be Safe!* gives very useful guidance on health and safety issues in primary science.

BACKGROUND

This section may briefly refer to the science concepts which underpin the teaching of individual lessons. It may also highlight specific concepts which children tend to find difficult and gives some ideas on how to address these during the lesson. Suggestions may be given for classroom displays as well as useful tips for obtaining resources.

VOCABULARY

There is a vocabulary list of science words associated with the lesson which children should use in discussing and presenting their work. Time should be spent defining each word at an appropriate point in the lesson.

STARTER

This introductory section contains ideas to build up interest at the beginning of the lesson and set the scene.

MAIN TEACHING ACTIVITY

This section presents a direct, whole-class (or occasionally group) teaching session that will help you deliver the content knowledge outlined in the lesson objectives before group activities begin. It may include guidance on discussion, or on performing one or more demonstrations or class investigations to help the children understand the work ahead.

The relative proportions of the lesson given to the starter, main teaching activity and group activities vary. If you are reminding the children of their previous work and getting them onto their own investigations, the group work may dominate the lesson time; if you are introducing a new topic or concept, you might wish to spend all or most of the lesson engaged in whole-class teaching.

GROUP ACTIVITIES

The group activities are very flexible. Some may be best suited to individual work, while others may be suitable for work in pairs or larger groupings. There are usually two group activities provided for each lesson. You may wish to use one after the other; use both together (to reduce demand on resources and your attention); or, where one is a practical activity, use the other for children who successfully complete their practical work early. You may even wish to use activities as follow-up homework tasks.

Some of the group activities are supported by a photocopiable sheet. These sheets can be found in the book as well as on the CD-ROM. For some activities, there are also accompanying differentiated ideas, interactive activities and diagrams – all available on the CD-ROM (for more information, see 'How to use the CD-ROM' on page 6).

The group activities may include some writing. These activities are also aimed at strengthening the children's science literacy and supporting their English literacy skills. They may involve writing labels and captions, developing scientific vocabulary, writing about or recording investigations, presenting data, explaining what they have observed, or using appropriate secondary sources. The children's mathematical skills are also developed through number and data handling work in the context of science investigations.

ICT LINKS

Many lessons have this section, in which suggestions for incorporating ICT are given. ICT links might include: using the internet and CD-ROMs for research; preparing graphs and tables using a computer; using the graphing tool, interactive activities and worksheets from the CD-ROM.

DIFFERENTIATION

Where appropriate, there are suggestions for differentiated work to support less able learners or extend more able learners in your class. Some of the photocopiable sheets are also differentiated into less able support, core ability, and more able extension to support you in this work. The book contains the worksheets for the core ability while the differentiated worksheets are found on the accompanying CD-ROM.

ASSESSMENT

This section includes advice on how to assess the children's learning against the lesson objectives. This may include suggestions for questioning or observation opportunities, to help you build up a picture of the children's developing ideas and guide your future planning. A separate summative assessment lesson is provided at the end of each unit of work. One may also be provided for a group of enrichment lessons if they form a section towards the end of a unit.

PLENARY

Suggestions are given for drawing together the various strands of the lesson in this section. The

lesson objectives and outcomes may be reviewed and key learning points may be highlighted. The scene may also be set for another lesson.

HOMEWORK

On occasions, tasks may be suggested for the children to do at home. These may involve using photocopiables or the setting of a research project, perhaps involving the use the books on display (as suggested in the background section) to broaden the knowledge of the topic being studied.

OUTCOMES

These are statements related to the objectives; they describe what the children should have achieved by the end of the lesson.

LINKS

These are included where appropriate. They may refer to subjects closely related to science, such as technology or maths, or to content and skills from subjects such as art, history or geography.

ASSESSMENT LESSONS

The last lesson in every unit focuses on summative assessment. This assessment samples the content of the unit, focusing on its key theme(s); its results should be used in conjunction with other assessments you have made during the teaching of the unit. The lesson usually comprises of two assessment activities, which may take the form of photocopiable sheets to complete or practical activities with suggested assessment questions for you to use while you are observing the children. These activities may include a mark scheme, but this will not be related directly to curriculum attainment targets and level descriptors. These tasks are intended to provide you with a guide to assessing the children's performance.

PHOTOCOPIABLE SHEETS

These are an integral part of many of the lessons. They may provide resources such as quizzes, instructions for practical work, worksheets to complete whilst undertaking a task, information, guidance for written assignments and so on.

Photocopiable sheets printed in the book are suitable for most children. The CD-ROM includes differentiated versions of many photocopiables to support less confident learners and stretch more confident learners.

How to use the CD-ROM

SYSTEM REQUIREMENTS
Minimum specifications:
● PC or Mac with CD-ROM drive and at least 512 MB RAM (recommended)
● Microsoft Windows 98SE or above/Mac OSX.1 or above
● Recommended minimum processor speed: 1GHz

GETTING STARTED
The accompanying CD-ROM includes a range of lesson and planning resources. The first screen requires the user to select the relevant country (England, Scotland, Wales, Northern Ireland, Eire). There are then several menus enabling the user to search the material according to various criteria, including lesson name, QCA unit, National Curriculum topic and resource type.

Searching by lesson name enables the user to see all resources associated with that particular lesson. The coloured tabs on the left-hand side of this screen indicate the differentiated worksheets; the tabs at the top of the page lead to different *types* of resource (diagram, interactive or photocopiable).

PHOTOCOPIABLES
The photocopiables that are printed in the book are also provided on the CD-ROM, as PDF files. In addition, differentiated versions of the photocopiables are provided where relevant:
● green indicates a support worksheet for less confident children;
● red indicates the core photocopiable, as printed in the book;
● blue indicates an extension worksheet for more confident children.

There are no differentiated photocopiables for assessment activities.

The PDF files can be annotated on screen using the panel tool provided (see below). The tools allow the user to add notes, highlight items and draw lines and boxes.

PDF files of photocopiables can be printed from the CD-ROM and there is also an option to print the full screen, including any drawings and annotations that have been added using the tools. (NB where PDF files are landscape, printer settings may need to be adjusted.)

INTERACTIVE ACTIVITIES
The CD-ROM includes twelve activities for children to complete using an interactive whiteboard or individual computers, as directed by the teacher. Each activity is based on one of the photocopiables taken from across the units. Activities include: dragging and dropping the body parts into the correct place; clicking on objects in the home to see if they light up and putting the baby animals next to their parents.

GRAPHING TOOL
The graphing tool supports lessons where the children are asked to gather and record data. The tool enables children to enter data into a table, which can then be used to create a bar chart, pie chart or line graph.

When inserting data into the table, the left-hand column should be used for labels for charts; the right-hand column is for numeric data only (see example below). The pop-up keypad can be used to enter numbers into the table.

DIAGRAMS
Where appropriate, diagrams printed in the book have been included as separate files on the CD-ROM. These include examples of tables and diagrams for children to refer to when undertaking experiments or building objects, such as the marble run in 'Pushes and pulls'. These can be displayed on an interactive whiteboard.

GENERAL RESOURCES
In addition to lesson resources, the CD-ROM also includes the planning grids for each unit, as printed in the book, and the relevant curriculum grid for England, Scotland, Wales, Northern Ireland and Eire. The curriculum grids indicate how elements of each country's National Curriculum are addressed by lessons in the book. The planning grids are supplied as editable Word files; the curriculum grids are supplied as Word and PDF files. Selection of a planning grid leads to a link, which opens the document in a separate window; this then needs to be saved to the computer or network before editing.

Lesson	Objectives	Main activity	Group activities	Plenary	Outcomes
Lesson 1 Body parts	• To know that there are different external parts of the human body.	Draw round a body and label it.	• Label a simple picture of a body. • Collage a body shape.	Recap on names of body parts. Compare two body outlines.	• Can locate and name the main external parts of the human body.
Lesson 2 Similarities and differences	• To know that there are differences and similarities between human bodies (hair, ears, eyes, and so on). • To draw and interpret a pictogram (of hair or eye colours).	Collect data about hair colour and make a class pictogram.	• Collect data about eye colour and make a group pictogram. • Make a self-portrait using a mirror.	Interpret and evaluate the pictograms. Discuss how individuals vary.	• Can describe how the external features of people vary. • Can make and interpret a pictogram.
Lesson 3 The senses	• To know about the human senses.	Name the five senses. Discuss how each is useful.	• Identify which senses would be useful in different contexts. • Describe a hidden object in sensory terms for others to guess what it is.	Discuss how our senses give us pleasure and warn us of danger.	• Can explain that we have senses to make us aware of our surroundings. • Are aware of the five senses: sight, hearing, smell, taste and touch.
Lesson 4 What's that smell?	• To identify familiar smells.	Smell pots to identify the contents.		Talk about the importance of the sense of smell.	• Can identify some familiar smells.
Lesson 5 A tasty surprise	• To identify familiar tastes.	Blindfolded tasting.		Make a 'yum' and 'yuk' chart. Discuss types of taste.	• Can recognise some familiar foods by taste. • Can identify some flavours.
Lesson 6 A sense of touch	• To know that the skin is sensitive to touch. • To know that we can feel all over our bodies.	Blindfolded feeling.		Discuss the skin as a sense organ.	• Know that the skin is sensitive to touch. • Know that we can feel all over our bodies.
Lesson 7 Sort it!	• To know how to distinguish a living thing from a non-living thing. • To know that living things have certain requirements.	Look at various items to compare the features of living things, no longer living things and things that have never been alive.	• Sort pictures of living and non-living things. • Make an observational drawing of a chosen object, living or non-living.	Review the group activity work.	• Can distinguish between a living thing, something no longer living and something that has never been alive. • Know that living things need food and water.
Lesson 8 Different but not so different	• To know that humans are more like each other than other animals.	Look at the similarities and differences between different humans, and humans and animals.	• Research another animal and say why it is different from a human. • Note similarities and differences between pairs of children.	Discuss the differences between humans and animals.	• Know that there are more similarities between humans than there are between humans and other animals. • Can identify similarities and differences between humans and other animals.
Lesson 9 Animals around us	• To recognise and name some common animals.	Look at pictures of animals. Go for an animal observation walk.	• Draw pictures of the animals seen on the walk. • Make a model animal.	Talk about what animals were found, and where.	• Can recognise and name some common animals.
Lesson 10 Animal body parts	• To recognise and name the main external parts of the bodies of animals.	Look at animal pictures and identify different features: wings, fins, beaks, shells, feelers etc.		Talk about similarities and differences between animals, and how they are adapted to where and how they live.	• Can name some external parts of animals such as wing, fin, tail, beak and feelers.
Lesson 11 What can they do?	• To know about how they have grown from birth to the present day.	A mother and baby visit the classroom. Discuss how the children have changed since birth.	• Match early to current pictures of children. • Identify what a child can do as a baby and later on.	Consider future growth and other changes.	• Can describe how they have grown from babyhood.
Lesson 12 The family	• To know that there are different stages in the human life cycle.	Use pictures and invited visitors to discuss phases in the human life cycle.	• Sequence a set of pictures of people at different ages. • Role play a family with three generations.	Consider ageing and other changes.	• Know about the different stages in a human life. • Can describe some of the changes.

Lesson	Objectives	Main activity	Group activities	Plenary	Outcomes
Lesson 13 Parents and babies	• To know that animals produce offspring and these offspring grow into adults. • To match adult animals with their offspring.	Match pictures or models of young animals to adults. Name adult and infant forms of some animals.	• Sort and match baby and adult animals in a model farmyard or zoo. • Match pictures of adult and baby animals.	Discuss adult animals that have different male and female names. Discuss young animals that are very unlike their adult form (for example, tadpoles).	• Know that animals produce offspring and that these offspring grow into adults. • Can match adult animals with their offspring. • Know the names of both the adult and infant forms of some common animals.
Lesson 14 Growing older	• To know that our appearance changes over time.	Discuss the different ages and stages a human being goes through.	• Draw pictures of people at different ages. • Children create portraits of what they will look like when they are old.	Discuss how people change with age.	• Can recognise that the appearance of humans changes over time. • Can describe some of the changes.
Lesson 15 Growing taller	• To be able to measure tallness and compare heights. • To make predictions about whether age and height are related.	Explore the range of heights in the class.	• Make actual-size collages of children in the class. • Make a display of paper strips to show children's heights.	Discuss how people grow at different rates.	• Know how to compare their measured height with that of other children. • Know that height and age do not necessarily correlate. • Can make simple predictions and relate their findings to them.
Enrichment Lesson 16 Fingerprint card	• To know that humans are similar in some ways and different in others.	Look at differences which help us to recognise people. Listen to a tape and identify voices.	• Fill in a fingerprint card and go on to make fingerprint pictures. • Decorate a measured ribbon with 'facts about me'. Display in size order.	Talk about similarities and differences.	• Can identify ways in which people are similar and different. • Know that people can be grouped in many different ways.
Enrichment Lesson 17 Guess who?	• To know that appearance may change but that people can still be recognised.	Face painting and hairdressing.		Discuss ways in which people who have been disguised can still be recognised.	• Can describe some of the ways in which appearance can be changed, but people can still be recognised.
Lesson 18 Joints	• To know that the human body can move in a variety of ways.	Examine a model or picture of a skeleton. During gymnastic activities, consider the action of joints.	• Play 'Simon says'. • Make a jointed paper figure.	Discuss the role of the skeleton in movement.	• Can demonstrate different ways in which the body can move. • Know that joints help us to move, and can name and indicate the main joints.
Lesson 19 Animal movements	• To know that animals can move and feed in different ways from humans.	Watch animals moving and feeding, live and on video. Notice how they swim, fly, run etc. Compare different ways of feeding.		Discuss which animals run, fly, crawl etc. Discuss which animals eat plants, insects, meat etc.	• Can describe how some animals move and feed.
Lesson 20 Food for life	• To know that food and water are needed for animals, including humans, to stay alive. • To carry out a simple survey.	Discuss how food and water are necessary to sustain life. Make a tally chart of favourite foods.	• Make a block graph of favourite foods. • Make models of favourite items of food.	Discuss the need to eat sensibly for health. If appropriate, discuss famine and drought.	• Know that animals need to eat and drink to stay alive. • Can undertake a simple survey. • Can construct a block graph.
Enrichment Lesson 21 Comparing classes	• To compare data from two classes.	Collect data from their own and another class, then draw two block graphs.		Interpret and compare the two graphs.	• Can compare data from two different graphs.

Assessment	Objectives	Activity 1	Activity 2
Lesson 22	• To assess whether the children can name parts of the human body, and identify the organs associated with the five senses. • To assess the children's ability to name some of the ways in which we move.	Match labels to body parts.	Show that they can move in a variety of ways.

SC1 SCIENTIFIC ENQUIRY

Exploring the senses

LEARNING OBJECTIVES AND OUTCOMES
- To explore, using the senses.
- To use first hand experience...to answer questions.

ACTIVITY
The children make observations using their senses to explore smell, sight, touch, hearing and taste and record on photocopiable page 39 (also 'The senses' (red), from the CD-ROM).

LESSON LINKS
This Sc1 activity forms an integral part of Lesson 3, The senses.

Lesson 1 ▪ Body parts

Objective
- To know that there are different external parts of the human body.

Vocabulary
arm, leg, hand, foot, head, body, elbow, knee, neck, shin, chin, shoulders, chest, hips, eyes, ears, mouth, nose forehead, thigh, abdomen

RESOURCES 💿
Main activity: Large sheets of plain wallpaper, chalk or large crayons, two sets of large labels of body parts (for back and front) as listed in Vocabulary.
Group activities: 1 Photocopiable page 38 (also 'Body parts' (red) available on the CD-ROM). **2** Collage materials, adhesive, scissors, Blu-Tack®.

BACKGROUND
None of the UK science curriculum documents, including the *QCA Scheme of Work for Science*, gives a definitive list of the parts of the body that children should be able to name. A decision has to be made about expectations for Year 1/Primary 2, particularly as Foundation Stage children will already have been working on identifying and naming parts of the body. Typically, they can sing 'Heads, Shoulders, Knees and Toes', play finger rhymes and point to the relevant parts of themselves. There is no reason why Year 1/Primary 2 children should not continue to sing a song that they enjoy; but less familiar body parts could be added, such as elbows and shins. It is important that as well as reinforcing what has been learned at the Foundation Stage, teaching should extend the children's knowledge of body parts.

You may feel that this would be a good opportunity to introduce the proper names for human genitals (such as 'penis', 'testicles' and 'vagina'). Male genitalia are obvious, but because female genitalia are less so, some little girls get quite worried that they have 'something missing'. Whether you discuss this with the children will depend on your school policy.

STARTER
Singing a familiar song such as 'Heads, Shoulders, Knees and Toes' is a good introduction to this lesson.

MAIN ACTIVITY
Talk to the whole class about familiar parts of the body. Ask the children to indicate each part on their own body. Discuss the fact that we usually have the same parts in the same places, and yet we all look different. Say some less familiar part names, such as 'shin', 'chin', 'elbows' or 'hips', asking the children to place a hand on the correct part of their body.

Look at one child from the back and front. Ask other children to come up, choose labels and stick them onto this child in the correct places. Have some spare labels on which to write the names of any extra body parts that the children may suggest.

Spread out four large sheets of plain wallpaper on the floor and choose

Differentiation
Group activity 1
To support children, give them 'Body parts' (green) from the CD-ROM, which includes only the most familiar body parts. For extension, give children 'Body parts' (blue), which asks them to label the body parts without providing the names.
Group activity 2
All children should be able to participate in this activity.

two children to lie on their backs on two of them. Using chalk or a large wax crayon, draw round each child. Then move the children to the other two sheets of paper, ask them to lie face down and draw round them again. If possible, choose two children who are physically different (for example, the tallest and the shortest in the class). Label the sheets 'front' and 'back'. From the selection of labels, ask a number of children to pick one and place it on the relevant part of any of the four outlines. If some of the labels have not been chosen, help the children to put them in the correct places. Have blank labels ready to add any other body parts that the children may suggest. Some labels may be repeated on both the back and front body pictures – for example, 'shoulder', 'neck' and 'thigh'. Labels such as 'back' and 'bottom' will only appear on the back view. While the labels are being placed, remind the children of the fact that we nearly all have the same body parts in the same places.

If appropriate, when all the ready-made labels have been placed, add some less familiar body parts to the list, such as 'knuckles', 'ankles', 'calf', 'forehead' and 'nostrils'.

GROUP ACTIVITIES
1 Give each child a copy of photocopiable page 38. Ask the children to find the correct word for each label on the body outline and write it in the appropriate box.
2 Ask the children, in groups of about six, to collage the big body outlines (back and front) for a display and attach all the body part labels identified by the class (use Blu-Tack, so that the labels can be removed and replaced).

ASSESSMENT
Note those children who can name all the main parts of the body. Note those who have made more progress and can name and place a range of less familiar parts.

PLENARY
Using the collaged figures, recap on the names of body parts. Remove and shuffle the labels, then replace them with the children's help in order to reinforce what they have learned, with particular emphasis on the less familiar names. Compare the pictures of the two children. Discuss the fact that they have the same body parts, even though they look quite different. Ask the children to think about how they are different. Invite the class to sing 'Heads, shoulders, knees and toes', replacing the usual words with the names of other body parts that they have identified.

OUTCOME
● Can locate and name the main external parts of the human body.

LINKS
Literacy: writing labels.

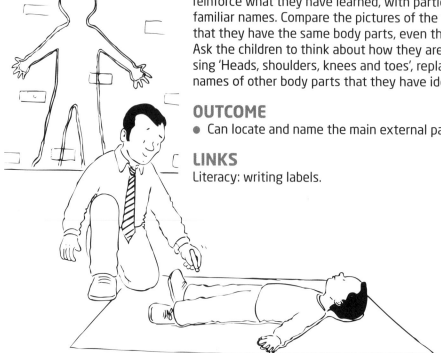

Lesson 2 ▪ Similarities and differences

Objectives
● To know that there are differences and similarities between human bodies (hair, ears, eyes and so on).
● To draw and interpret a pictogram (of hair or eye colours).

Vocabulary
different, same, similar, pictogram, data, hair, eyes, ears, skin, self-portrait, unique, identical twins

RESOURCES
Main activity: Large sheets of paper (for pictograms), small squares of paper (for recording hair colour).
Group activities: 1 Large sheets of paper, small squares of paper, plastic mirrors. **2** Plastic mirrors, drawing and colouring or painting materials.

BACKGROUND
It is important that the children know that humans usually have two eyes, two ears, two legs and so on, whatever their race or skin colour. This lesson provides a good opportunity to talk sensitively about those of us who might differ in some way or have a disability. Differences in skin colour are the result of adaptation to the level of sunlight found in different parts of the world. The children should realise that although the body parts are the same, there are subtle differences that enable us all to be recognised as individuals. Making a graph or chart of the eye colours of children is a good activity, but don't suggest that they chart the eye colours of the rest of their family. Some children who are adopted or not living with both biological parents may be unaware of the fact at this stage.

STARTER
Remind the class that we nearly all have the same features in the same places - eyes, ears, mouth, hands, feet and so on - and that we talked about this in the previous lesson.

MAIN ACTIVITY
Compare two or three children with different colouring. Ask the other children to identify similarities and differences between them. Reinforce the fact that we all have the same features in the same places, but that we are all different from each other - even those with similar colouring. Compare two or three children with similar colouring: *How are ___ and ___ the same? How are they different? How do we recognise them as individuals? Look at the shape of their eyes, noses or mouths. Are they all the same height? Can you identify some other differences, such as the shape of their teeth? Even if they had the same colour hair and eyes and the same sort of haircut, would we still be able to recognise them as individuals? If so, how?* Discuss the fact that we are all unique - even identical twins, who might be mistaken for each other physically, show differences in their movement, expression and behaviour.

Sort the children into groups according to whether they have fair or dark hair. Line them up and count how many are in each group. Look at each group and ask the children whether it could be split into smaller groups - and if so, how. Perhaps there could be separate groups for light brown, dark brown and black hair, or for blonde and red hair. Line the children up again and re-count. Talk to the children about how this 'living graph' could be recorded on paper. Ask them to suggest ways of doing this. Discuss the purpose of a graph or pictogram and how it can give us information.

Ask each child to draw a small picture of his or her own head, showing the hair colour. Make a class pictogram of hair colour under the colour headings decided on during the discussion.

Differentiation

Group activity 1
Some groups may be able to substitute coloured squares for pictures and make a block graph of their eye colours.
Group activity 2
This activity is accessible to all children.
Plenary
Some children will need more support in interpreting the data on the pictograms.

GROUP ACTIVITIES

1 Remind the children how they made the pictogram showing their hair colour. Ask them to look carefully in a mirror and draw a picture showing their eye colour, then work together to agree on colour headings and make a pictogram with the eye pictures.
2 Ask the children to look in a mirror and draw or paint a self-portrait, including as much detail as possible.

ICT LINK 💿

The children could use the graphing tool from the CD-ROM to create a block graph of their results.

ASSESSMENT

Note those children who are able to construct and interpret a pictogram relatively independently. Are there others who require much more help, and will need further opportunities to work with graphs in order to develop their understanding?

PLENARY

Ask the children questions about the information on the graph (pictogram) to assess their ability to interpret the data. *What can you find out from this graph? How many people have dark brown hair? How many blondes are there?* Invite a visitor (such as your headteacher) to the classroom. Encourage the children to ask him or her questions about the graph. *How much could the visitor find out about the hair colours in the class if the children weren't there?* This will help the children to understand the purpose of gathering data and making graphs. *Can you think of any way the graph could have been made better, to give even more information?* Look at the self-portraits and discuss how the children vary. Compare those with the same colouring. Ask the children to identify some unnamed self-portraits. Reinforce the idea that we are all unique and that even though some of us may have virtually identical skin, hair and eye colouring, we could never be mistaken for each other (except in the case of identical twins).

OUTCOMES

● Can describe how the external features of different people vary.
● Can make and interpret a pictogram.

LINKS

Maths: graphing data in a practical context.

Lesson 3 ▪ The senses

Objective
● To know about the human senses.

Vocabulary
look, see, sight, hear, listen, taste, flavour, smell, sense, feel, touch, light, sound

RESOURCES 💿

Main activity: A picture of a garden.
Group activities: 1 Photocopiable page 39 (also 'The senses' (red), available on the CD-ROM). **2** A card screen, a collection of different objects or materials.
ICT link: 'The senses' interactive, from the CD-ROM.

BACKGROUND

We see because light enters the eye and signals are sent along the optic nerve to the brain, which interprets the signals so that we 'see' images. Many children believe that light comes out of the eye and focuses on whatever they are looking at, so that they can see it. Help your class to understand that we need light in order to be able to see by asking them how much they can see when it is dark.

Differentiation 💿
Group activity 1
For support, give children 'The senses' (green) from the CD-ROM, which asks them to match pictures of sense organs (eg nose, mouth) to the five senses. For extension, use 'The senses' (blue). In this activity, as well as matching pictures to senses, children are asked to think of and draw other objects and match these to the senses.
Group activity 2
All children should be able to participate in this activity.

Sounds are made by things vibrating. Our ears change the vibrations into signals that are sent to the brain, which interprets them as sounds.

Taste is situated on the tongue, and can vary between individuals. One person might judge a food too sweet while another thinks it is not sweet enough. Using a magnifying glass, you can actually see the small papillae ('taste buds') on the tongue that are responsible for tasting. We smell things because olfactory sensors in our noses can detect minute particles in the air, released during various processes or for various purposes. Like taste, smell is subjective: different individuals may be more or less aware of various smells and react differently to them.

Children are used to touching and feeling things with their fingers, but may not really appreciate that the whole of their skin is sensitive to touch. Sensitive cells (touch receptors) just below the skin enable them to feel things all over their bodies, though there is a particular concentration of such receptors at the fingertips.

STARTER
Ask the class whether they know the names of the five senses, and where each sense is located on the body. Ask them to respond to: *We see with our... We hear with our...* and so on.

MAIN ACTIVITY
At this stage, many children will still be developing the language that enables them to describe their observations. List some of the words that they might use, referring to particular senses. For example: 'rough', 'smooth' or 'cold' would go with touch; 'light', 'dark' or 'colour' would go with sight. Using one of the following contexts, think about which sense would tell you most about where you were or what was happening:
● Role play someone cooking for the children. *Which sense would tell you something was cooking? What could it tell you about the ingredients? Could it tell you if the food was burning?* Other role-play situations that could be explored include: listening to a radio or Walkman; doing a jigsaw; a doctor using a stethoscope; eating an ice cream or a bar of chocolate; stroking a cat or a dog.
● Present a picture of a garden. *Which senses would you use here?* Sight would help you to appreciate all the colours and shapes in the garden, while smell would tell you more about things in the garden (such as flowers or new-mown grass).

GROUP ACTIVITIES
1 Give each child a copy of photocopiable page 39. Ask the children to match each picture to the sense that would be most useful. Some children may match more than one sense to a particular picture; if so, ask them to give their reasons for doing this.
2 Invite the children to take turns to hold an object behind a screen and describe it by its smell, its appearance, the sound it makes and so on. Can the others guess what it is?

ICT LINK 💿
Using 'The senses' interactive from the CD-ROM, ask the children to drag and drop the objects onto the sense it relates to.

ASSESSMENT
Check the children's work on matching senses to pictures. Which of them need more opportunities to do this in order to develop their understanding? Are some children able to describe their 'behind the screen' object easily, while others need more practice in putting their thoughts into words and

developing their vocabulary?

PLENARY
Talk about how our senses tell us about our surroundings. They may give us pleasure, or they may warn of danger.
Discuss some pleasurable experiences and which senses are employed. *How do our senses warn us of danger?* Consider sirens, bells, burning smells, a stone in a shoe, bad food, traffic lights and so on.

OUTCOMES
● Can explain that we have senses to make us aware of our surroundings.
● Are aware of the five senses: sight, hearing, smell, taste and touch.

LINKS
Unit 1c Lesson 2, Many materials.

Lesson 4 ▪ What's that smell?

Objective
● To identify familiar smells.

RESOURCES
Rubber, lemon juice, soap, vinegar, talcum powder, coffee, fresh sawdust; small pots with lids, cotton wool, labels. Make very small holes in the lids. Put a few drops of each liquid on cotton wool to prevent liquids spilling; cover powders with a thin layer of cotton wool to prevent them being inhaled.

MAIN ACTIVITY
Place small amounts of the materials in the pots. Invite the children to smell the pots and identify the contents. They could match labels to the appropriate pots.

Differentiation
Some children may need to experience the materials first and then choose a given material from the selection. Others may be able to guess the materials from previous experience.

ASSESSMENT
Note those children who are able to identify the substances correctly.

PLENARY
Talk about smells: favourite smells; nasty smells; smells that remind us of people or places; smells that may warn us of danger.

OUTCOME
● Can identify some familiar smells.

Lesson 5 ▪ A tasty surprise

Objective
● To identify familiar tastes.

RESOURCES
Small pieces of orange, lemon, ginger biscuit, carrot, apple, crisp and so on. (Fruit gums are a fun alternative.) Be aware of any food allergies (for example, to artificial colourings or nuts) or dietary restrictions.

MAIN ACTIVITY
With eyes closed or blindfolded, the children taste a familiar food and try to identify it. (With sweets, they try to identify the flavour.)

ASSESSMENT
Note those children who are able to identify the substances correctly.

PLENARY
Talk about likes and dislikes. Make a collective 'yum' and 'yuk' chart. Discuss
vocabulary such as 'sweet', 'sour' and 'salty'.

OUTCOMES
- Can recognise some familiar foods by taste.
- Can identify some flavours.

Lesson 6 ▷ A sense of touch

Objectives
- To know that the skin is
sensitive to touch.
- To know that we can feel all
over our bodies.

RESOURCES
Blindfolds for half the class.

MAIN ACTIVITY
The children work in pairs and take turns to blindfold each other. The child
without the blindfold gently touches the other child on the cheek, hand,
arm, leg, shoulder, foot and top of head. The blindfolded partner says when
he or she can feel the touch and where it is.

ASSESSMENT
During the plenary session, ask the children where they could feel a touch
on their bodies and where they felt it most clearly.

PLENARY
Discuss the fact that we can feel all over our bodies; that we feel with our
skin; and that the most sensitive parts of our bodies include our fingertips
and mouth. Explain that in these parts there are more of the special cells
that enable us to feel.

Differentiation
All the children should be able
to take part in this activity.

OUTCOMES
- Know that the skin is sensitive to touch.
- Know that we can feel all over our bodies.

Lesson 7 ▷ Sort it!

Objectives
- To know how to distinguish
a living thing from a non-living
thing.
- To know that living things
have certain requirements.

Vocabulary
dead, alive, move, grow,
breathe, feed, eat, drink, food,
water, feel, see, hear

RESOURCES 💿
Main activity: A collection of living and non-living things (stones, buttons,
fridge magnets, a living fish, mouse or gerbil, a snail, a woodlouse, a
collection of plants in pots, a wooden spoon, a dried flower, cornflakes).
Group activities: 1 Photocopiable page 40 (also 'Sort it!' (red) available on
the CD-ROM), A3-sized paper, scissors, adhesive. **2** Art paper, drawing
materials.
ICT link: 'Sort it!' interactive, from the CD-ROM.

BACKGROUND
There are seven basic requirements for life: respiration, reproduction,
excretion, movement, nutrition, sensitivity and growth. Children do not need
to know all of these at this stage; they might, for example, use the word
'breathing' for respiration and 'eating and drinking' for nutrition. They may
find these requirements easy to recognise in animals, but not so easy when
it comes to plants. Allow them to take responsibility for caring for plants or
animals in the school. Having an animal in the classroom permanently is not
something that many teachers are willing to do. It takes a great deal of
commitment, and finding someone to look after creatures at weekends and
in the holidays is not always easy. Unless you are really committed, it is

better to borrow animals for a day or two, so that the children have a chance to observe, discuss and look after them without the difficulties of looking after them full-time. Children must be made aware, from the beginning, that all living things should be treated with respect. Many adults do not set a good example in this respect, showing aversion to creatures such as spiders and wasps, often killing them for no good reason. Try not to pass on your particular aversions - remember, one person's feared animal is another person's best friend!

Beware of reinforcing misconceptions when talking about plants. We say that we are 'feeding' a plant when we give it a dose of fertiliser, but in fact we are only providing trace minerals that help it to make its own food by the process of photosynthesis. Plants do not 'move' in the sense of travelling, but many will grow quickly towards a light source; there are time-lapse videos that show this very well. Plants, like animals, take in oxygen and give out carbon dioxide in the process of respiration - but they also take in carbon dioxide and give out oxygen in the process of photosynthesis (during the hours of daylight). They reproduce by producing seeds or spores, which do their 'travelling' for them.

STARTER
Look closely at the items collected. Add a child to the collection. Why do the children think some of these things are alive?

MAIN ACTIVITY
Talk to the children about how we might know whether something is alive or not. Encourage the children to volunteer their ideas. This is a good way of finding out the level of their understanding and whether they have any misconceptions. Ask them what we need to do to keep animals and plants alive and healthy. Remind them that humans are animals too.

Ask the children to sort the things that are living from those that are not. Choose one correct thing from each set, such as a fish and a stone. Compare the two things. Look closely at the living thing. *What does it do?* Encourage the children to describe such processes as moving, breathing, drinking and feeding. *Do all animals do these things?* Think of a different animal and check that it does the same things. Humans are animals too. *Do they do all these things? What would happen to animals if they were not able to feed and drink?* Now look at the stone. *Is it alive? Why not? How is it different from the living thing you have just looked at? Can it move? What does it eat? Does it have babies?*

Next, look closely at a plant. *Is it alive? What does it need to keep it alive and healthy?* (Light, water and air.) *What would happen if it had no water?*

Look at all the things and check that each one has been sorted into the right set. *Should anything be in a different set?* Pick up the dried flower. *What about this? It is not alive - but has it ever been alive? Can you find anything else in the set that was once alive?* (The cornflakes and the wooden spoon.) Suggest that these go in a different set. Label the three sets 'Living', 'No longer living' and 'Never been alive', and leave them out as part of a class display. The children might add to the display over the next few days. (Remember that borrowed pets must go back fairly soon.)

GROUP ACTIVITIES
1 Ask the children to cut out the pictures from photocopiable page 40 (or choose pictures from old magazines or catalogues), sort them into sets of 'Living', 'No longer living' and 'Never alive', then stick the sets onto appropriately labelled sheets of A3 paper.
2 Ask the children to choose an object from the collection (either living, no longer living or never alive) and draw it very carefully. Use their pictures for a suitable display.

ICT LINK

Using the 'Sort it!' interactive from the CD-ROM, ask the children to sort the illustrations into groups of living, no longer living and never alive.

ASSESSMENT

Observe how the children sort the things. Use their work in group activity **1** to assess their understanding.

PLENARY

Look at some of the work the children have produced from group activity **1**. Ask them to explain why they have sorted the pictures in the way they have. Look at some of the observational drawings and draw the children's attention to any significant details that have been observed (such as whiskers on a mouse or the grain on a piece of wood).

OUTCOMES
● Can distinguish between a living thing, something no longer living and something that has never been alive.
● Know that living things need food and water.

LINKS
Art: observational drawing.
Maths: sorting into sets.

Differentiation
Group activity 1
To support children, use 'The senses' (green) from the CD-ROM, and ask them to sort the pictures into 'living' and 'never alive'. To extend children, use 'The senses' (blue), which contains a wider range of items for the children to sort.
Group activity 2
All children should be able to participate in this activity.

Lesson 8 ▪ Different but not so different

RESOURCES
Main activity: Collections of pictures of different animals (try to include pictures of animals with fur, feathers, scales, tails, trunks, and so on), flipchart or board.
Group activities: 1 Reference books, CD-ROMs, writing materials. **2** Writing and drawing materials, pictures of a range of different animals.

BACKGROUND
Each type of creature is adapted to its environment and lives and feeds in a particular way. Year 1 children can begin to think about the more obvious differences between species, and identify that all humans are much more similar to each other than they are to any other types of animal. Most animals, including humans, have certain attributes in common (such as possession of eyes and a mouth), but these are not always present. Some burrowing creatures, and others that live in totally dark caves or the depths of the sea, have no eyes. Some species of moth, such as Atlas moths, have no mouthparts as their lifespan is very short: they emerge, mate and die without the need for feeding.

STARTER
Remind all the children of the work they did in Lesson 2 (Similarities and differences) about humans being animals and about the similarities and differences between people.

Objective
● To know that humans are more like each other than other animals.

Vocabulary
same, similar, similarities, different

MAIN ACTIVITY

Tell the children to look carefully at their neighbour. Ask: *Who can tell me some of the ways in which humans are all the same as each other?* (We all have a head, a body, two legs, two arms, two eyes and so on.) Make a list of the children's suggestions on the flipchart and add to their list if they have forgotten anything significant. Discuss further similarities between humans that other animals definitely don't have. (Humans can talk to each other in words, they can read and write and make music on musical instruments, they use tools and care for their young for about 16 years from birth.) Say: *Now think of some of the ways in which we are different and tell me what they are.* (We have different-coloured hair, eyes and skin; the shapes of our bodies, faces and features are different.)

Show the children the collection of pictures of animals. Ask them to tell you some of the ways in which they are different from humans. (Some have fur, feathers, scales, tails, fins; some live underwater, some live in trees, some can fly, some lay eggs, many have four legs, some have no legs.) Again discuss any additions to the children's list if necessary. Ask: *Are there any ways in which animals are similar to us?* (They have two eyes, most have two ears, they generally have mouths with teeth in them, some have two legs.) Hold up a picture of a bird and ask two children of different hair colour to come and stand beside you. Say: *Look at the picture of the bird, then look at your two classmates. In what ways is the bird the same as the humans?* (It has two legs and two eyes. It also has ears but you generally can't see them. Some children may know that it is warm-blooded.) *Now tell me ways in which it is different from us.* (It has a beak with no teeth in it, it has wings instead of arms, it has feathers, it can't talk, it lays eggs.)

Tell the children to look at their two classmates again. Point out that their hair colour is different but that in most ways they are very similar. Ask the children: *Are they more like each other than like the bird? Are we all more like each other than the bird?* Repeat this process with other animals, pointing out that humans are more like each other than other animals.

GROUP ACTIVITIES

1 Organise the children into pairs, or groups of three, and give each group a reference book or CD-ROM. Ask them to choose an animal and then find out as many things about it as they can that make it different from humans. They should also note if there are any similarities. Tell the children to record what they find out in note form to remind them of what they have learned, because they are going to report back to the rest of the class.

2 Put the children in pairs. If possible place a boy with a girl, or pair children with different-coloured hair, eyes and so on. Ask the children to look at each other very carefully. (They could draw pictures of each other, including as much detail as possible.) They should then write down in two columns as many differences and similarities between them as they can think of. (They should include things like the ability to talk, walk on two legs and so on). *Are there more similarities than differences?* Give each pair a picture of an animal and ask them to note the similarities and differences between that animal and human beings. *Are there more differences in this case?*

ASSESSMENT

Use the children's work to assess the level of their understanding. During the plenary session, note those who report clear differences between their given animal and humans.

PLENARY

Remind the children about what they learned in the main activity. Ask groups to report some of the differences between their animal and humans to the class. *Were there any similarities?* Reiterate the fact that humans are more like each other than they are like other animals.

OUTCOMES
● Know that there are more similarities between humans than there are between humans and other animals.
● Can identify similarities and differences between humans and other animals.

Lesson 9 ▪ Animals around us

Objective
● To recognise and name some common animals.

Vocabulary
caring, feeding, animal names as appropriate

RESOURCES
Starter activity: Photocopiable page 41 (also 'Animals around us' (red), available on the CD-ROM), pictures or photographs of animals that the children might recognise, including humans, a dog, a cat, a goldfish, a butterfly and a familiar bird such as an owl or parrot.
Group activities: 1 Appropriate reference books; drawing, collage and painting materials. **2** Modelling materials.
ICT link: 'Animals around us' interactive from the CD-ROM.

BACKGROUND
Many children will not realise that humans are part of the animal kingdom, and that the animal kingdom includes insects, birds, fish and so on as well as mammals. Each type of creature is adapted to live and feed in a particular way, and children at this age can begin to think about the more obvious differences between species and how they are adapted to their habitats. For example: fish have fins to help them swim in water; birds have wings so that they can fly and various types of beaks to get seeds or nectar from plants, catch insects and so on; ducks' feathers are waterproof so that the duck does not become waterlogged and sink.

PREPARATION
If possible, a few days before the lesson place a few half grapefruit shells under a hedge or in a garden area to attract snails and slugs. A piece of bark in a shady place will attract woodlice and spiders, but this will need to have been there for some weeks for best results. Some small creatures such as snails, spiders or woodlice can be kept in a vivarium for a few days and then returned from whence they came.

The ASE booklet *Be Safe!* gives a comprehensive list of animals that are suitable for the classroom, together with advice on how to care for them. However, unless you are fully committed to caring for an animal over a long period, don't try! A goldfish is easy to look after and will provide interest. Be aware that you may have children in the class who are allergic to fur and feathers. There may also be a school policy about keeping animals in the classroom, which you will need to consult.

STARTER
Look at some pictures of animals (see Resources). How many can the children name? How many of these animals have they actually seen? Many children may recognise a giraffe or elephant, but never have seen one; they may have no real idea of the size of the creature. Hand out copies of photocopiable page 41 for the children to complete.

MAIN ACTIVITY
Ask which of the animals we might find in the locality. *What else might we find there?* In small groups, go outside and look for animals (especially any you have elicited – see Preparation). Look for birds in trees or on rooftops. If you have a birdtable, it may be better to observe it from a suitable window: it is unlikely that you will get any visitors while the children are in the vicinity, though the children should be encouraged to sit or stand quietly to

make their observations. They can look under stones or logs, or under
window ledges, for small creatures. If there are flowers, the children may
see butterflies or bees. Can they see any cats or dogs in the street? Make a
list of all the animals found.

GROUP ACTIVITIES

1 Draw pictures of the different animals seen on the walk. Use the pictures
to make a class frieze showing where the various animals were found: birds
in trees and on roofs, snails under stones and in the grass, a cat on the wall
and so on.
2 Make a model animal. For example, use clay to make models of dogs and
cats. Each child can cut out two fish shapes from thick paper and staple
them together, leaving a small gap so that the fish can be stuffed with
crumpled newspaper. Invite the children to decorate the fish with silver
paper scales. The group can then put together a fish mobile to hang from
the ceiling.

ICT LINK

Let the children play the activity 'Animals around us' from the CD-ROM on a
computer or interactive whiteboard.

ASSESSMENT

Ask the children to name some of the animals they found on their walk. Can
they describe any of them?

PLENARY

Talk about the variety of different animals found. *Where were they found?
How were they different?* Talk about how some animals are only found in
certain places - for example, woodlice prefer dark, damp places.

OUTCOME

● Can recognise and name some common animals.

Lesson 10 ▪ Animal body parts

RESOURCES

An animal (if available); pictures of animals or a collection of model animals
(including fish, insects and birds).

MAIN ACTIVITY

Look at an animal (if possible), then at models or pictures of various animals,
and ask the children to name parts. Ask them what parts various animals
have in common with humans (such as ears, eyes or legs), and how some
animals differ from humans (number of legs, fins rather than arms and legs,
wings instead of arms and so on). *What other parts do some animals have?*
(Feelers, shells, beaks, tails and so on.)

ASSESSMENT

Note which children are able to name the parts of animals in the main
activity.

PLENARY

Talk about how all animals are basically the same: they all grow, feed and so
on. Talk about how different animals are adapted to their way of life and
habitat (for example, fish have fins for moving through the water; birds have
wings for flying through the air).

OUTCOME
● Can name some external parts of animals such as wing, fin, tail, beak and feelers.

Lesson 11 ▸ What can they do?

Objective
● To know about how they have grown from birth to the present day.

Vocabulary
baby, grow, crawl, walk, run, feed, milk, bottle, birth, born, talk, physical independence, confidence, taller, change, womb, abdomen

RESOURCES ◉
Main activity: If possible, a baby brother or sister to visit the class with his/her mother or father; a tape measure, bathroom scales.
Group activities: 1 Photographs of the children now and as babies, home videos (if available), measurements taken of the children at birth (if available) such as weight and height. **2** Photocopiable page 42 (also 'What can they do? (red), available on the CD-ROM).

PREPARATION
Send a note home a week or so before this lesson, asking to borrow recent and early photographs and similar records (see Resources) of the children for use in this lesson.

If you are able to invite a parent with a small baby into the classroom, it may be possible to arrange for the baby to be bathed so that the children can appreciate how tiny they once were. This could also provide an opportunity to introduce the correct names for the external genitalia. (You will need to consult your school's policy on sex education beforehand.)

BACKGROUND
Children should be helped to understand that the changes that happen to them as they grow are not simply physical. For example, not only do they become taller, have larger hands and become able to run faster, but they also increase in independence and confidence, understand more and know more. Not everyone develops at the same rate, and there may be children at different stages of development within the same class. One of the most notable changes during these early years is the acquisition of language skills: children can now begin to communicate their own ideas to others. Cognitive development is accelerated when ideas can be put into words. Children should be encouraged to express and explain their ideas at every opportunity.

STARTER
Ask all the children to stand up and look at each other. Compare heights, colouring and so on fairly quickly (see Lesson 2, Similarities and differences). Now ask them to sit quietly for a moment with their eyes closed and think about what they were like when they were babies.

MAIN ACTIVITY
Ask the children: *How have you changed?* Invite individuals to tell the class about some of the things they can do now that they could not do when they were smaller. *How many of you have younger brothers and sisters, and how are they different from you? What do your baby brothers and sisters need to have done for them that you can do for yourself? Did you have to be fed and washed and have your nappies changed when you were a baby? What were some of the other changes in your life from birth to now? Are any of you already losing your milk teeth? Do babies have teeth when they are born?*

Invite a baby brother or sister of one of the class to visit the classroom with his/her mother or father. Choose one or two of the children to measure the length of the baby and the height of the baby's big

Differentiation
Group activity 1
All the children should be able to join in this activity.
Group activity 2
Support children by using 'What can they do?' (green) from the CD-ROM. Read through the statements with the children and ask them to put a tick or cross in the box to show what they could do as a baby and what they can do now. For extension, use 'What can they do?' (blue) which challenges children to select activities from a list.

brother or sister. Take various other measurements of the baby, such as the circumference of the head, the weight and the size of the hands and feet, and compare these measurements with those of the sibling. Some children may have similar sets of measurements from when they were born: how do these compare with the baby in the class and with themselves now? Look for other differences between the children in the class and the visiting baby, such as teeth and nappies.

Look at pictures of the children when they were babies and pictures of them now. *How have you changed? What has helped you to grow?* Talk about the need for food, drink, exercise and warmth: explain that all these things have helped them to grow, and will continue to keep them growing healthy and strong. Ask the children to list some of the things they can do now but could not do when they were babies. Do you need looking after as much now as you did when you were born?

GROUP ACTIVITIES

1 Play 'Who's who?' The children have to match pictures of each other as babies to present-day pictures. Discuss how they have changed.
2 Give each child a copy of photocopiable page 42 or use a whiteboard for a class activity. Ask the children to put ticks and crosses in the appropriate boxes.

ICT LINK
Display 'What can they do' photocopiable (red) from the CD-ROM on the interactive whiteboard. Use the drawing tool to add ticks or crosses.

ASSESSMENT
Review the photocopiable sheets from group activity **2**. Note which children have correctly identified changes between babyhood and their own age. Which children were able to add categories of their own?

PLENARY
Discuss the fact that we were all born and that we have all grown from babyhood. Even the oldest adult we know was once a baby in his or her mummy's womb, was born, grew up and became old. Explain that a womb is the special place in a mother's abdomen where babies grow until they are ready to be born. Recap on what we need to grow up strong and healthy. Ask the children what will happen to their bodies next. Ask them to think about the children in Year 2/Primary 3: *How are they different from you? Can they do anything that you can't do?* Talk about losing early teeth ('milk teeth') and getting taller: *Do we all do that?* Talk about brothers and sisters who are even older than Year 2/Primary 3 children: *How are they different? How have they changed?*

OUTCOME
● Can describe how they have grown from babyhood.

Lesson 12 ▸ The family

Objective
● To know that there are different stages in the human life cycle.

RESOURCES
Main activity: Photocopiable page 43, enlarged to A3 size (also 'The family - 1' (red), available on the CD-ROM).
Group activities: 1 Photocopiable page 44 (also 'The family - 2' (red), available on the CD-ROM), scissors, adhesive, colouring materials, blank paper. **2** Props for role play,

Vocabulary
grow, child, adult, ageing, independent, help, old, mother, father, grandparents, brothers, sisters, son, daughter

such as a walking stick, spectacles, hats, a feeding bottle, a feeding cup, a rattle, a shopping basket, a skipping rope, a card book, a picture book, a novel and so on.
ICT link: 'The family' interactive, from the CD-ROM.

PREPARATION
If possible, ask a cooperative parent with a small baby and an older person (perhaps a grandparent) to visit. If you are able to invite adults in, ask them to bring photographs of themselves as children.

If you wish, you could prepare two or three sets of sequencing cards from page 44 by photocopying them onto stiff card and laminating them for durability. They could be used to play Snap-type games.

BACKGROUND
For most young children, anyone over 20 is ancient: they cannot really imagine that they will ever be that old.

Different people develop and age at different rates. Our body shape changes during puberty, and secondary sexual characteristics appear. The texture of hair and skin may change. The change in pitch of a boy's voice is very noticeable, but a girl's voice will also change. Our roles may change from being cared for to caring. We do not continue to grow in height after our early adult height has been achieved, but we do continue to change. As we get older still, our hair colour may change (though this is often disguised); men may lose their hair. Our movements slow down as our bodies lose their suppleness, and the roles of caring and cared-for person may once more be reversed. Some children may have experienced the death of a family member, and this may be an opportunity to talk sensitively about death. Care should be taken, as some children get very worried about death and think, for example, that if it has happened to Granny, it might happen just as soon to Mummy.

STARTER
Look at a picture of an extended family and identify the different members: mum, dad, grandad, grandma, sons, daughters and so on.

Differentiation
Group activity 1
For children who need support, use 'The family - 2' (green) from the CD-ROM, which omits the toddler and the young adult from the range of people to sort into correct age order. To extend children, use 'The family - 2' (blue). In this activity, children must arrange the pictures and then place word cards alongside them.
Group activity 2
All the children should be able to take part in the role play. Some will be able to demonstrate more subtle changes or differences between the ages and stages within a given role.

MAIN ACTIVITY
Ask the class how they know that the people in the picture on photocopiable page 43 are different ages. Who do they think is the youngest and who is the oldest? Ask the children how old they think the different people might be. Can they guess what the relationships between the people might be?

Introduce the visitors (if you have them). Allow the children to ask them questions about some of the things that they can no longer do as well as they used to - for example, run up the stairs, thread a needle or read without spectacles. Can they hear as well as they used to? Are their joints as supple as they used to be? Is there anything they do better? For example, they are taller and can reach higher objects than when they were children.

Compare the different ages of the people in the picture. What are the differences? The baby is smaller and moves differently from the grown-ups. It needs looking after. The parents are bigger, can look after the baby and can talk. The father grows hair on his chin and talks in a deep voice. The mother has breasts so that she can feed the baby. The grown-ups can do things for themselves. Some people always wear spectacles to help them see better; nearly all old people need them, at least for reading. Old people may not hear very well, and they may have difficulty moving. Their faces may show more lines and wrinkles. They may not have all their teeth. Some very old people may need to be looked after because they can no longer look after themselves.

GROUP ACTIVITIES
1 Give each child a copy of photocopiable page 44 or a set of sequencing cards (see Preparation). The children can cut out and sequence the pictures, then paste them into a book or onto paper. They could also play 'Snap' with the cards.
2 Encourage the children to take part in structured role play, acting as three different generations within a family group.

ICT LINK
Using 'The family' interactive from the CD-ROM, ask the children to sort the illustrations of people of different ages into the correct order.

ASSESSMENT
Note which children know the stages in the human life cycle – and in particular, order the pictures correctly.

PLENARY
Talk about the way in which people grow up, grow old and eventually die. Discuss the fact that our bodies change as we grow up and continue to change as we age, and that this is quite natural. Ask the children to describe how they think they will change as they grow. Emphasise that people may change in different ways and at different rates.

OUTCOMES
● Know about the different stages in a human life.
● Can describe some of the changes.

Lesson 13 ▪ Parents and babies

Objectives
● To know that animals produce offspring and these offspring grow into adults.
● To match adult animals with their offspring.

Vocabulary
calf, cow, chick, hen, cockerel, foal, horse, duckling, duck, cub, tiger, pup, seal

RESOURCES
Main activity: Models of adult and baby animals (very good, reasonably priced models are now available). They can be used for a range of sorting and naming activities, and will more than repay the investment. You will also need pictures of adult and baby animals, books about animals, videos of animals with babies. The pictures should include a human adult and baby, horse and foal, cow and calf, hens and chicks and so on, as well as cases where the babies are very different from the adult (caterpillar and butterfly, tadpole and frog).
Group activities: 1 Model animals, a model farmyard or zoo (or a layout of one on a large sheet of paper). **2** Photocopiable page 45 (also 'Parents and babies' (red), available on the CD-ROM), scissors, adhesive.
ICT link: 'Parents and babies' interactive, from the CD-ROM.

PREPARATION

It may be possible to invite someone with a baby animal, such as a lamb, to
visit the classroom.

BACKGROUND

Although all creatures have young, they don't always look like the adult. Not
all baby animals are cared for by their parent (or parents). Some, such as
snakes, most fish, crocodiles and spiders, are independent at birth and fend
for themselves immediately (though crocodiles do sometimes carry their
newly hatched young in their jaws from their nest in the sand to the water).
Most warm-blooded creatures are cared for by at least one parent, and in
many cases by both parents. All creatures need to be treated with care and
sensitivity, and children should be made aware of this from the beginning.
Hatching chicks in the classroom is fascinating for the children, and a good
lesson in caring for living things. It is possible to keep the chicks until they
begin to fledge, so that the children can see the change from fluffy yellow
ball to adult cockerel or hen. An incubator can sometimes be borrowed from
a secondary school or from a Local Education Authority loan service.

Alternatively, several schools in a cluster could combine to buy one. It is
vital, though, that arrangements are made for the chicks to be returned to a
suitable environment when they are no longer needed in the classroom.

STARTER

Remind the children about when they were babies and how they have
grown up. Talk briefly about how they have changed.

MAIN ACTIVITY

Discuss the fact that all animals have babies. Draw the children's attention
to the fact that the babies often have different names from their parents –
for example, tadpole and frog. Ask them whether they know the names of
some animals and their babies (such as sheep and lamb, duck and duckling).
Look at pictures or models of adult animals and ask the children to identify
them. Look at a corresponding set of baby animals. Invite the children to
match each baby to the appropriate adult. Can they give the babies their
proper names? Introduce pictures of a frog and a butterfly. Do any of the
children know what their babies are called and what they look like? Ask
them to match pictures of a tadpole and a caterpillar to the correct parents.

GROUP ACTIVITIES

1 Ask the children to sort baby animals and match them to their parents,
using models in a model farmyard or zoo. Encourage them to label both the
adult and the baby as they sort, especially where the baby animal has a very
different name from the adult (as in the horse and foal or the sheep and
lamb).
2 Give each child a copy of photocopiable page 45. Ask the children to cut
out the pictures of the baby animals and stick each one onto the picture
next to its parent.

ICT LINK

Using the 'Parents and babies' interactive from the CD-ROM, ask the children
to place the baby animals next to their parents.

ASSESSMENT

Observe how the children have sorted the model animals. Use the
photocopiable sheet to assess their understanding.

PLENARY

Discuss what the children have done. Show the animal pictures and models
again, and ask the children to match adults and babies. Can they name the

parents and their babies, including parents that have different male and female names? Some children could select the correct labels to put with the various family groups (for example, 'cow', 'bull', 'calf'). Talk about the fact that adults and babies often don't look alike (for example, a baby chick and a mother hen). Ask the children whether they can name any animals whose babies are very different from their parents (for example, a tadpole and a frog). *Do human babies look like grown-ups? How are they the same? How are they different?* Finish the session by singing 'Old MacDonald Had a Farm'. Encourage the children to suggest the names of baby animals and then the parents to match them in each successive verse.

OUTCOMES
● Know that animals produce offspring and that these offspring grow into adults.
● Can match adult animals with their offspring.
● Know the names of both the adult and infant forms of some common animals.

LINKS
Maths: sorting and matching.

Lesson 14 ▪ Growing older

Objective
● To know that our appearance changes over time.

Vocabulary
human, life cycle, stages, appearance, lifetime

RESOURCES ⊙
Main activity: Flipchart or board.
Group activities: 1 Photocopiable page 46 (also 'Growing older' (red), available on the CD-ROM), writing and drawing materials.
2 Plastic mirrors, paper; drawing, colouring or painting materials (depending on how you wish to approach this activity).

BACKGROUND
Some of the differences and changes in the appearance of human beings are very obvious, others are much less so. Discuss some of these more subtle differences with the children as the lesson progresses. Babies have round faces and snub noses because their complete bone structure has yet to develop. They have snub noses to make suckling easier. Their heads are quite large in proportion to their bodies as heads grow less, proportionally, during development than other parts of the body, such as the limbs. Although some babies are born with thick hair, they often lose most of it in the first few weeks of life so, generally, babies have less hair than a fully grown adult. Other changes in bodies are due to puberty and hormonal differences, such as the growth of body and facial hair in young men, and the development of genitalia and breasts.

   Other changes as people age are also due to hormonal changes or 'wear and tear' – hair loss in men and thinning hair in women; the skin becomes less elastic and develops more wrinkles. Other changes, such as the tendency for everything to sag are due, in part, to the effects of gravity, as well as wear and tear!

STARTER
Remind the children of the work on ageing that they did in previous lessons. Ask: *What do you remember about some of the things we talked about?* (How they had grown from babyhood to the age of 5 or 6 and about different stages in the human life cycle.) Say: *Now we are going to think about how people's appearance changes as they grow old.*

Group activity 1
For children who need support, use 'Growing older' (green) from the CD-ROM, which does not require any writing. To extend children, use 'Growing older' (blue). In this activity, the children are asked to select words from a list and put them in correct age order, as well as drawing the pictures.

Group activity 2
All children should be able to participate in this activity.

MAIN ACTIVITY

Ask the children what stages they think a human being goes through from birth to death, and list these on the flipchart, leaving room to note the children's ideas about appearance next to, or under, each stage. Possibilities include: baby, toddler, schoolboy/girl (children may want to say 'infant' and 'junior'), teenager, young adult, parent, granny or grandpa, very old person. Help the children to make a full list if they leave any out. Read through the list again and ask them to think about the different stages that they have identified. Take each stage in turn and say: *Think about some of the people you know at this stage. What do they look like? How will they have changed when they get to the next stage?* Remind the children to focus on how people look at the various stages of their lives, not on what they can or can't do, which was the focus of previous lessons. (Babies and toddlers have very round faces, no lines, little snub noses and sometimes a little hair. Later the shape of the face is less round, the nose becomes more prominent, the head is a smaller proportion of the height and people have more hair. Later still lines begin to appear, people may stoop, the hair becomes thinner again and may go grey or white. See Background for further ideas.) Write the children's ideas about appearance against each stage.

GROUP ACTIVITIES

1 Give each child a copy of photocopiable page 46. Ask them to draw a picture of a person at each of the stages showing the differences in appearance. The children may be able to write one or two differences under, or near, each picture.

2 Ask the children to think of a very old person that they know, and what they look like. Say: *Now look carefully at yourself in the mirror and try to imagine what you may look like when you are very old too. Draw what you think you will look like then.* Remind the children of some of the things listed against 'very old person' in the main activity.

ICT LINK

Display 'Growing older' (red) on an interactive whiteboard and complete the illustrations as a class, using the drawing tools provided on the CD-ROM.

ASSESSMENT

Use the children's completed photocopiable sheets to assess the level of their understanding and note which children are able to respond correctly to questions asked during the plenary session.

PLENARY

Ask the children to name some of the differences in human appearance during the various stages from birth to old age (see main activity). Hold up some of the children's work and discuss the changes that they have drawn and written about. You may wish some of the children to explain their work to the rest of the class.

OUTCOMES
- Can recognise that the appearance of humans changes over time.
- Can describe some of the changes.

Lesson 15 ◾ Growing taller

Objectives
● To be able to measure tallness and compare heights.
● To make predictions about whether age and height are related.

Vocabulary
tall, short, height, measure

RESOURCES

Strips of paper or lengths of ribbon, large sheets of paper, collage materials, scissors and glue.

BACKGROUND

Children should be helped to understand that one of the changes that happen as they grow older is that they increase in height, but that not all individuals grow to the same height or at the same rate. Children often think that the older you are, the taller you are. Genetic factors, diet and general health all have a bearing on how tall an individual will eventually become. Historically it can be shown that as diets and better understanding of nutrition and health care has developed, people in general have got taller and bigger. For example, the suit of armour worn by the Black Prince and other surviving costumes from the Middle Ages are very small and show that the people were generally much shorter than we are today.

STARTER

With the whole class, talk to the children about how they are growing taller. Ask the children to predict who is the tallest in the class. *Do you think the tallest people are the oldest? Do any of you know how tall you are? Do you measure yourselves at home? Do you have any brothers or sisters who are taller or shorter than you? Who is the tallest in your house?*

MAIN ACTIVITY

Ask the whole class to stand up and sort themselves into height order. They may need some help with this! Ask the children to sit down where they are and talk about the factors which may influence their height. *Who has a tall/ short parent or grandparent? What types of food do you think will help you to grow tall?*

Compare the heights of the tallest and shortest child. Some children may be sensitive about their height, either tall or short, so this is a good opportunity to talk about the wide range of heights that are all to be expected in children of this age. Talk about the fact that children grow at different rates and that you are going to compare heights again later in the year to see if things have changed. Sometimes children have 'a growth spurt' and grow quite quickly in a short space of time.

Ask the tallest child to lie down on a large sheet of paper and draw round them with a marker pen or chalk. Repeat the process with the shortest child. Use a metre stick to measure the height of each picture

GROUP ACTIVITIES

1 Use collage to fill in the outlines of the tallest and shortest children with clothes. Make labels to show their names, heights and ages and use as a class display.
2 Put the children into pairs. Ask one child to lie on a paper strip (or ribbon) while their partner marks where their head and feet come. Cut the strip to the correct length and change places. Make sure that the child's name is on their strip. When each child has finished their strip, arrange them in height order.

ICT LINK

Use the internet to find the tallest person on record. Make a strip of that length to add to the class display

Differentiation
Group activity 1
All children should be able to take part in this activity.
Group activity 2
To challenge children, ask them to measure their strip in centimetres and write their measurement on the strip.

for comparison. Some children may be able to use IT to make a simple database of the height information.

ASSESSMENT
Assess the children's understanding from their responses in the plenary session.

PLENARY
Ask the children to look at the strips on the wall display and get themselves into the right order. Remind them of their earlier predictions about whether the oldest child in the class would be the tallest. Were they right? Ask them if they think the strips would be in the same order if the measurements were done again later in the year. Remind them that all people are different and will grow at different rates.

OUTCOMES
● Know how to compare their measured height with that of other children.
● Know that height and age do not necessarily correlate.
● Can make simple predictions and relate their findings to them.

LINKS
Maths: measuring, bar charts, data collection.
Art: collage, design.

ENRICHMENT
Lesson 16 ▪ Fingerprint card

Objective
● To know that humans are similar in some ways and different in others.

Vocabulary
similar, different, features, humans, subtle, obvious, individual, measurement, recognise

RESOURCES 💿
Main activity: A tape recording of all the children saying the same very short sentence or phrase (see Preparation, below), cassette player, enlarged copy of the key (see Preparation), flipchart or board.
Group activities: 1 Washable inks or similar (black for the fingerprint cards and other colours for the pictures), copies of photocopiable page 47 (also 'Fingerprint card' (red), available on the CD-ROM), paper for the fingerprint pictures, pictures of pointillist art. **2** The height strips from Lesson 15.

PREPARATION
Make a tape recording of all the children (and you) one by one, saying exactly the same short sentence or phrase. Make a key that lists the order of people speaking.

BACKGROUND
The fact that all humans usually have the same features (ears, eyes, noses and so on), whatever their race or colour, was discussed in Lesson 2 and revisited in Lesson 8. This lesson can therefore be used to review and reinforce this, and also to concentrate on other less obvious features that are 'the same but different', such as our voices, our teeth, the shape of our faces and whether we have freckles or not. Children should realise that, although the body parts are the same, there are differences, some very much more subtle than others, that enable us all to be recognised as individuals. You can often recognise people from a distance simply by the way they move or by a particular mannerism – for example, the way they walk, or the way they use their hands while talking. This lesson also provides a good opportunity to talk sensitively about those of us who might differ in some way or have a disability. Take care not to focus too closely on similarities between parents and children as some children may be adopted, or not living with both biological parents, and may be unaware of this.

Differentiation
Group activity 1
All the children should be able to participate in this activity.
Group activity 2
Some children will include more subtle facts about themselves on their ribbon. They should also be able to include more accurate measurements.

STARTER

Gather the children around you and remind them of what they learned in Lessons 2 and 8 of this unit. Ask: *Can anyone tell me about some ways in which we are all the same and some ways in which we are different?* (We all have two eyes and ears, one nose, hair and two legs; but we are not the same height, and eyes and hair may be different colours.)

MAIN ACTIVITY

Ask the children if they can think of something else, less obvious than two eyes, that we all have but that is different from person to person. Suggest that we all have skin, but some of us have freckles and some don't. We all have hair, but some is naturally curly and some is not. All of us have teeth, but different people's teeth are different in shape and size. Ask the children to stand up in pairs and look carefully at their partners. What else can they see that is the same, but different? (Perhaps they have different-shaped faces, their hands and feet may be a different size from their partner's, their partner's neck may be longer or shorter than theirs.) Tell the children that all these subtle differences, although we have the same features, enable us to recognise people for who they are. We don't look at other people and mistake one for another – because of these differences we know who they are.

Ask the children to sit down again and listen very carefully to the tape you are going to play. Challenge them to see if they can tell who is speaking (remind them that we all have voices, but they sound different). Ask: *Have you ever answered the phone and recognised who is speaking by their voice even though you couldn't see him or her?* Tell them this is what you are going to try to do now. As the children guess who is speaking, list the suggestions on the flipchart. At the end, pin up the prepared key to the speaking order and run through it with the children. Discuss how accurate they were.

Invite the children to stand up. Remind them that they have been thinking about some of the things that all humans have but that are slightly different so people can be recognised as individuals. Ask them now to think of ways in which they could be grouped, such as: freckles/no freckles; straight hair/curly hair and so on. Each time a suitable group is named, ask the children with the attribute mentioned to join the group. Discuss the fact that the children can be grouped in lots of ways and that they fit into more than one group.

GROUP ACTIVITIES

1 Give each child a copy of the fingerprint card on photocopiable page 47. Ask them to complete the card by putting their fingerprints on it for both their right and left hands. When this is done, ask them to pair up and compare their fingerprints with a partner, looking for similarities and differences. They could then compare their right hand with their left hand. Ask: *Are there any differences?* Show the children some pointillist pictures and explain that these are done using hundreds and hundreds of little dots. Ask them to make a picture in the same sort of way, using just their fingerprints to make the dots.
2 Using the height strips from Lesson 15, each child should write his/her name very clearly at the top and decorate it with pictures and facts about themselves. It is a good idea to run through some of the appropriate facts that could be put onto the ribbons such as: weight, shoe size, hand span size, circumference of head, colour of skin, eyes or hair. They could also record any achievements such as: 'I can swim', 'I belong to...', and so on. When the ribbons are finished, lay them out on the floor or pin them on the wall in height order. They can then form the basis of a class display.

ASSESSMENT
During the plenary session, ask the children to tell you some of the things that humans all have that are the same, but different. Look for more subtle answers, as detailed above. Ask the children if they remember some of the ways in which they could be grouped.

PLENARY
Talk to the children about what they have learned. Ask them to remind you of some of the less obvious ways in which they are the same, but different. Look at the 'Facts about me' ribbons and discuss them. Can the children identify any patterns? For example, has the shortest child also got the smallest hands and shoe size? Talk about some of the similarities and differences illustrated by the ribbons.

OUTCOMES
- Can identify ways in which people are similar and different.
- Know that people can be grouped in many different ways.

LINKS
Art: pointillism.

ENRICHMENT
Lesson 17 ◗ Guess who?

Objective
- To know that appearance may change but that people can still be recognised.

RESOURCES
Pictures of people with changed appearance (including people wearing make-up, different hairstyles, dyed hair); face paints, make-up (adult help would be useful for this); combs, ribbons, hair grips, ponytail holders, wigs, mirrors.

MAIN ACTIVITY
Show the pictures to the children and talk to them about the people in them. Some of them are wearing make-up. Do the children think that they can still be recognised? Some have elaborate hairstyles – can they be recognised? Ask the children if they think that their classmates would still recognise them even if they had a different hairstyle or wore make-up. *What about a clown's make-up, or face paints? Would your friends still know you?* Ask the children to change their appearance in some way with the items you have provided.

ASSESSMENT
During the plenary session, ask the children to describe some of the ways in which appearance can be changed but people can still be recognised. Note those children who are able to respond, and the quality and level of detail of their responses.

PLENARY
Gather the children together and look at each other. Ask: *How have people changed their appearance? Can they still be recognised? How?* (Their voices are the same, their faces are the same shape, they move in the same way.)

OUTCOME
- Can describe some of the ways in which appearance can be changed, but people can still be recognised.

Differentiation
All children should be able to take part in this activity according to their ability.

Lesson 18 ◗ Joints

Objective
● To know that the human body can move in a variety of ways.

Vocabulary
walk, run, jump, skip, hop, roll, balance, climb, hang, twirl, bend, stretch, crawl, skeleton, joint, hip, knee, ankle, shoulder, elbow, wrist

RESOURCES ◉

Main activity: Space to move around, a model human skeleton or picture of a skeleton, a *Funnybones* story by Janet and Allan Ahlberg (Mammoth).
Group activities: 1 Space to move around. **2** Photocopiable page 48 copied to A3 size onto thin card for each child (also 'Joints' (red), available on the CD-ROM), paper fasteners, scissors, single hole punches, materials for decoration.
ICT link: 'Joints' interactive, from the CD-ROM.

BACKGROUND

Learning to look after our bodies cannot begin too early, and understanding something of how the body works is a necessary part of this. Young children can begin to think about how their joints are different and how the joints help them to move. Knees and elbows are hinge joints, allowing the limb to bend in one direction and lock when straight. If our knees bent in both directions, we would be unable to stand or walk. Hips and shoulders are ball and socket joints, which allow a greater degree of movement. The skeletons of young children are more cartilaginous than those of adults, which gives them greater flexibility: their joints are more supple, allowing them to move in ways that most adults can only dream of!

Many children at this stage will still be exploring their bodies and what they can do. Some children will be more adventurous than others, and appear to be totally unaware of any danger. Others will be more timid and reluctant to try anything different. It is important that children are allowed to develop at their own pace. The daredevils need to be made aware of how their movements may affect both their own safety and that of others. The reluctant may be gently encouraged to spread their wings with a little support. Holding a hand as the child takes his or her first steps along a balance beam can help to inspire the confidence for a solo attempt.

STARTER
Build on work done at the Foundation Stage: ask the children to quickly name different ways of moving. Read one of the *Funnybones* stories to the children.

MAIN ACTIVITY
Look at a model or picture of a human skeleton. Identify some of the joints. Can the children find the same joints on their own bodies? If you have a model skeleton, move some of the limbs and demonstrate how the joints work. What do the children notice about the way in which the elbow works, compared with the shoulder? Talk about the different types of joints (see Background).

Look specifically at walking. Ask the children to think about how their legs move: *Do they bend? Where do they bend? What are these joints called?* (Hip, knee, ankle.) *How easy is it to walk without bending your legs? Will your legs bend backwards? What would happen if they did?*

Ask the children to bend and stretch their arms. *Will they bend backwards? What about the joints at your shoulders?* Ask them to touch their hands together in front of them, and then see how far back they can move their arms. *Can you touch your hands behind you?* Ask them to sit on the floor or stand and hold on to something, then see how far and in which directions they can move their legs, swinging them from the hip. *Which limbs do you use to climb the climbing frame? Which joints do you use?*

GROUP ACTIVITIES
1 Play 'Simon says' (run, skip, hop, jump and so on). The children should obey the instruction only if told that 'Simon says' to do so.
2 Give each child a copy of page 48, copied onto thin card. They should cut out the pieces, punch holes where indicated (using a single hole punch) and join the limbs together with paper fasteners, so that they can make the figure move. They could decorate their figure, giving it a face and so on.

ICT LINK ⊙
Let the children use the 'Joints' interactive from the CD-ROM, to join the parts together to create a jointed figure.

ASSESSMENT
During the plenary session, ask the children to indicate a number of joints on their bodies. Can they all name and locate the main joints: hip, shoulder, knee, ankle? Ask them to describe how these joints help us to move.

PLENARY
Ask the children: *Why do we need to move in different ways? Why don't our legs bend backwards?* Look at a model or picture of a skeleton and talk about how our skeletons help us to move. This may provide an opportunity to talk sensitively about people who cannot move so easily for one reason or another. You may have a child in the class who has suffered a broken limb and can tell the class what it felt like.

OUTCOMES
● Can demonstrate different ways in which the body can move.
● Know that joints help us to move, and can name and indicate the main joints.

LINKS
Unit 1e Lesson 1, Movement tally.

Lesson 19 ▸ Animal movements

Objective
● To know that animals can move and feed in different ways from humans.

RESOURCES
Snails, worms or fish in a tank; videos of animals moving and feeding; a birdtable.

MAIN ACTIVITY
Watch videos of animals moving. *How do animals without legs move?* Watch worms, fish or snails in a tank. In a PE session, ask the children to move smoothly like a snail; quickly like a spider; with a slow, slinky movement like a cat stalking, and so on.

Watch snails (live or on video) feeding on lettuce leaves, and compare with humans feeding. *Do we sometimes eat the same things? Do animals cook their food? How do animals put food in their mouths?* Elephants use their trunks, but monkeys and humans use their hands.

ASSESSMENT
During the plenary session, ask the children to describe how particular animals move and feed.

PLENARY
Discuss different movements made by animals. Talk about animals that run, hop, skip, jump, fly, swim and crawl. Discuss different ways that animals feed on plants, insects, fish and so on.

OUTCOME
● Can describe how some animals move and feed.

Differentiation
All children should be able to take part in this activity.

LINKS
Unit 1e Lesson 1, Movement tally.

Lesson 20 ▸ Food for life

Objectives
● To know that food and water are needed for animals, including humans, to stay alive.
● To carry out a simple survey.

RESOURCES
Starter: A selection of pictures of foods, food packets and food wrappers.
Main activity: Pictures of well-nourished and malnourished children; a large sheet of paper (or board). Many aid organisations produce useful teaching packs containing information and photographs.
Group activities: 1 Squared paper for graphs. **2** Paper plates, a variety of materials for collage or modelling (for example: tissue paper to roll into peas, sugar paper to make lettuce or cabbage leaves, foam sheeting to cut into chips, red and brown paint for tomato ketchup and brown sauce, felt for meat slices, string for spaghetti).

BACKGROUND
It is difficult to demonstrate to children that we need food and drink to stay alive, since a 'fair test' would logically mean feeding one group a

Vocabulary
favourite, graph, fruit, vegetable, food, life, living, essential, death, malnourished, starvation, famine, drought, hunger, thirst

wholesome, nutritious diet and starving another group until they became very ill or died. However, most children will have seen pictures on television of children involved in wars or natural disasters who are starving, and many aid organisations produce information packs dealing with food or water shortages. Take care not to reinforce the stereotypical view that all starving children come from Africa or India.

Growth requires good nutrition, and a balanced diet is needed to maintain good health. There are no 'bad' foods, just some that we should eat or drink in moderation. Children need to know that they need to drink in order to replace fluids lost through excretion, and that they should drink lots of water and not just sweet drinks. Some children may become distressed if certain foods are labelled as 'bad' or 'not to be eaten'; since these may be the foods they are given. Not all children of this age have a choice about what they eat. Conduct any discussion sensitively - for example, some children may come to school without breakfast; some may only have one meal a day; and some may feed themselves with whatever they can find in the house. Others may eat far too much or live on sweets, crisps and fizzy pop. It is important that children learn the need for a balanced diet, but it is equally important not to make very young children feel guilty about what they eat or do not eat.

STARTER
With the whole class, look at the pictures of foods and the packets and wrappers. Name some familiar items. Are there any foods the children don't recognise?

MAIN ACTIVITY
Ask the children what they like to eat. *What is your favourite meal? Why? What is your favourite drink? Do you know any living thing that doesn't eat or drink?* Explain that plants make their own food, but still need water. This provides an opportunity to think about things that are living and non-living (see Unit 1B Lesson 2, Living or non-living?). Ask whether anyone in the class has a pet. *How do you care for your pet? What would happen if it were not fed and given water to drink?* Discuss the children's ideas about why we need to eat and drink. *What do you think might happen to us if we had no food or drink?* Look at the pictures and compare the malnourished people with those who look well fed. *What has happened to those who have not had enough to eat?*

Ask the children if they have ever felt really hungry. *What does it feel like?* Explain the difference between just feeling hungry and real starvation: that some people in situations of famine may have nothing to eat for days on end, and may die from lack of food.

When the children are hungry, what do they like to eat best? Use the board (or a very large sheet of paper) to create a tally chart. Ask each child for one food that they like to eat when they are hungry, and mark the chart accordingly. If you wish, you could restrict the choice of foods to one category (such as breakfast cereals).

GROUP ACTIVITIES
1 Working in groups of two or three, the children can use the survey data collected in the tally chart to make a block graph of favourite foods
2 Using the materials provided, individuals can model the various components of their favourite meal and stick them onto a paper plate.

ICT LINK
Use a whiteboard to create your class tally chart. The children could create a block graph using the graphing tool from the CD-ROM.

Differentiation
Group activity 1
Support children by asking them to make a graph using the data for just five or six most popular foods.
Group activity 2
As an extension, allow children to work independently to select materials for a model meal.

ASSESSMENT

Can the children say (in simple terms) why we need food and water to stay alive? Check their block graphs to see whether they have been able to transfer the information from the tally chart of favourite foods.

PLENARY

Review the fact that all animals need to eat and drink to stay alive. Discuss the need to eat sensibly in order to grow and stay healthy. It may be appropriate to talk about children who do not have enough to eat, or who do not have access to clean drinking water. Beware of giving the impression that this only happens in third-world countries: there are many families in the western world who live in less than adequate conditions.

OUTCOMES
- Know that animals need to eat and drink to stay alive.
- Can undertake a simple survey.
- Can construct a block graph.

LINKS
Unit 1b Lesson 2, Living or non-living?; Lesson 9, Where does it come from?

ENRICHMENT
Lesson 21

Objective
- To compare data from two classes.

Differentiation
The children should work in mixed-ability groups in order to help each other collect the data and construct the graphs.

Comparing classes

RESOURCES
Tally charts, clipboards, cooperation of a second class.

MAIN ACTIVITY
Discuss the data that the children are going to collect – for example, favourite drinks or foods. Different groups could collect different data. The children should collect data from their own class and another class using tally charts, then construct two block graphs.

ASSESSMENT
From the children's work, note those who have been able to make a tally chart and transfer the data to a block graph.

PLENARY
Ask the children to interpret the data gathered from another class and compare it with the data collected in their own class.

OUTCOME
- Can compare data from two different graphs.

Lesson 22

Objectives
- To assess whether the children can name parts of the human body, and identify the organs associated with the five senses.
- To assess the children's ability to name some of the ways in which we move.

Assessment

RESOURCES
Assessment activities: 1 Photocopiable page 49 (also 'Assessment-1' (red), available on the CD-ROM), writing materials. **2** Photocopiable page 50 (also 'Assessment -2' (red), available on the CD-ROM), writing materials.

STARTER
You may wish to start by singing 'Heads, Shoulders, Knees and Toes', 'Put Your Finger on Your Nose' or another familiar song about body parts.

Vocabulary
see, hear, smell, taste, feel, shoulder, leg, elbow, fingers, foot, head, hand, toes, arm, neck, chest, knee, walk, run, hop, skip, jump, crawl, roll, bend, stretch, twirl

ASSESSMENT ACTIVITY 1

This activity may be done with the whole class, or with groups over a period of time. In the latter case, organising the children into ability groups will give you the opportunity to focus on those children who need extra help with reading. Give each child a copy of photocopiable page 49. Read through the words with the children, asking them to put their finger on each word as you read it out. Ask them to draw a line matching each word to the appropriate part of the body.

ANSWERS

Senses: see - eye; hear - ear; smell - nose; taste - mouth; feel - skin (some children may draw a line to a hand, while others may draw it to any exposed area of skin). Body part labels: check that the label lines are reasonably close to the part being identified, particularly less obvious parts such as the elbow, knee or shoulder.

ICT LINK

If discussing the answers as a class, display 'Assessment - 1' photocopiable (red) from the CD-ROM on the interactive whiteboard. The line tool could then be used to link the senses and body parts to the relevant part of the illustration of the body.

Alternatively, use the filled box tool to cover the words and see which parts of the body the children can label without seeing the words listed.

LOOKING FOR LEVELS

Most children should be able to label ten of the body parts and four of the sense organs correctly. Some may get all the answers right; others may only label the more obvious parts, such as the head, arm, leg, hand and foot and only identify one or two sense organs.

ASSESSMENT ACTIVITY 2

Write the following movement words on the board: walk, run, hop, skip, jump, crawl, roll, bend, stretch, twirl. Give each child a copy of photocopiable page 50. Borrow a child (who can skip) from another class. Read through the words on the board with the children. Explain that as they see each movement, they should write its name in the spaces on the sheet - starting with 1 and going down to 10. Whisper the name of a movement from the list to the borrowed child and ask him/her to demonstrate that movement to the class. Repeat until all the movements have been carried out. Be careful to say the movements in a different order from that on the board, but take a note of which order you said them in.

ANSWERS

The children should have written the names of the movements in the appropriate order.

LOOKING FOR LEVELS

Most children will be able to identify the more common movements such as walk, run, hop, skip, jump and crawl. Some children will know all the movements; others may have difficulty with all but the most familiar (such as walk, run and jump).

PHOTOCOPIABLE

Body parts

■ Choose the correct word to write in each label box.

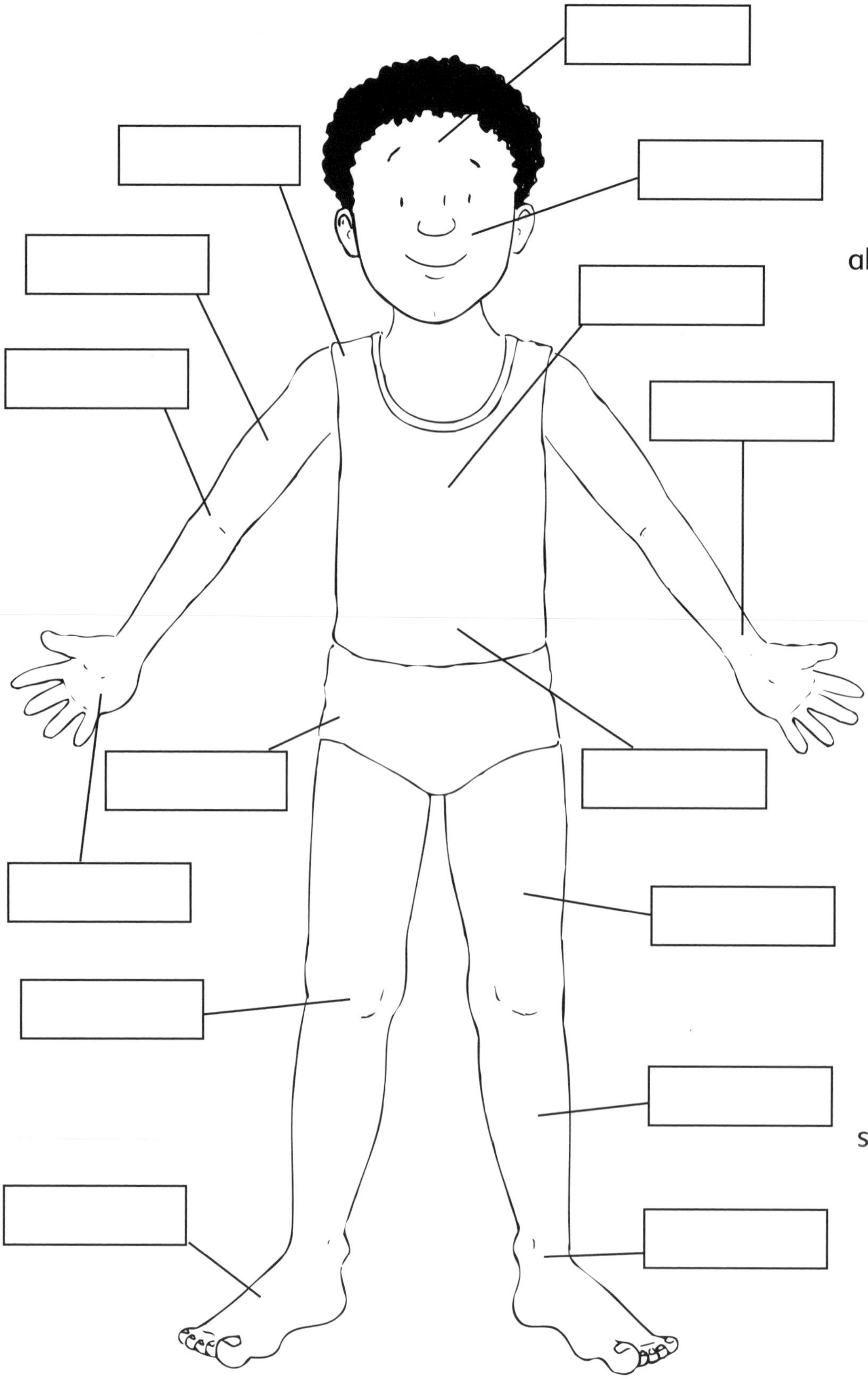

arm
leg
head
abdomen
face
hand
foot
chest
knee
elbow
ankle
wrist
hip
thigh
shoulder

Illustration © Kirsty Wilson

The senses

◼ Draw a line to match each thing to the sense or senses you would use for it.

taste

smell

touch

sight

hearing

Illustration © Kirsty Wilson

PHOTOCOPIABLE

Sort it!

◼ Cut out the pictures and stick each one in the right set: living, no longer living or never alive.

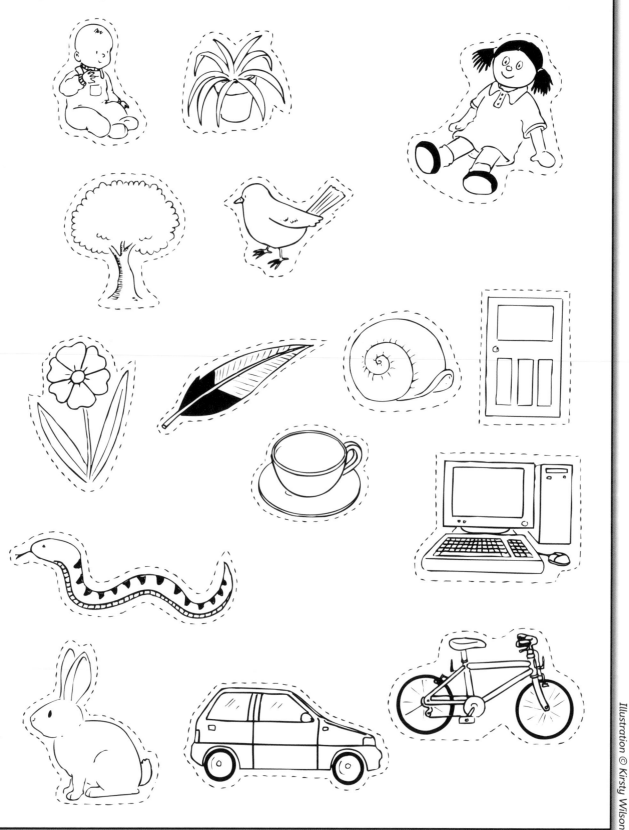

Illustration © Kirsty Wilson

Animals around us

■ Cut out and stick the labels in the correct spaces, or choose the right word and write it in the box by each picture.

fly	human	rabbit	robin	frog	goldfish
squirrel	sheep	mouse	horse	cat	dog

Illustration © Kirsty Wilson

What can they do?

✔ or ✗ what each child does.

☐	crawls	☐
☐	cries	☐
☐	walks	☐
☐	talks	☐
☐	laughs	☐
☐	feeds himself	☐
☐	eats using teeth	☐
☐	waves	☐
☐	wears a nappy	☐
☐	takes himself to the toilet	☐

Illustration © Kirsty Wilson

■ SCHOLASTIC

The family – 1

Illustration © Kirsty Wilson

The family – 2

◼ Cut out these cards and arrange them in the right sequence.

■SCHOLASTIC

Parents and babies

■ Cut out each baby animal and place it in this farmyard picture next to its parent.

Illustration © Kirsty Wilson

PHOTOCOPIABLE

Growing older

■ Draw pictures of a person as they grow older and write a few words to explain how they change.

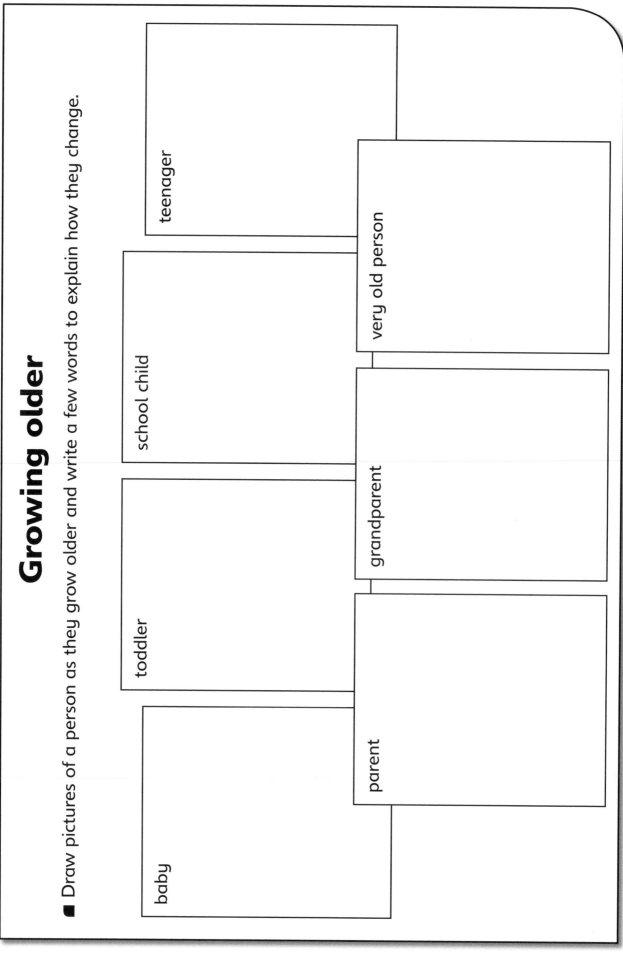

baby

toddler

school child

teenager

parent

grandparent

very old person

Fingerprint card

Left hand		Right hand	
little finger		thumb	
ring finger		index finger	
middle finger		middle finger	
index finger		ring finger	
thumb		little finger	

PHOTOCOPIABLE

Joints

■ Cut out the pieces, then join them together with paper fasteners to make a jointed figure.

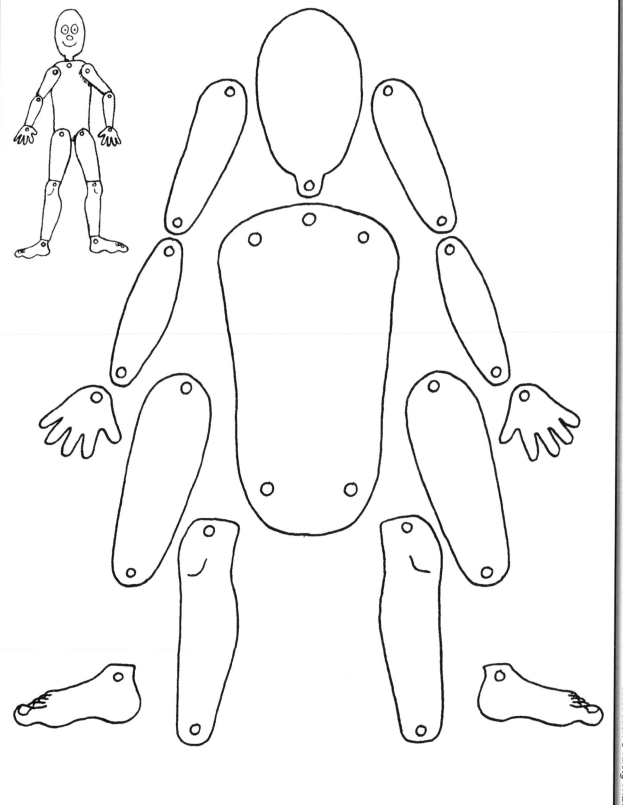

Illustration © Kirsty Wilson

Assessment – 1

 Draw a line to the part of the body with which we:

see

hear

smell

taste

feel

 Draw a line to match each name to the body part:

shoulder

leg

elbow

foot

head

hand

arm

neck

knee

Illustration © Kirsty Wilson

PHOTOCOPIABLE

Assessment – 2

1	
2	
3	
4	
5	
6	
7	
8	
9	
10	

CHAPTER 2 Growing plants

Lesson	Objectives	Main activity	Group activities	Plenary	Outcomes
Lesson 1 Plant spotters	• To recognise and name some common plants. • To understand that all living things should be treated with respect.	Go for a walk to observe different plants in the local environment.	• Identify plants found. • Make a collage of plants.	Review the children's observations; compare plants seen.	• Can recognise and name some common plants.
Enrichment Lesson 2 Living or non-living?	• To know how to distinguish a living thing from a non-living thing. • To know that living things have certain requirements.	Look at various items to compare the features of living things, no longer living things and things that have never been alive.		Review the differences between living and non-living things. Explore the things plants need to keep them alive.	• Can distinguish between a living thing, something no longer living and something that has never been alive. • Know that living things need food and water.
Lesson 3 Make a flower	• To know that plants have roots, stems, leaves and flowers.	Look closely at some flowering plants and their parts, both in and out of their pots.	• Draw and label a picture of a plant. • Make a model plant.	Label a large plant picture. Discuss the functions of plant parts.	• Know that flowering plants have roots, stems, leaves and flowers.
Lesson 4 Seed diary	• To know that most plants grow from seeds.	Look at and sort seeds. Sow seeds in a garden or in pots; follow up by observing growth.	• Grow cress seeds or mung beans to observe germination. • Make a seed collage.	Recall what happened when they planted their seeds, and the sequence of events.	• Can describe how a seed germinates and grows into a plant. • Know that different plants come from different types of seed.
Lesson 5 Bean race	• To observe the changes in a growing plant. • To make simple measurements. • To take information from a chart.	Observe, measure and 'train' the growth of peas or beans. Record growth on a chart.	• Keep a diary of a plant's growth. • Make a class book about a plant's growth.	After plant growth, mark dates on a calendar; draw a timeline; discuss how the plant grew and changed.	• Can describe the growth of a plant. • Can make simple measurements. • Can take information from a chart.
Lesson 6 Roots	• To know that roots change as they grow. • To know that different plants can have different types of roots.	Plant bean seeds in jars of gravel or pebbles. Observe and record the changes. Look at the roots of some common plants.	• Cut open and examine some root vegetables. • Make a 3D frieze of trees with roots.	Examine the roots and shoot of a bean.	• Can describe how the roots of a plant grow. • Know that different plants may have different root systems.
Lesson 7 Water for growth	• To know that plants need water to survive.	Investigate what happens to a plant deprived of water.	• Draw a picture of what the plant might look like after more time without water. • Use reference materials to find out about plants that grow in deserts.	Discuss why plants need water to survive.	• Know that plants need water to survive.
Lesson 8 In the dark	• To know that green plants need light to grow. • To carry out a simple investigation.	Observe the changes in a plant kept in the dark, compared with one kept in the light.	• Make an observational drawing of the plant kept in the dark.	Consider the arrangement and function of leaves in a healthy plant.	• Know that light is necessary for green plants to grow healthily. • Can carry out a simple investigation with help.
Lesson 9 Where does it come from?	• To know that plants provide a range of foods. • To be able to match some foods to their plant of origin.	Relate various foods often eaten by children to the plants from which they come.	• Draw a chart of the foods, matched to the original plants. • Devise a menu for a meal consisting of foods made from plants.	Discuss the importance of plants in the diet of humans and other animals.	• Know that plants provide a range of food. • Can match some foods to their plant of origin.
Enrichment Lesson 10 A medley of fruits	• To know that some foods are prepared directly from plants. • To know that there is a wide variety of fruits.	Sort a collection of fruits. Make a fruit salad.		Discuss how plant foods may be eaten raw, processed or cooked.	• Know that some foods are prepared directly from plants. • Know that there is a wide variety of fruits. • Be able to handle knives safely.
Lesson 11 From plant to plate	• To know that some foods are processed by humans, and some are taken directly from the plant.	Discuss the contents of a cress sandwich, their origin and how they have been changed. Make and enjoy!		Consider other plant foods used in sandwiches, and how they have been changed.	• Know that some foods that are made from plants have been processed and changed by humans, and some are taken directly from the plant.

Lesson	Objectives	Main activity	Group activities	Plenary	Outcomes
Lesson 12 All around us	• To know that the environment is the surroundings in which plants and animals live.	Walk around the outside of the school, looking at different areas and what lives there.	• Draw or paint their favourite area seen on the walk. • Contribute to a large class picture of the school's environment.	Review the idea of the environment. Discuss how to improve the environment within and around the school.	• Know that the environment is all around us, and that it is where plants and animals live.
Lesson 13 My weather chart	• To know that there are simple features of the weather that can be observed. • To use data collected to construct a pictogram or block graph.	Keep a simple class weather chart, including comparative judgements of temperature.	• Make and keep a weather diary. • Find out about extreme weather conditions in other parts of the world.	Use the data collected on the weather chart to make a pictogram or block graph.	• Know that there are different types of weather. • Can enter simple information on a chart. • Can use the information from a chart to construct a pictogram or block graph.
Enrichment Lesson 14 Measuring rainfall	• To measure rainfall over a period of time.	Make a simple rain gauge and use it to measure rainfall each day.		Draw conclusions from data over a week.	• Know how to use a simple rain gauge. • Can enter information on a simple chart.
Lesson 15 When the wind blows	• To make and use a simple wind meter to measure the strength and direction of the wind.	Make and use a simple wind meter to indicate the direction and relative strength of the wind.		Discuss other ways of telling the direction of the wind.	• Know that the strength and direction of the wind can be measured.
Enrichment Lesson 16 The seasons	• To know how the environment changes as the year passes through the seasons (autumn).	Look outdoors for signs of autumn. Draw round a shadow. Begin a 'seasons hoop' mobile.	• Add autumn pictures to the seasons mobile. • Record observations on a photocopiable page.	Review work done and predict changes in the next season.	• Can describe some changes associated with autumn.
Enrichment Lesson 17 Winter	• To know how the environment changes as the year passes through the seasons (winter).	Look at the changes in the environment, including day length. What are the signs of winter?		Review work done and compare with previous season.	• Can describe some changes associated with winter.
Enrichment Lesson 18 Spring	• To know how the environment changes as the year passes through the seasons (spring).	Look at the changes in the environment. What are the signs of spring?		Review work done. Compare with autumn and winter; try to explain the changes.	• Can describe some changes associated with spring.
Enrichment Lesson 19 Summer	• To know how the environment changes as the year passes through the seasons (summer).	Look at the changes in the environment. Complete the seasons hoop.		Review the changes over the year; try to explain them.	• Can describe some changes associated with summer. • Know that we have four seasons each year.
Enrichment Lesson 20 Our tree	• To know that plants change according to the seasons.	'Adopt' a tree in the local area; observe and record its seasonal changes.	• Fill in a simple record sheet. • Find out what type of tree it is and compare it with other trees.	Discuss what was observed and the usefulness of keeping a record.	• Know that plants change according to the seasons.
Enrichment Lesson 21 Growing plants indoors	• To know how to care for growing plants indoors.	Work in groups to create a tiny indoor garden.		Discuss how small plants should be cared for when being kept indoors.	• Can describe what needs to be done to care for plants indoors.

Assessment	Objectives	Activity 1	Activity 2
Lesson 22	• To assess whether the children recognise how the environment changes according to the season. • To assess whether the children know that plants have roots, stems, flowers and leaves.	Draw or describe a tree and the weather in spring, summer, autumn and winter.	Draw a plant and label the flower, stem, leaf and root.

SC1 SCIENTIFIC ENQUIRY

Thirsty plants

LEARNING OBJECTIVE AND OUTCOME
● To ask questions...and decide how they might find answers to them.

ACTIVITY
Children are asked to suggest ideas for finding out whether or not a plant needs water. They leave a plant without water for a day or two and make observations of the condition of the plant as it dries out. They then water the plant and observe again as it revives.

LESSON LINKS
This Sc1 activity forms an integral part of Lesson 7, Water for growth.

Lesson 1 ▸ Plant spotters

Objectives
● To recognise and name some common plants.
● To understand that all living things should be treated with respect.

Vocabulary
collect, sample, leaf, bud, flower, seed head

RESOURCES
Main activity: A nice sunny day; an area where there is a range of common plants for the children to see (for example: grass, daisies, dandelions, trees, buttercups, according to the time of year); small containers/trays for collecting, magnifiers, pictures of common plants and simple reference books, camera.

BACKGROUND
This activity is best done in spring or summer to be sure of finding a reasonable range of plants. At this time you may find plants with buds, flowers and seed heads which will aid identification. If flowers are absent it may be possible to identify a plant by its leaf shape.

It is wise to visit your chosen site a few days in advance to familiarise yourself with what the children are likely to find and also to make a risk assessment of the area. Try to choose an area with a variety of plant life, including trees. Trees are also flowering plants but children often do not recognise this fact. They may recognise the candles on a horse chestnut tree but miss the relatively insignificant green flowers on an oak tree. Many trees such as hazel and pussy willow are pollinated by the wind and flower before they produce any leaves so that the leaves do not impede the wind. Plants that rely on insect pollination usually flower a little later when it is warmer and the insect population has increased.

Make sure that the children understand that it is illegal to pick some wild flowers or dig up the plants. They should be encouraged to pick only one sample of even common flowers such as dandelions and daisies. Children should understand that all living things - including plants - should be treated with respect. Use a camera to record findings instead of taking too many samples.

It is often useful to let the children work in groups of two or three so that responsibility for equipment can be shared. For example, one child could be responsible for the magnifier while the other holds the collecting container. Clipboards and paper are often more trouble than they are worth with small children and add little to the exercise. Children will probably get more from this exercise if they concentrate on looking and finding; discoveries can then be noted and discuss back in the classroom.

STARTER
Before you leave the classroom, remind the children about the rules of picking and the need to show care and respect for the plants. Show them

Differentiation
Some children may need to be reminded to look carefully all around them. Some may be able to recognise not only that there are different types of trees, but that trees are flowering plants.

pictures of common plants you might expect to see. Talk about observing closely, looking for similarities and differences.

MAIN ACTIVITY
Go for a walk and look at the plants all around. Draw the children's attention to the great variety of plants even in a small area. Identify some common varieties such as daisies, dandelions and buttercups. Emphasise that trees and grass are also flowering plants. Remind the children that plants are living things, that they must be treated with care and sensitivity and that we must not dig up wild flowers or spoil them. Ask them to observe closely and find as many different-shaped leaves and different-shaped and coloured flowers as they can. Talk about how plants make our world look beautiful. Use a camera to record what the children find. Collect a few specimens to identify back in the classroom.

GROUP ACTIVITIES
1 Ask the children to use reference books to identify plants that they don't recognise.
2 Use collage materials or photographs to make a wall display of plants found and label appropriately.

ICT LINK
You may be able to find a list of all the flora and fauna that can be found in your county on the internet, using a search engine such as Google.

ASSESSMENT
During the walk, note those children who can recognise and name some of the plants. Back in the classroom, note who can recognise pictures of plants seen and name them.

PLENARY
Ask the children if they can remember and name any of the plants seen on their walk. Ask: *What did you notice about them? Can you remember some of the ways in which these plants were the same or different? Were there lots of each type or only a few? Did you find anything unusual?*

OUTCOME
● Can recognise and name some common plants.

LINKS
Art: collage and drawings.

ENRICHMENT
Lesson 2 ▪ Living or non-living?

Objectives
● To know how to distinguish a living thing from a non-living thing.
● To know that living things have certain requirements.

RESOURCES
A collection of plants in pots, buttons, stones, paper clips, a wooden spoon, a dried flower, cornflakes.

MAIN ACTIVITY
Ask the children to look at the collection of objects carefully and challenge them to sort the objects into sets of living and non-living things. Afterwards, ask them to tell you why they have sorted as they have done. Discuss what

plants need to keep them alive and healthy (light, water and warmth). *What would happen if a plant had no water?* Look at the things that were once alive (wooden chopping board, bamboo cane, breakfast cereal) and ask the children if they should go in a different set and if so, why. Talk about the differences between things that are living, things that were once living and things that have never been alive.

ASSESSMENT
Note how the children sort the collection and during the plenary observe whether they have understood the concept of living, not living and never been alive. Look at the new sets that the children have created.

PLENARY
Ask the children to tell you the differences between things that are alive, things that are no longer living and things that have never been alive. Can they describe the things that living plants need to keep them alive and healthy?

OUTCOMES
● Can distinguish between a living thing, something no longer living and something that has never been alive.
● Know that living things need food and water.

Differentiation
Some children may need to sort the original set several times with adult help before grasping the concept.
Some children may be able to draw alternative sets of things living, never living and once living from looking at pictures and catalogues. Some children may also be able to draw the sets of things from the main activity and add one or two things to each set.

Lesson 3 ▪ Make a flower

Objective
● To know that plants have roots, stems, leaves and flowers.

Vocabulary
leaf, stem, root, flower, petal, (also plant names).

RESOURCES 💿
Main activity: A small collection of three or four flowering plants in pots (try to find a selection of plants that have a different number of petals, different-shaped leaves and so on); newspaper or a plastic sheet.
Group activities: 1 Drawing materials, art paper. **2** Photocopiable page 85 (also 'Make a flower (red), available on the CD-ROM), art straws, string, adhesive, small tubs.
Plenary: A large picture of a flowering plant, labels for the parts, Blu-Tack.

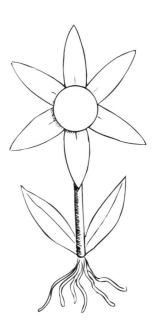

PREPARATION
Photocopy the shape templates provided on photocopiable page 85 onto thick paper or light card. Cut out the shapes to make a sufficient number of petals in a selection of colours (each child will need at least six petals), leaves (at least two per child), and central discs in yellow, black or dark brown (one per child). Cut string into short lengths for roots (four to six per child), and cut art straws in half (one piece per child). It is always wise to have a few spares in case of accidents!

BACKGROUND
The collection of plants available will depend on the time of year: for example, primulas or pansies in spring or busy lizzies, pot marigolds and geraniums in summer. Many children do not realise that trees are flowering plants (or even, in many cases, that they are plants at all). If these activities are being done at a time when no trees are in flower, it is a good idea to add books containing pictures of trees in flower to the collection of resources available.
　　Plants are essential to us: without them, there would be no life on the

planet. Plants (and marine algae) are the world's oxygen producers; they also absorb carbon dioxide, thus helping to control pollution. Virtually all non-marine food chains start with a green plant. Flowers attract pollinating creatures such as insects (and in some countries, hummingbirds and bats) with their colours and nectar. These creatures perform an essential service in carrying pollen from one plant to another, enabling fertilisation to take place and seeds to grow. Most plants are not self-pollinating (because of the need to maintain genetic variety), and would not produce fertile seeds without the pollinating creatures. The wind also plays an important part in the pollination of plants, especially trees. For this reason, most plants that are wind-pollinated flower before they produce leaves, so that the wind can pollinate them easily without the leaves getting in the way. Some plants, such as ferns and fungi, do not produce flowers: they reproduce by producing spores (asexual reproductive cells), which grow into plants that are genetically identical to the parent plant.

STARTER
Remind the children what they did in Lesson 2, Living or non-living? *Can you remember whether plants are living or not living?* Reinforce the idea that all living things need to be treated with care and respect.

MAIN ACTIVITY
Look at the collection of flowering plants in pots and ask the children to name the visible features. *Are all the leaves the same shade of green and the same shape? Are all the flowers the same shape and colour? Do they all have the same number of petals? What might be below the ground?*

Carefully take each plant out of its pot, place it on a plastic sheet (or newspaper) and look at the roots. Discuss the purpose of each part of the plant. Petals are usually coloured to attract bees and insects to assist with pollination; leaves help the plant to make its food; the stem holds the flower up; roots help to anchor the plant in the ground and keep it steady, as well as absorbing the water that the plant needs to keep it healthy. Compare and contrast the various plants, noting how they grow. *Are they stiff and woody or soft and pliable? Do they all have roots?* Having examined the plants closely, replant them carefully and remind the children of the need to care for all living things.

GROUP ACTIVITIES
1 Let the children work individually to draw and label a plant that has been taken out of its pot. Remind them that their drawing should fill the paper provided. Encourage them to label the parts (independently if possible): flower, stem, leaf, root, bud (if present).
2 Ask the children to make a model flower. Provide tubs of petals, centres, stems, leaves and roots for them to choose from. They can choose the flower colour and the number of petals to stick to the back of a central disc, which they can then attach to an art straw before adding leaves and string roots to complete their plant. The model plants could be used for a 'Mary, Mary, Quite Contrary' class display.

ASSESSMENT
Use the children's labelled drawings from group activity **1** to assess their knowledge of the parts of a plant.

PLENARY
Present a large picture of a flowering plant. Hold up some large labels naming the main parts of the

plant, and ask the children to indicate where they should go on the big picture. Can they explain the purpose of each part? The picture could then form part of a whole-class display.

OUTCOME
● Know that flowering plants have roots, stems, leaves and flowers.

Lesson 4 ▪ Seed diary

Objective
● To know that most plants grow from seeds.

Vocabulary
grow, plant, seed, poisonous, germinate, root, shoot

RESOURCES ⊙
Main activity: Plant pots, compost, plant labels (lolly sticks or pieces cut from yoghurt pots), a watering can or jug, white paper plates, newspaper or plastic sheets, a camera (optional), photocopiable page 86 (also 'Seed diary' (red), available on the CD-ROM); a variety of seeds including a coconut, conkers, acorns, beans, and seeds for onion, French marigold, mustard, cress and radish. Beware: some of the most impressive seeds can be very poisonous! The ASE booklet *Be Safe!* gives a comprehensive list of seeds that are suitable for use in the classroom and seeds that should be avoided. Children should always be taught that they must never eat any seeds they find in the wild or in gardens.
Group activities: 1 Cress seeds and kitchen towel (or mung beans, blotting paper and a glass jar), saucers, a magnifier. **2** A selection of seeds of different sizes and colours, such as beans, lentils, dried edible peas, sunflower seeds, popping corn and melon seeds; stiff paper, PVA glue. Seeds such as those mentioned are available from garden centres for growing, but you could try a local health food store or pet shop for larger quantities to use in craft work.
Plenary: A calendar.

BACKGROUND
After the lesson, the growing plants will need to be revisited over a period of time to make observations. Some seeds, such as cress or mung beans, germinate very quickly: you can usually see some results within a few days. Most annuals germinate quite quickly, but will take several weeks before they produce flowers and then seeds. French marigolds will produce seeds before the summer holidays if started off in a warm place in February or March. This will allow the children to see the whole life cycle of a plant, from a growing seed to an adult plant producing seeds. If this is not possible, you could produce 'the one I made earlier' by buying bedding plants (of a similar variety to those sown by the children) from a garden centre, where they will have been forced into growth much earlier than is normal.

The children will also enjoy collecting acorns, horse chestnuts and citrus seeds. These will all germinate, but will take a longer time to do so than the seeds of an annual plant. Acorns and conkers usually need to spend the winter outside, where they are exposed to frost, before they can germinate in the next spring.

Differentiation 💿
Children who need support can use the simple writing frame in 'Seed diary' (green) from the CD-ROM, to keep a record of their plant's progress. To extend children, give them 'Seed diary' (blue). This resource can be made into a book, which the children can use to record the progress of their plants in pictures and words of their own.

In order to avoid reinforcing misconceptions, it is important to remember that before they can grow, seeds need to germinate. This is the process whereby the seed produces its first shoot (plumule) and root (radicle), using its stored food reserves. We all talk about seeds 'growing'; but to be correct, we should talk about seeds germinating and plants growing. The plant does not really begin to grow until it has produced its first green leaf and begun to photosynthesise. Most plants need moisture and warmth to germinate and water, warmth and light to grow successfully. Soil is not a requirement for growth. For example, many tomato crops are now grown hydroponically (with their roots suspended in a liquid nutrient). Think of all the hyacinths grown in water pots on classroom window sills, and the cress seeds germinated on cotton wool or blotting paper.

A classroom window sill may not be the best place to keep any plant. A botanist friend of ours believes it to be one of the harshest habitats in the world: the plants cook in full sunlight during the day, then freeze when the heating goes off at night. All plants need some light, but most do not require full sunlight shining through a window.

STARTER
Look at some of the seeds you have collected. *Where do acorns and conkers (horse chestnuts) come from?* Do the children appreciate that a coconut is actually a seed from a palm tree? Look at some much smaller seeds, such as cress or onion seeds.

MAIN ACTIVITY
Put a variety of seeds on white paper plates, so that they can be seen easily. Provide a plate for each group. Make sure the children understand that they must not eat any of the seeds. Discuss the different types of seeds. *How do we know what the different seeds will grow into?* Look at the pictures on the seed packets. *Do we believe that is what the seeds will grow into? How could we find out?* Ask the children to suggest how the seeds could be planted.

If you have a garden area, some seeds could be sown directly into the ground. Different groups of children could choose a different variety to sow and care for, write labels and mark where the seeds are. Remind them to 'water in' the seeds on planting. Before they start handling soil or compost, make sure that any cuts the children may have are covered. If you are working indoors, make sure that the tables are well covered with newspaper or plastic sheets. Encourage the children to fill the plant pots with compost and put a small number of seeds in each pot, then water them in and make sure that each pot is labelled with the seed type and date of sowing. They can put the pots in a safe but accessible place and wait, checking daily for the appearance of any shoots.

The children could use photocopiable page 86 to keep a simple record of the progress their plants make. If you have access to a camera, the growth of the plants could be recorded in a series of photographs for a class book or display.

GROUP ACTIVITIES
1 Ask the children to put some cress seeds on a damp kitchen towel (or some mung beans on damp blotting paper lining a glass jar), then watch them closely over the next few days. Children can use a magnifier to watch for the first signs of the root and shoot. Tell them that when they appear,

the seeds have 'germinated': taken the first step towards becoming plants. **2** Allow the children to use lots of different seeds to create a group collage: either a picture (such as a big flower) or a pattern. They should draw their picture or pattern first, then choose an appropriate type of seed to fill in each area. Do not provide pieces of paper that are too large, or the children will use too many seeds!

ICT LINK
If you have a digital camera, the children could download a pictorial record onto a computer which could be displayed on a whiteboard.

ASSESSMENT
During the plenary session, ask the children to describe what they would do if they wanted to grow (for example, some radishes). How would they plant them and care for them?

PLENARY
Ask the children to recall the sequence of events involved in planting the seeds. Talk about what they think will happen next. *How long do you think you might have to wait before you see anything happening?* Look at a calendar and estimate when you might see the first shoots, and when the flowers might appear. Mark the estimated date; later, mark the actual date. *How accurate was our estimate?*

OUTCOMES
● Can describe how a seed germinates and grows into a plant.
● Know that different plants come from different types of seed.

LINKS
Unit 1b Lesson 21, Growing plants indoors.
Art: collage.

Lesson 5 ▪ Bean race

Objectives
● To observe the changes in a growing plant.
● To make simple measurements.
● To take information from a chart.

Vocabulary
grow, plant, seed, poisonous, germinate, root, shoot

RESOURCES
Main activity: A version of the 'Jack and the Beanstalk' story; a large plant pot or tub, compost, pea or bean seeds, three or four 1.5m canes, a plant pot to cover the tops of canes for safety, garden twine, a camera (optional), newspaper or a plastic sheet.
Group activities: 1 Strips of thick paper or card (about 15cm × 40cm) to make zigzag books, drawing materials. **2** Paper to make a large class book.
Plenary: A calendar.

BACKGROUND
Peas or beans are a good choice of seed for this investigation, since they germinate and grow quite quickly and the adult plants are quite tall, allowing the children plenty of opportunities for measuring and recording. (Beware: most pea seeds have been treated with fungicide, and children should not be allowed to handle these.) If you make a wigwam of canes in a large pot, you can have a competition between three beans to see which gets to the top of the canes first. Since germination can never be guaranteed, plant two beans by each cane; if both germinate, remove the weaker-looking plant to leave one bean per cane. Bean plants will twine themselves around the cane. However, peas will need a little more support

for their tendrils to hang on to: either use twiggy branches instead of canes or make a web of string around a wigwam of canes, so that the pea plants can be woven in and out.

Peas and beans will both grow indoors, but don't do well in hot conditions. They tend to be healthier if you can grow them outside, or at least put them outside during the day. The children need to take great care as they tend the plants, and particularly when they are measuring them, that they don't knock off the tips of the shoots. If this happens, the plant will shoot again from lower down; but this will take time and the measurements will become somewhat confusing. If you grow the plants indoors, you (or the children) will need to act as bees if you want a crop. Use a soft paintbrush to transfer pollen gently from one flower to another. You will need to do this on several occasions to ensure a good set of seeds. If you can grow the plants outside, then nature will take care of itself. Choose an early variety and sow the seeds between mid-March and early April if you intend to get a crop before the summer holidays. Keep the young plants indoors until all danger of frost has gone.

STARTER

Science lessons are often very effective if started off with a story stimulus. Read the story of 'Jack and the Beanstalk' to the children. *Are there really such things as magic beans? Do bean plants really get that big or grow that quickly? How could we find out?* Have the resources that you are going to use for the activity available, so that the children can begin to make suggestions about what to do.

MAIN ACTIVITY

You will need one initial lesson to set up the investigation, with shorter periods each day to chart the progress of the plants.

Spread some newspaper or a plastic sheet on the floor and have the children sitting around it. Choose two or three to fill a large pot or tub with compost and construct a wigwam from three or four canes to support the growing plants. Choose different children to plant two seeds at the base of each cane, asking them to water them well. Discuss with the children why they are planting two seeds rather than just one. (One seed may not germinate, so you have a 'spare'.) If both germinate, take the weaker one out. You could then have a little fun by putting a different coloured flag (red, blue, green) at the top of each cane and letting the children predict which bean will reach the top of its cane first. Make a chart with the children's names under the colour they have chosen. (Watch out for sabotage if the race gets close!)

Discuss how you are going to measure the growth of the plants. *What equipment will you need? How are you going to record the measurements? Will you need to make a chart? What else will you need to notice?* For example, if you use beans, the children might count the number of leaves each time they measure the height (peas grow too many leaves after a while). They might also record the date on which they see the first flowers. *Why does a plant have flowers? Why do bees and other insects visit flowers?* Talk about how the flowers need to be pollinated if the tiny eggs inside the plant are to be fertilised and grow into seeds (beans or peas).

In subsequent shorter lessons, watch how the

shoots uncurl as they come out of the compost. Note how the leaves are curled at first, and how they unfold and become flatter. Later, note how the bean shoots twine around the canes or how the peas hold on to the sticks with little curly tendrils. Look carefully to see how the new leaves come from the tip of the shoot, while the 'old' leaves at the bottom gradually get bigger. Look for the first flower buds and watch how they open. The children can add entries to their diaries or a class book (see below) when there is something significant to record. Daily records can be kept on a simple chart, and information from this used to update the diaries or class book from time to time.

GROUP ACTIVITIES

1 The children can make a simple zigzag book and use it as a diary to record the growth of the plants. They should make sure all entries are dated. Discuss with them what it will be appropriate to record in their diaries, and how often they are going to check the plants. Every second or third day should be sufficient to note changes, but the plants may need watering

more often if they are in a warm environment.

2 Make a class book about the beans or peas, with children contributing drawings, writing, poems and facts they have found out along with any photographs taken.

ASSESSMENT

Use the children's diaries or contributions to the class book to assess their understanding. Ask them to describe how the plants grew.

PLENARY

After the initial lesson, you may wish to recap on what you have done and organise the first groups to make the observations. The final plenary may occur when you harvest the first peas or beans, or at the end of the topic if time runs out. The discussion will vary, depending on the maturity of the plants. Look at the records and mark the dates on a calendar to see how long the plants took to grow. Make a timeline to show when the first shoots appeared, the first flowers and so on. Talk about how the shoots changed as they grew, and how the leaves changed in size and number.

Differentiation
Organise the children into small mixed-ability groups to take turns to measure the plants.
Group activity 1
Some children may need help in making their zigzag book and may present their observations or thoughts in a pictorial way.
Group activity 2
Some children may contribute written records or stories to the class book.

OUTCOMES
● Can describe the growth of a plant.
● Can make simple measurements.
● Can take information from a chart.

LINKS
Literacy: writing records and stories.
Maths: measuring, counting.

Lesson 6 ▪ Roots

Objectives
● To know that roots change as they grow.
● To know that different plants can have different types of roots.

Vocabulary
root, shoot, seek, absorb

RESOURCES 💿
Main activity: A clear container, gravel or small pebbles, four or five germinated bean seeds, black paper, an elastic band, water, photocopiable page 87 (also 'Roots' (red), available on the CD-ROM), coloured pencils, saucers. Useful containers can be made from plastic soft-drink bottles: simply cut off the top to the desired height and bind the new rim with sticky tape to cover any sharp edges. For Session 3: some weeds, such as dandelions and groundsel, dug up carefully to show the roots (or small pot plants if you do not have access to weeds); a clear container, water.
Group activities: 1 A collection of root vegetables (carrots, parsnips and so on). **2** A display board, old (clean) tights, newspaper, paints and brushes, blue and brown sugar paper, textured wallpaper, different shades of green paper, scissors, pastel paints or crayons.
Plenary: Kitchen towel, a ruler, black paper.

PREPARATION
About a week before the lesson, put some beans (enough for each group to have four or five each) on a damp kitchen towel to germinate. For group activity **2**, cover a display board (or other suitable large area) with brown sugar paper at the bottom and blue sugar paper at the top, representing the ground and the sky.

BACKGROUND
Not all plants have the same root systems. Some plants develop a strong main root or tap root that grows deeply into the ground, while others may have many fine roots that spread out just below the surface. A tap root anchors the plant firmly in the ground. Common examples of this type of root are carrots and parsnips. Dandelions also have a long tap root, which explains why they are so difficult to pull up. Roots usually grow downwards, towards water and in the dark. Their job is to absorb water and nutrients from the growing medium, which is usually soil or compost. The water then passes up through the plant and out through pores (stomata) on the underside of the leaf. As well as absorbing nutrients, the roots anchor the plant securely in the ground to prevent it being blown or washed away. They also play a part in helping to prevent soil erosion by holding the soil together and preventing it from being blown or washed away. Evidence shows that where wholesale logging has taken place without the trees being replaced, the soil has quickly been eroded and the land has become barren.

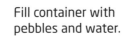

Fill container with pebbles and water.

Wrap in black paper and fasten with elastic bands.

STARTER
Look at the germinated beans and talk about the roots and shoots that have emerged. *How are the roots different from the shoots?*

MAIN ACTIVITY
You will need to revisit this activity over a period of time to observe the changes. Three sessions (to be undertaken by the whole class, working in groups) are suggested below.
Session 1. Talk with the class about what roots do and why they are important. Ask the children for their ideas. Help them to understand that the roots take up water and help to anchor the plant in the soil.
   Each group should fill a clear container with gravel or small pebbles, then fill it with water to just below the top of the pebbles. They should place four or five germinated beans on top of the pebbles, round the edge of the jar, making sure that the beans do not get waterlogged (see illustration). They should wrap black paper around the container to keep out the light, fasten it firmly in place with an elastic band, then place it somewhere safe and leave it for a week.
Session 2. Ask the children to remove the black paper from the jar and look carefully at what is happening. *In which direction are the shoots growing? What is happening to the roots? How much have they grown?* They should start to fill in the record sheet (photocopiable page 86), using a coloured pencil to draw the roots. They should put the black paper back around the container and leave it for a few more days.
Session 3. Let the children look at the roots again. *How have they changed now?* Ask the children to fill in the changes on the record sheet.
   Working with the whole class, dig up some weeds (being careful not to damage the roots). Include a dandelion if possible (but be warned: the roots can go down a surprisingly long way). Gently wash the roots in water to get rid of all the soil or compost, and spread them out on a saucer so that the pattern of growth can be seen. (Alternatively, the roots show up very well if you fill a clear container with water and allow the plant to sit on top.) Gently remove one of the beans from the jar and place it on a saucer. Compare the different root systems. *How are they different? How are they the same? Is there one main root, or are there lots of branches?*

GROUP ACTIVITIES
1 With the group, look at a carrot, a parsnip, and some other root vegetables. Invite the children to use a magnifier to see the smaller roots coming from the central tap root. Cut across one tap root, then cut another lengthways. Observe the difference. Ask the children to draw what they see.
2 Make a large 3D wall display showing views above and below ground. In

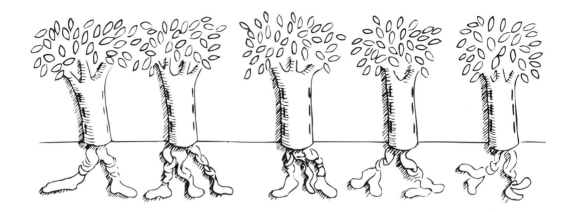

groups, the children can stuff pairs of old brown tights with scrunched-up pages of newspaper, and then paint them roughly with streaks of brown, green and grey. Twist the tights together and staple them to the brown sugar paper to look like thickly growing, gnarled and twisted roots. The children can use appropriately painted textured wallpaper to make tree trunks and branches. Staple these loosely to the blue part of the display board, and stuff behind them for a 3D effect. Ask the children to cut leaves from paper in different shades of green, adding details with pastel paints or crayons. Add these to the picture.

ICT LINK
Display a copy of the record sheet on a whiteboard so that the roots may be drawn in as they grow.

ASSESSMENT
Ask the children to draw a simple plant including the roots. Can they say what roots do? (Absorb water and keep the plant in the ground.)

PLENARY
Discuss how the roots of the beans have grown. Take a bean plant from the jar and gently dry the roots on some kitchen towel. Lay the whole plant on some black paper. *Which is longer, the root or the shoot? Why do roots branch into lots of smaller rootlets?* (So that there is a bigger surface area to absorb water and nutrients.)

OUTCOMES
- Can describe how the roots of a plant grow.
- Know that different plants may have different root systems.

LINKS
Art: making a frieze, 3D modelling.

Lesson 7 ▪ Water for growth

Objective
- To know that plants need water to survive.

RESOURCES
Main activity: A flowering pot plant, such as a busy lizzie (Impatiens), which reacts quickly to a lack of water; a bowl or tray, a watering can, a camera (if available).
Group activities: 1 Drawing materials, paper. **2** Simple picture reference books and CD-ROMs with information about plants growing in deserts.

BACKGROUND
Most plants need a steady supply of water to survive, although many plants

are adapted to living in very dry and arid parts of the planet. Plants take in water through the roots, from where it travels up the stems and into the leaves. Special tubes within the stem (called xylem vessels) carry the water up to the leaves, where it is used in the process of photosynthesis. The water also helps to keep the plant cells turgid (firm), keeping the plant upright so that it can make maximum use of the sunlight. Having served its purpose, excess water is excreted through pores (called stomata) on the underside of the leaves: the water evaporates through the pores and more water is automatically drawn up through the xylem vessels (a process called transpiration). If conditions change and the plant becomes short of water, the leaves will droop or wilt in order to preserve water within the plant. A busy lizzie plant will react quite quickly. If you start the experiment fairly early in the day, you may well have a result before home time - especially if you can put the plant on a warm, sunny window sill. The rates of transpiration and photosynthesis are increased in bright conditions, so the plant will lose water at a faster rate. Most plants revive quite quickly if water becomes available again within a short time, but will die if deprived for long periods. Some plants can survive longer than others. Plants such as succulents and cacti are specially adapted to store water in fleshy stems or leaves. They can withstand the extreme conditions found in deserts (or on classroom window sills!) for long periods of time.

STARTER
Look at a healthy flowering pot plant such as a busy lizzie. Note how the stems are stiff and straight, and how the leaves are crisp and fresh. Are the flowers standing up from the leaves? Feel the compost in the pot: it should be damp.

MAIN ACTIVITY
Talk with the whole class about the things a plant needs to keep it healthy. Ask the children why they think a plant needs water. *What do you think might happen if the plant was left without water?* Suggest that you could carry out an investigation to find out, and ask the children for ideas about how you could do it. This is a simple investigation, and most children should be able to tell you that you simply leave the plant unwatered for a day or two and watch what happens. Discuss where you might leave the plant during this time. Remind the children that they often feel thirsty when they are hot and sweaty. *Do you think plants might be the same? Where would be a hot, bright place to put the plant?* (Perhaps by a sunny window or near a radiator.) Place the plant in the chosen place, checking it every hour or so throughout the day.

Encourage the children to observe what happens as the plant begins to dry out. *How have the leaves changed? Why have they gone floppy and droopy? Are the stems still stiff and upright? How could we revive the plant and make it look crisp and healthy again?* If possible, take photographs of the plant 'before' and 'after'.

Encourage the children to water the plant (the best results are achieved by standing the pot in a bowl of water). *How long does the plant take to revive? Do all the leaves recover?* Sometimes weaker or older leaves will not recover, and will be shed. Busy lizzies are an ideal plant to use as they are very quick to take up water and revive almost miraculously, as long as they have not wilted too far.

Differentiation
Group activity 1
All the children should be able to take part in this activity.
Group activity 2
Most children will appreciate that water is necessary for plants to live. Some children may need help to access reference books or CD-ROMs. They could work in mixed-ability groups in order to help each other.

GROUP ACTIVITIES

1 Ask the children each to draw a picture of what they think the plant would look like after some time without water. Remind them to think carefully about how the leaves will look. *Will they still be crisp, or will they be limp and droopy? Will some of the flowers drop off? Why do you think this will happen?*

2 The children can work in small groups, using reference materials to find information about and pictures of plants that grow in deserts and need little water. Each group should report back to the class on what they have found out.

ASSESSMENT

Assess the children's understanding from their responses in the plenary session.

PLENARY

Talk about what happened to the plant when it was deprived of water. Ask the children why they think the leaves hang down on a plant when it is short of water. It is not necessary for children at this stage to know about transpiration or photosynthesis in detail, but they may know that plants wilt in order to try and save water. Talk about what happened when the plant was watered again. Ask them to explain why the leaves perked up. Remember, at this stage we are not looking for accurate scientific explanations but for the children's own ideas.

OUTCOME

● Know that a plant needs water to survive.

Lesson 8 ▶ In the dark

Objectives
● To know that green plants need light to grow.
● To carry out a simple investigation.

Vocabulary
light, dark

RESOURCES 💿

Main activity: Card for a countdown calendar; a small collection of pot plants; two small plants of a similar type (or two small trays of cress); a dark cupboard or black bin bag.

Group activity: Photocopiable page 88 (also 'In the dark' (red), available on the CD-ROM), drawing materials.

PREPARATION

If small trays of cress will be used, sow three of these (it is always useful to have a spare tray in case of accidents) about ten days before they are required. Make a 'countdown calendar' (see illustration opposite), so that the children can tick off the days until they take the plant out of the cupboard or bag.

BACKGROUND

There is often confusion between growing plants and germinating seeds. Seeds do not generally need light to germinate. They are usually in the soil, where it is dark. The initial germination uses the food reserves in the seed. However, green plants need light if they are to grow. They are the only living things that are able to make their own food. They do this through the process of photosynthesis in the leaves. Plant leaves are green because of the presence of chlorophyll, a pigment that traps light energy and so allows photosynthesis to take place. Water is absorbed through the roots; carbon dioxide is absorbed through the leaves. Using these in the presence of light

Differentiation 💿
Group activity
For children who need support
use 'In the dark' (green) from
the CD-ROM, which asks them
to draw 'before and after'
pictures of the plant that is
placed in the cupboard. For
extension, use 'In the dark'
(blue), which challenges
children to write a few words
to describe the appearance of
the plant alongside their
drawings.

energy, plant cells are able to synthesise sugars, which are then stored as starch.

The by-products of photosynthesis are also important to life on Earth. Large forests are often called 'the lungs of the Earth'. They can absorb vast quantities of carbon dioxide, which is given off by animals and produced by many of our power stations, vehicles and manufacturing processes. As they photosynthesise, plants give off oxygen, which animals need to sustain life. All green plants - including green algae floating near the surface of the world's oceans - also carry out this process.

At this stage, children do not need to understand the above information; but it is useful knowledge for you to have in order not to reinforce any misconceptions.

We put the plants in the cupboard on _____

We will take them out on _____

Mon	Tue	Wed	Thur	Fri	Sat	Sun

STARTER
Talk about where plants usually grow: in the garden, in the house, in fields, in forests and so on.

MAIN ACTIVITY
You will need two sessions for this activity: one to set up the investigation and another to observe the results. This is a whole-class investigation, but it could be done by groups if you have the space and resources.
Session 1. Look at a collection of healthy green plants in the classroom. Ask the children where the plants are greenest (the leaves). Talk about how healthy the plants are, and recap on the names of the different parts. Ask the children what we need to do to help these plants grow healthily. *We need to water them - but not too much. Where is the best place to put them? Does it make a difference whether they are put in a bright place or a dark corner? Do you think the plants will grow better and keep healthier in the light or the dark? Could we do an experiment to find out? Do you have any ideas about how we could carry out an investigation using the classroom plants?* One plant could be put in a really dark cupboard that is not opened very often, or put in a black plastic bin bag (make sure it is well labelled to avoid accidents). Ask the children to explain why another plant should be kept out in the classroom. Make sure they understand that they need a plant that is grown in the light to compare with the one in the dark. If the plants are well watered before the experiment, there should be no need to water them again (unless the room is very warm) during the few days that it takes for some changes to take place. Decide how long you are going to leave the plant in the cupboard. (A week should be long enough.)
Session 2. On the agreed day, take the 'dark' plant from the cupboard or bag. Compare it with the plant left out in the light. *How are they different? How has the plant kept in the dark changed?* (It will have turned yellow, and may have grown longer and more straggly in the search for light.) *What do you think has caused the change?* Leave the plant in the light for a few days and note how well it recovers. (It should turn green again quite quickly.) Review the list of things that a plant needs in order to grow healthily. Remind the children that their previous invesigation showed that plants need water.

GROUP ACTIVITY
Give each child a copy of photocopiable page 88. Ask them to draw and colour the plant (or tray of cress) before it is put in the dark. They should use the same sheet to record the changes at the end of the experiment.

ICT LINK

If you have a digital camera, the children could take photographs at each stage of the experiment and download them onto a computer to keep a pictorial record. Some children may be able to annotate the photographs.

ASSESSMENT

At the end of the experiment, ask the children to describe what would happen to a plant that was left in the dark (or use their recordings to assess their understanding of how a plant needs light to remain healthy).

PLENARY

Talk about how the absence of light has made a difference. Look closely at the healthy plant, and observe how the leaves are spread out so that they can all receive as much light as possible. Look at some different plants: are their leaves arranged in the same way? Ask whether anyone knows why light is so important for plants. Tell the children that green plants can make their own food, but they need light to help them do this.

OUTCOMES

- Know that light is necessary for green plants to grow healthily.
- Can carry out a simple investigation with help.

Lesson 9 ▪ Where does it come from?

Objectives
- To know that plants provide a range of foods.
- To be able to match some foods to their plant of origin.

Vocabulary
food, plant, processed, raw, cooked, changed, origin

RESOURCES ⊙

Main activity: A collection of foods and the plant parts that they are made from. For example: cornflakes or popcorn – a corn on the cob; a tin of baked beans – dried beans; bread, wheat, cereal or pasta – ears of wheat or another cereal; crisps or chips – potatoes; a jar of jam or tin of fruit – the corresponding fruit.

Group activities: 1 Photocopiable page 89 (also 'Where does it come from?' (red), available on the CD-ROM), writing and drawing materials, hand lenses. **2** Cards, writing and drawing materials.

BACKGROUND

Many young children do not realise that a high proportion of the foods they eat are derived from plants. In fact, many do not know that the carrots, peas and so on that come from the supermarket have grown from plants. If possible, take the children somewhere where they can see vegetables growing. If there are allotments in the area, it is worth getting in touch with the local allotment society; it is likely that an allotment holder will be willing for the children to go along and maybe even pick a vegetable or two. If this is not possible, try to buy some vegetables from the organic section of the supermarket, or in the local market, that still have their leaves on and maybe have some earth still clinging to them.

It is possible to grow enough potatoes in a bucket for the class to cook and share. Half-fill a large bucket or pot with compost and plant one seed potato. Place the bucket in good light and keep it watered. As the shoots appear, add more compost to cover them until the bucket is full. Leave for six to eight weeks. When the potatoes are ready, empty the bucket on to a large plastic sheet and harvest your crop!

STARTER

Ask the children what they had for breakfast or lunch. Make a list. Can the children say how many of these foods were made from plants (wholly or in part)? *What about a chocolate biscuit, the bread in a sandwich, rice pudding? Do any of you have a piece of fruit in your lunchbox?* Add 'Yes' or 'No' to each food on the list, according to whether there is plant material in it. Ask the children: *Can you name any of the plants? Can you think of any plants or parts of plants that you eat raw? Are these sometimes cooked as well?*

MAIN ACTIVITY

Put out the foods collected (see Resources) and ask the children to name them. Discuss when they are eaten, and how often the children eat them. *Do you all eat the foods in this collection? Do you all like them? Which are your favourites?* Talk about the fact that these foods are all made from plants. Now put out the plants. Can the children match each food to the plant that it is made from? Can they think of any other foods made from some of the plants?

GROUP ACTIVITIES

1 Give each child a copy of photocopiable page 89. Ask them to draw a chart of some of the foods in the collection, matched to the original plant parts. Remind them to look carefully at the plants and draw as much detail as they can. They might like to look more closely with a hand lens.
2 Challenge the children to devise and create a menu card for a meal consisting of foods made from plants. There should be more than one course. For example, fruit juice, cereal and toast with jam or marmalade would be a suitable three-course breakfast. If they include a pizza or a salad, they should list the toppings that are on the pizza and say what is in the salad.

ICT LINK 💿

Display 'Where does it come from?' (red) on an interactive whiteboard. Complete the worksheet as a class, adding notes onto the interactive whiteboard, using the drawing tools provided on the CD-ROM.

Alternatively, a teaching assistant could work with a small group, or individual children, using 'Where does it come from?' (green) on an individual computer.

ASSESSMENT

Ask the children to name some foods made from plants. Use the photocopiable sheet to assess their understanding of how particular foods are linked to their plant of origin.

PLENARY

Recap on the various foods and their plant of origin. Talk about why plants are so important in our diet; explain that they are not only healthy, but that they add variety and colour too. Ask the children whether humans are the only animals that eat plants. *Can you name some others?* (Sheep, cows, rabbits and so on.) *What do they eat? Do they only eat plants, or do they eat other things like meat, fish, eggs and cheese?* Discuss the fact that many people in the world do not eat meat or fish, but are able to remain healthy.

OUTCOMES
● Know that plants provide a range of foods.
● Can match some foods to their plant of origin.

LINKS
Unit 1a Lesson 20, Food for life.

ENRICHMENT
Lesson 10 ▪ A medley of fruits

Objectives
● To know that some foods are prepared directly from plants.
● To know that there is a wide variety of fruits.

RESOURCES
A range of fruits (such as apple, pear, banana, kiwi fruit, mango, orange and pineapple), chopping boards, school dinner knives, a fruit salad bowl, dishes, spoons and fruit juice.

MAIN ACTIVITY
Look at the collection of fruits. Ask the children to identify them, then to sort them by various criteria (colour, shape, whether we peel them and so on). Remind the children of the importance of washing their hands before preparing food and show them how to use the knives safely. Some hard fruits, such as a pineapple, may have to be cut ready for the children to cut into smaller chunks. Cut up the fruit together and prepare the fruit salad. This could be tasted at the end of the lesson, or later on in the day.

ASSESSMENT
As the children are sorting, note how many fruits they can identify. Observe how safely they handle a knife.

PLENARY
Remind the children that the fruit salad has been made directly from the fruits, which have not been cooked or changed (except by chopping). Draw a contrast with some other foods from plants that the class have looked at.

Differentiation
This activity is accessible to all. Some children may be able to find out where the various fruits come from, using reference materials.

OUTCOMES
● Know that some foods are prepared directly from plants.
● Know that there is a wide variety of fruits.
● Be able to handle knives safely.

Lesson 11 ▪ From plant to plate

Objective
● To know that some foods are processed by humans, and some are taken directly from the plant.

RESOURCES
Cress (grown in the classroom or purchased), bread, a spread made from vegetable oil, empty bread packets.

MAIN ACTIVITY
Discuss the various foods that go into making a cress sandwich. Explain that they are all foods from plants. *Which one looks like the plant? Which ones don't? Why?* Make the sandwiches and share them.

Differentiation
Some children may be able to examine the bread packets to find out what else is in the sandwich bread in addition to wheat.

ASSESSMENT
During the plenary session, note which children can distinguish between foods taken directly from plants and foods that have been processed.

PLENARY
Ask the children to think of and name some of the other foods from plants that they sometimes have in sandwiches, such as jam, peanut butter, tomatoes, salad or chocolate spread. Which ones can they still recognise as being parts of plants?

OUTCOME
● Know that some foods that are made from plants have been processed and changed by humans, and some are taken directly from the plant and are not changed.

Lesson 12 ◗ All around us

Objective
● To know that the environment is the surroundings in which plants and animals live.

Vocabulary
environment, habitat, sheltered, damp, warm, dark, sunny, clouds, windy, up, down, around

RESOURCES
Main activity: The school grounds and the surrounding area.
Group activities: 1 Drawing and painting materials, paper. **2** A display board, collage materials, scissors, adhesive, drawing and painting materials, paper.

BACKGROUND
The environment consists of everything around us - indoors and outdoors - and children need to be made aware of this. They might begin by looking at their classroom and thinking about the area in which they work, which is a small part of the wider environment. Children may only be familiar with one or two aspects of the environment, such as school, home and the immediate surrounding area. It is useful, therefore, to visit different areas (such as woods, the seaside, a local park, a farm or a shopping centre and so on) in order to give the children a wider experience, so that they can make comparisons.

Children very often do not realise that people have had a great impact on the environment, and that the buildings and other structures that we have made are as much a part of our environment as woods, fields, mountains and rivers. Even at Key Stage 1, they can start to be aware that they have a role in caring for the environment - for example, by always putting litter in bins provided (or taking it home), and keeping the classroom and cloakroom tidy and pleasant. It is important for the children to understand that they should not cause damage to trees or street furniture (for example), as this can make the environment less pleasant for other people and other living things.

STARTER
Ask the children to look around the classroom. *What do you notice about the classroom environment? Is it too hot or too cold, or just right? Is it light enough for you to work comfortably? Can you find things when you need them? Do the displays, plants and collections make the room attractive? Is there anything you would change to improve the environment of your classroom?*

MAIN ACTIVITY
Talk to the children about going out for a walk to look at the environment outside the school. Stress that the environment means everything that is all around us. Discuss the things they might look for. They need to look down at their feet and notice the different surfaces they walk on. They need to

look around at bushes, flowers, walls, buildings and hedges. They need to see where shadows fall, and which places might be windy or sheltered from the wind. They need to look up and notice the trees and the sky above them. Remind them never to look directly at the Sun, as this can damage their eyes.

Walk around the school and look at the different areas and the conditions within them. Look for shady areas. *Why are they shady? What is making the shadows? Which places are sunny? Are there any windy places? Does litter collect in a particular corner? Where would you go to get out of the wind? Are some areas warmer or cooler than others?* Look for different surfaces – for example, the playing field, playground, paths, pond, wildlife area and areas under trees where the grass is thin. Have a look at a tree that might be suitable for the class to 'adopt' later (see Lesson 20, Our tree). *Is it making shadows? Is anything growing underneath it? What are the leaves like?* Talk about the fact that the environment is all around us, and almost every area is home to some plants or animals. Turn over some damp leaves and wood. Are there any woodlice? (Make sure that you put back anything you may have moved.) Look at the lichen on the path. Even though this is a hard, dry surface where people walk, something lives there and it is part of the environment.

GROUP ACTIVITIES

1 Ask each child to draw or paint a picture of their favourite area from the walk. Encourage them to put in as much detail as possible.
2 Make a large picture of the school's environment on a display board. This could be collaged or painted by small groups of children. Other children could then paint or make pictures of flowers, birds, animals, children playing and so on; these could be cut out and added to the big picture.

ASSESSMENT

Ask the children to describe some features in the environment, indoors or outside. Ask: *What is the environment? What lives in it?* (The environment is all around us and is where plants and animals live.)

PLENARY

Reinforce the idea that the environment is all around us. Remind the children that plants and animals, including humans, live in the environment. Ask the children to say what they have seen. *Which was your favourite area? Was there an area that you didn't like? Why didn't you like it? What could be done to make it better? Could we do anything to make the classroom a better, more attractive environment?*

Talk about the tree that the class has looked at as being a habitat (that is, a particular 'home' area) within the environment for many small creatures, to whom it offers shelter and food. Talk about where the children live, play and go to school – this is their habitat, and is part of their environment.

OUTCOME

● Know that the environment is all around us, and that it is where plants and animals live.

LINKS

Unit 1b Lesson 20, Our tree.

Lesson 13  My weather chart

RESOURCES 💿

Main activity: A large thermometer with a comparative scale; a weather chart and symbols. A range of commercially produced weather charts are available, or you may prefer to make a simple one of your own. You may choose to have one that is changed daily, or one that can be used to record the weather over a week or a month. This lesson plan assumes that the chart used will be similar to photocopiable page 90 (also 'My weather chart' (red), from the CD-ROM).

Group activities: 1 Small notebooks for diaries, or paper for children to make their own. **2** Reference books about weather in other parts of the world, particularly where conditions are extreme (for example in deserts, the Arctic and rainforests).

Plenary: A large outline for a pictogram or block graph.

BACKGROUND

The weather has a profound effect on people's lives. It affects what we wear, how we travel, how we do our work, and sometimes even the type of work that we do. The weather can affect how people feel and how they behave. The UK has a 'temperate' (mild or moderate) climate. The Gulf Stream, bringing warm water from the tropics, moderates our temperature; and being an island, we have sufficient rainfall to keep the land green and fertile. The prevailing winds are from the west, so the western areas (such as Ireland, Wales, Cumbria and the Western Isles) tend to have a higher average rainfall than, for example, East Anglia. Because the UK has such a varied weather pattern, keeping a weather record can be fun: the weather is rarely the same two days running! However, we do get more settled periods of weather in the summer, so this may not be the best time of the year to carry out a weather survey if the objective is to look for changes.

Children may have seen reports on TV about floods and hurricanes in other parts of the world, and know that these are caused by extremes of weather. They may be aware that some parts of the world are always very hot or very cold.

STARTER

If possible, go outside and make first-hand observations of the weather. Talk about what the weather is like today. *Is it hot or cold? Is it wet or dry? Are there any clouds in the sky? Is there any wind?*

MAIN ACTIVITY

Show all the children the weather chart and explain how it works. Discuss how often the chart needs to be changed. *How can we make sure that the record is fair? Do we need to record the weather at the same time each day?* Look at the symbols you are using and discuss what each one means (alternatively, the children could suggest symbols and make their own). Encourage the children to think again about what the weather is like today. Ask them to select the symbols that will best represent this weather.

Talk about what is meant by 'warm' or 'cold' weather. *How do we know it is warmer or colder than yesterday?* Present a large thermometer with a comparative scale: *cold, colder, warm, warmer, hot.* A large standard thermometer can be adapted by sticking a strip of paper or card down the side and writing on the appropriate words. Record the temperature word for today on the chart.

Differentiation
Group activity 1
To support children, use 'My weather chart' (green) from the CD-ROM. The activity involves simply cutting and pasting weather symbols onto the chart. To extend children, use 'My weather chart' (blue), which asks the children to record the temperature in degrees Celsius.
Group activity 2
Encourage the children to work in small mixed-ability groups and help each other.

Ask the children if any of them have seen a weather forecast on television. *Why is it important to know what the weather is going to be like? Who might need to know?* The children might need to know if they were planning a picnic or a barbecue. Farmers need to know if they are planning to spray or harvest their crops. Fishermen and seafarers need to be warned of impending storms, and pilots need to know whether it will be safe to fly. *Who else might need to know, and why?*

GROUP ACTIVITIES

1 Give the children a copy of photocopiable page 90 and ask them to keep a weather diary to record the weather each day.
2 Let the children use simple reference books to find out about weather in parts of the world that are very hot or very cold, or that have a lot of rain or no rain at all.

ICT LINKS

The children could use the graphing tool from the CD-ROM to create a block graph of the results of their weather chart.

ASSESSMENT

Ask the children to describe different types of weather. Look at their weather diaries. Note those children who are able to take information from the pictogram or block graph (see below).

PLENARY

This might take place at the end of the week, when there are several days' records to consider. Discuss what the weather has been like during the week. *How has it changed? How do we know? What has helped us to remember?* (The weather chart.) Help the children to transfer the information on the weather chart to a large pictogram or block graph. Ask: *Is it easier to find out now how many cloudy days we had in the week, or how many days it rained?* Encourage the children to use the graph to find out these things.

OUTCOMES

● Know that there are different types of weather.
● Can enter simple information on a chart.
● Can use the information from a chart to construct a pictogram or block graph.

LINKS

Maths: drawing block graphs.
Literacy: keeping a diary.
Geography: weather.

ENRICHMENT

Lesson 14 ◗ Measuring rainfall

Objective
● To measure rainfall over a period of time.

RESOURCES
A watering can, a rain gauge (use a commercially produced one or make a simple one from an empty, clear plastic bottle – see illustration below), a measuring cylinder, a rain chart (or the weather chart from Lesson 13), felt-tipped pens.

MAIN ACTIVITY
Discuss the fact that we have different amounts of rain on different days, and sometimes it is important to know how much rain has fallen. Use a watering can to demonstrate how a rain gauge collects the rain as it falls. Choose a suitable place to put the gauge outside. Make sure that it is firmly fixed so it cannot tip over. Make a chart to record the rainfall each day (or add this to the class weather chart).

ASSESSMENT
Note those children who are able to measure the rainfall and transfer the information to their chart or the class chart. Note those who can take information from the chart at the end of the period.

Differentiation
Some children could mark the side of the rain gauge with a different-coloured felt-tipped pen for each day, and use this to note the days on which the most and least rain fell. Others may be able to measure the amount of rainfall in millilitres, using a measuring cylinder.

PLENARY
Find out on which days you had the most and the least rain. *How much rain has fallen altogether during the week?*

OUTCOMES
● Know how to use a simple rain gauge.
● Can enter information on a simple chart.
● Can retrieve information from a chart.

Lesson 15 ◗ When the wind blows

Objective
● To make and use a simple wind meter to measure the strength and direction of the wind.

RESOURCES
Strips cut from three or four different weights of plastic sheeting (carrier bags, freezer bags etc), several short pieces of dowel or cane (or large curtain rings), a simple compass.

MAIN ACTIVITY
Tie three or four plastic strips (one of each weight) to the top of each short stick (or to each curtain ring). Go outside with the children and hold these wind meters up high. *How hard is the wind blowing? Which way is it blowing? Does it always blow in the same direction? Is the strength of the wind always the same?*

Differentiation
Some children may be able to use a compass to find the direction in which the wind is blowing, while others may note that it is blowing (for example) towards the school gate.

ASSESSMENT
During the plenary, note which children are able to say how we know which way the wind is blowing and understand that the heavier the 'streamer', the more wind is required to move it.

PLENARY
Talk about other signs that tell us which way the wind is blowing, such as washing on a line, trees bending or smoke from a chimney.

OUTCOME
● Know that the strength and direction of the wind can be measured.

ENRICHMENT
Lesson 16 ▪ The seasons

Objective
● To know how the environment changes as the year passes through the seasons (autumn).

Vocabulary
spring, summer, autumn, winter, lighter, darker, longer, shorter, day length

RESOURCES ◉
Main activity: Pictures showing each of the four seasons (preferably depicting the same scene; ideally photographs scanned onto computer and then displayed on an interactive whiteboard), a camera, chalk, emulsion paint (optional), a large PE hoop, a small practice ball, a piece of wire or paper clip, a large yellow ball or balloon (if you use a balloon, it will need replacing as it gets old and deflates), crêpe paper in four seasonal colours.
Group activities: 1 Drawing materials, paper, thin card, adhesive.
2 Photocopiable page 91 (also 'The seasons' (red), available on the CD-ROM), drawing materials.

PREPARATION
Divide a large hoop into four sections and wrap each section in different-coloured crêpe paper appropriate to each of the four seasons. Hang the hoop horizontally from the ceiling or other suitable place. Use a piece of wire or a paper clip to make a hook by which to attach the practice ball to the hoop. The practice ball represents the Earth, and the hoop its orbit. Hang the yellow ball in the centre of the hoop to represent the Sun. Make small labels for the months of the year and attach them to the hoop within the appropriate seasons. (See diagram below.) Using the hoop helps the children to appreciate that the seasons are cyclical and come round each year. (A similar hoop method can be used to demonstrate the orbit and position of the planets in other lessons.)

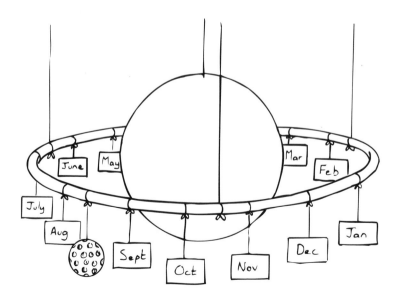

BACKGROUND

The changing seasons affect our lives in many ways. However, these days, the traditional four seasons are becoming increasingly hard to distinguish. Climate changes have resulted in much milder, less 'seasonal' weather throughout the year. Although the changes in trees and other plants still give a some indication of the seasons, blossom in winter, and trees shedding their leaves in summer are becoming more common. We notice changes in temperature and rainfall, but the change that has the greatest effect on us is probably that of the length of the day (that is, the number of daylight hours). This change is also the same from year to year, not being affected by climate change and global warming

As the days lengthen in the spring, plants are stimulated into growth and many animals (such as birds and frogs) mate and prepare to raise their young. We have the seasons because of the tilt of the Earth's axis, not because we are nearer to the Sun at any particular time (the Earth's orbit around the Sun is slightly elliptical; those in the northern hemisphere are actually nearer to the Sun in the middle of January). Summer occurs in the northern hemisphere when the North Pole is tilted towards the Sun. The South Pole is obviously tilted away from the Sun at this time, so the southern hemisphere experiences winter. Six months later, halfway through the Earth's annual orbit of the Sun, the positions are reversed: the South Pole is tilted towards the Sun and the North Pole away from it, giving summer in the southern hemisphere and winter in the north. The change in day length is less noticeable in the tropics, but becomes greater the nearer to the poles you go. Few people live in the Antarctic, but the people living in the Arctic regions experience 24 hours of daylight in midsummer, while in midwinter the Sun does not rise at all.

Five- and six-year-old children will have had little experience of seasonal change that they can remember, so it is important to help them notice the changes that occur as each season comes round, such as leaves falling from the trees, snow on the ground and so on. It is helpful to go on the same walk, or visit the same areas in each season, so that the children can observe specific changes. Try to go at the same time of day if possible, especially if you choose to look at the shadows.

STARTER

Show the children the pictures depicting the four seasons (see Resources). Talk about what is in each picture and point out the differences between them. Ask the children to name each season.

MAIN ACTIVITY

Carry out this lesson in autumn. Ask the class: *Which season do you think we are in now? Which picture looks the most like how it is outside?* Go outside and look together for some of the things in the picture. Look at the colour of the leaves on the trees. *What is happening to the leaves?* Take some photographs. *Do any of the trees have fruits or berries?* Look for acorns, conkers, apples, blackberries and the seed heads of different plants. Ask the children to collect a few, so that they can set them in plant pots and watch them grow; but tell them not to collect many fruits or seeds, as the birds and small creatures will depend on them for food in the winter. Autumn is a good time to look for spiders' webs, particularly if you go out on a misty morning when the dew clings to them like tiny diamonds. You may see flocks of birds gathering ready to fly off to warmer lands. *Why do they need to leave?* (Think about what they eat: many live on insects that are not available here in the winter, so they have to travel to where they can find food.)

Look at the shadows. *How long are they?* If you have a suitable surface, you could draw round a child's shadow with chalk and fill the shadow in with emulsion paint so that it lasts for a while.

When does it begin to get dark in the evening? Can you play outside until

bedtime, or do you have to come in sooner? Is it light when you wake up in the morning? The children may not have noticed, so this could be a small homework task.

Back in the classroom, show the children the hoop and explain, very simply, that we have different seasons because the Earth travels around the Sun. Explain that each section of the hoop shows a different season. Add the photographs to the autumn section. Show the children the picture of a tree in the four seasons, from the CD-ROM.

GROUP ACTIVITIES
1 Remind the children of some of the things they have seen. Ask each child to choose one of the things and draw a picture of it. Make sure that the children don't all choose the same thing to draw. Cut out the pictures and mount them on card; hang some of them from the autumn section of the hoop, and use the rest as a wall display.
2 Give each child a copy of photocopiable page 91 to complete.

ASSESSMENT
Ask the children to name the four seasons. Can they describe some of the changes they might find in autumn?

PLENARY
Talk about the things you have seen, and ask the children what else happens at this time of year. Some children may have birthdays that can be added to the hoop as they come round. Some may celebrate Harvest Festival or Bonfire Night. Ask the children which season comes next. *What changes might we expect in that season? What will the weather be like? What will look different?*

OUTCOME
● Can describe some changes associated with autumn.

Lesson 17 ◻ Winter

Objective
● To know how the environment changes as the year passes through the seasons (winter).

RESOURCES
Autumn and winter pictures (or appropriate reference books), chalk, emulsion paint (optional), a camera, the 'seasons hoop' from Lesson 16.

MAIN ACTIVITY
Remind the children of the autumn picture on the CD-ROM and discuss what they saw. Look at the winter picture and talk about any changes. *What will you expect to see outside?* Go outside and revisit the places looked at in the autumn walk. *How have things changed?* If possible, draw a new shadow outline on top of the old one and paint it in a different colour. *How has the shadow changed?* Take photographs. Add new photographs to the seasons hoop. Take a photograph, outside, of the children dressed and ready to go home at the end of the school day. *What time does it get dark? Is it dark when you get up?*

ASSESSMENT
During the plenary, ask the children to describe some changes from autumn to winter.

Differentiation
Some children may not remember everything, so give them a specific area (for example, a tree or flower bed) to look for. Other children could take some weather readings (see Lesson 13).

PLENARY
Talk about what you have seen. Look at the photographs taken in the autumn, and compare them with what the children have just seen. *How have things changed? What has happened to the shadows? What do you think has caused these changes?*

OUTCOME
● Can describe some changes associated with winter.

Lesson 18 ◻ Spring

Objective
● To know how the environment changes as the year passes through the seasons (spring).

RESOURCES
Winter and spring pictures (or appropriate reference books), a camera, chalk, emulsion paint (optional), the 'seasons hoop'.

MAIN ACTIVITY
Remind the children of the winter picture. Look at a spring picture and talk about the differences the children can see. Go out and revisit the places looked at in autumn and winter. *How have the places changed?* Take more photographs for the collection. Draw a new shadow outline. *Is it still dark when you get up in the morning and go to bed at night?* Add photographs to the spring section of the hoop. Take another 'home time' picture.

ASSESSMENT
During the plenary, ask the children to describe some changes from winter to spring.

Differentiation
Where children need support, focus their attention on a specific area outside. To extend children, ask them to measure the lengths of the three shadows and begin to think about the changes: How have they changed? Why have they changed? Where might the next one be?

PLENARY
Talk about what you have seen. Compare the photographs taken in spring and winter. Talk about how the hoop is filling up. *How many seasons are left? What will that season be like?*

OUTCOME
● Can describe some changes associated with spring.

ENRICHMENT
Lesson 19 ◖ Summer

Objective
● To know how the environment changes as the year passes through the seasons (summer).

Differentiation
Allow children who need support to compare the changes to one specific area over the year. Extend children by asking them to make a block graph of the shadow lengths, and to use a compass to find in what direction the shadows lie.

RESOURCES
Pictures of all seasons (or appropriate reference books), a camera, chalk, emulsion paint (optional), a compass, the 'seasons hoop'.

MAIN ACTIVITY
Remind the children about what they saw in the spring. Look at the spring picture and photographs, then look at the summer picture. Discuss the differences. Retrace the walk taken in previous seasons. Note changes and take photographs. Draw a new shadow outline. Was the children's prediction from the last time correct? Add new photographs to the seasons hoop. Take another 'home time' picture.

ASSESSMENT
During the plenary, ask the children to describe some of the changes from spring to summer. *What will happen after that? Which season will it be?*

PLENARY
Look at the four season pictures and the photographs taken throughout the year. *What changes have taken place? What is going to happen next? Why have these changes taken place?*

OUTCOMES
● Can describe some changes associated with summer.
● Know that we have four seasons each year.

ENRICHMENT
Lesson 20 ◖ Our tree

Objective
● To know that plants change according to the seasons.

Vocabulary
spring, summer, autumn, winter, seasons, change, grow, flower (verb), die, tree, plant, bush, branches, leaves, flowers

RESOURCES 💿
Main activity: A tree in the locality, paper or books for diaries, a measuring tape, a camera (if possible), blank paper, chunky wax crayons.
Group activities: 1 Photocopiable page 92 (also 'Our tree' (red), from the CD-ROM). **2** Simple reference materials about trees.

PREPARATION
Find a tree in the locality that will make a suitable subject for the children to observe in each season. You will need a deciduous tree, not an evergreen. If you can, choose a tree that changes dramatically through the year – for example, one that has very obvious blossom or fruits, or has brightly coloured leaves in the autumn, such as an apple tree or horse chestnut.

BACKGROUND
Children often have very stereotypical ideas about what trees look like in the various seasons, and have never looked closely to make observations.

Trees are flowering plants, and many of them are wind-pollinated. Wind-pollinated trees (such as the silver birch) often develop flowers before the leaves appear, so that the wind can carry the pollen through the bare branches to other trees. Many trees have relatively insignificant flowers, and the children will have to look closely to find them.

Trees are the biggest living things on the planet, and modern methods of dating have proved that some living trees are more than 1000 years old. In Britain, we have a rich heritage of very old trees – so much so that we tend to take them for granted. Because there are so many of them, they are often not protected; whereas in some countries that have far fewer ancient trees, they are all mapped and have rigorous protection orders on them.

Big, old oak trees are frequently hollow. This is not because they are beginning to die: it is part of the way in which the tree continues to thrive. The fact that the tree is hollow means that it is more pliable and can bend slightly with the wind, so there is less danger of it being blown over. The organic material from the core of the tree falls to the ground, and the nutrients it contains are recycled. This material provides food and habitats for many insects and other small creatures. Some hollow trees are nearly big enough for a whole class to stand inside - but for obvious reasons, this should not be attempted!

STARTER

Before leaving the classroom, remind the children of the need for sensitivity towards and care of all living things. Remind them that plants are living things. Recap on the fact that trees are flowering plants. Explain that the children are going to look closely at the tree and find out as many things about it as they can. Talk about the things they should look for: the shape and condition of the tree, the bark, any leaves, flowers or fruits. A good way of ensuring that they do note and discuss what they see is to tell them that each group is going to report back to the class and tell everyone what they have observed.

MAIN ACTIVITY

Take the children outside to look at the tree that they are going to 'adopt'. Look at the chosen tree from a distance and ask the children what they notice. Go close up to the tree and make more observations. *What is the bark like? Is it rough or smooth? Are there leaves, flowers or fruits? What shape are they? Do they smell? What colour is the bark? Is the bark on the trunk a different colour from that on the branches? Is the trunk a different colour on one side from the other? Could that be because the wind and rain come mainly from one direction? Is there any fruit on the tree?* Encourage

the children to measure the circumference of the tree using a tape measure. They can collect any leaves already shed by the tree or take rubbings of the bark, including different bark areas (being careful not to damage any growth on the bark).

Take the children out to look closely at the tree in the spring, summer, autumn and winter. If possible, take photographs of the tree on every visit so that the changes can be compared in the classroom. The children should keep a 'tree diary' to record their observations over the year.

GROUP ACTIVITIES

1 Give each child a copy of photocopiable page 92 to complete for the appropriate season. Remind them about what they saw when they were looking at the tree.
2 The children can work in small groups with reference materials to find out what type of tree the 'adopted' tree is and compare it with other types of tree. For example: *Do all trees lose their leaves? Are they all the same size? Are they all the same shape?* Each group could report their findings back to the rest of the class.

ASSESSMENT

Use the photocopiable sheet for assessment. When the children report back their findings, note whether they have observed a range of details (such as shape and condition of tree, bark, leaves, flowers or fruits).

PLENARY

After each visit to the tree, talk to the children about what they have observed. After the first visit, draw their attention to the fact that they needed to make a record of their observations so that they will be able to make comparisons on future visits. For example, they will be able to compare times when the twigs were bare, had leaves, had flowers and so on.

OUTCOME

● Know that plants change according to the seasons.

LINKS

Unit 1b Lesson 3, Make a flower.
Maths: measuring.
English: speaking and listening.

ENRICHMENT
Lesson 21 ◗ Growing plants indoors

Objective
● To know how to care for growing plants indoors.

RESOURCES
Plastic trays, such as those used for cat litter or school drawers; compost, small plastic mirrors, stones, grass seeds, twigs, lolly sticks, a small hand-held garden spray, small plants or cuttings.

MAIN ACTIVITY
The children work in groups, using the materials provided to design and make a model garden in a tray. They can use small mirrors for ponds, and use small stones to build walls, paths and rockeries. Garden seats can be made from lolly sticks, and trees from twigs. They can sow grass seeds and watch the lawn grow. Other small plants could be planted. The gardens will need daily care to keep the plants healthy (cutting the grass, removing dead flowers and leaves, spraying with water to keep fresh). The children could also be encouraged to bring in their own materials as part of a homework activity.

ASSESSMENT
Note the children's responses during the plenary session. Do they show an understanding of the care needed to create and maintain their indoor gardens?

PLENARY
Discuss how the children made their gardens, and what they will need to do to help the plants grow and keep them healthy.

Differentiation
All the children should be able to access this activity.

OUTCOME
● Can describe what needs to be done to care for plants indoors.

Lesson 22 ◗ Assessment

Objectives
● To assess whether the children recognise how the environment changes according to the season.
● To assess whether the children know that plants have roots, stems, leaves and flowers.

RESOURCES ◉
Assessment activities: 1 Plain paper, divided into four sections, pencils, crayons. **2** Photocopiable page 93 (also 'Assessment' (red), available on the CD-ROM), pencils.

STARTER
Talking to the whole class, ask the children to tell you about some of the things they have learned in this unit. *What can you remember about plants and seasons? Do plants need water? Do plants look the same throughout the year? What different kinds of weather can you think of? When in the year is it coldest? When is it hottest?*

ASSESSMENT ACTIVITY 1
Tell the children to add the headings Spring, Summer, Autumn and Winter to the sections of their paper. They should then draw or describe the appearance of a tree or a flower and the weather under each heading, to show how plants and their environment change throughout the year according to the season.

ANSWERS
Accept any drawing or description showing some differences between the seasons.

LOOKING FOR LEVELS

Most children will be able to describe some changes between at least two seasons. For example: cold in winter and warmth in summer; bare trees in winter and leafy trees in summer. More able children will be able to draw or describe changes in more detail and will notice more subtle changes between the seasons. For example, some children may show blossom on the trees in spring, and leaves and fruit on the trees in summer.

ASSESSMENT ACTIVITY 2

Give each child a copy of photocopiable page 93. Read through the words with the children and ask them to draw the picture of a plant, following the instructions on the photocopiable.

ICT LINK

Display 'Assessment' (red) on an interactive whiteboard. Complete as a class or use as part of the plenary to discuss the children's responses to the assessment task.

ANSWERS

Accept any drawing of a recognisable plant showing all the features on the list.

LOOKING FOR LEVELS

The expectation for Year 1/Primary 2 children is that they should all be able to name the main parts of a flowering plant.

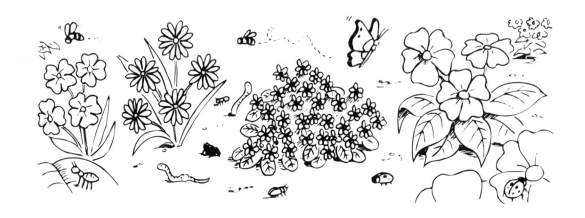

Make a flower

petals

leaves

PHOTOCOPIABLE

Seed diary

Our seeds were _____

They should grow to look like this:

We sowed the seed on _____

We did this by _____

_____

The first proper leaves appeared on _____

They looked like this:

We saw the first flower buds on _____

They were the colour _____

The first flower opened on _____

It was the colour _____ and looked like this:

We collected some seeds on _____

We are going to save some and
sow them next year.

Stick your seeds
here

SCHOLASTIC

Roots

■ Look carefully at the roots of the bean. Draw how they have grown.

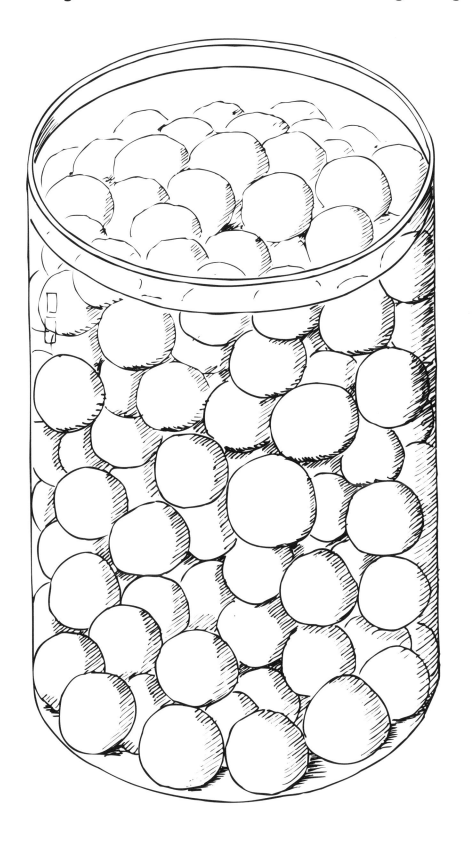

Illustration © Kirsty Wilson

PHOTOCOPIABLE

In the dark

Our plant looked like this before it went in the dark. It has leaves that are

the colour _____

After _____ days in the dark, it looked like this.

It has leaves that are the colour _____

■SCHOLASTIC

Where does it come from?

◼ Draw and label the food and the plant that it came from.

Food	Plant it came from

My weather chart

	Week 1	Week 2	Week 3
Monday			
Temperature			
Tuesday			
Temperature			
Wednesday			
Temperature			
Thursday			
Temperature			
Friday			
Temperature			

Illustration © Kirsty Wilson

■SCHOLASTIC

The seasons

In _____

We collected these things

The trees looked like this

The weather was usually

PHOTOCOPIABLE

Our tree

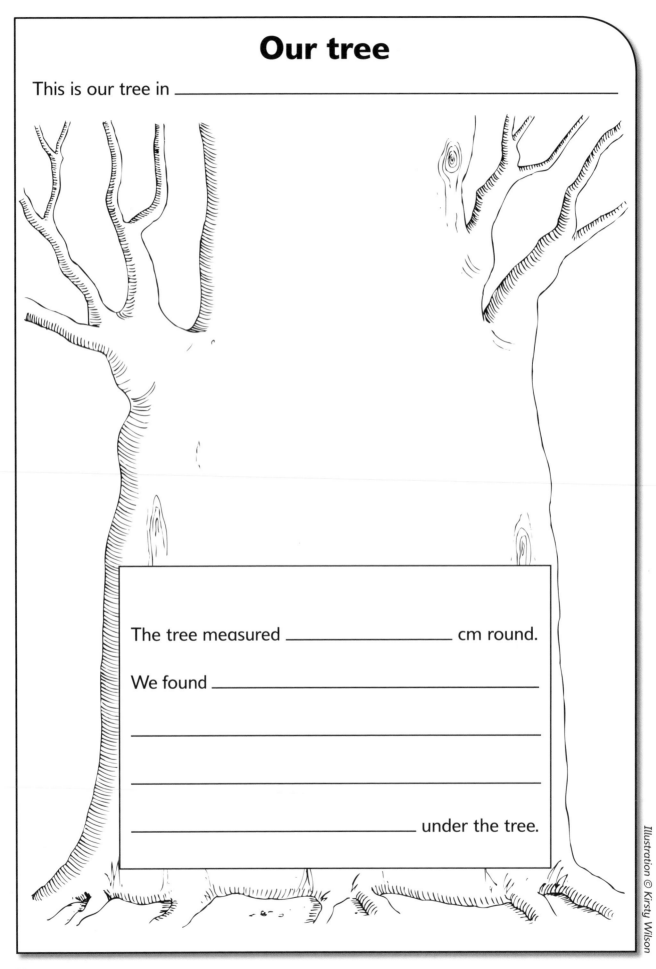

This is our tree in _____

The tree measured _____ cm round.

We found _____

_____

_____

_____ under the tree.

■SCHOLASTIC

Assessment

◼ Draw a plant with all these things labelled:

flower

stem

leaf

roots

◼ Put a bud on a stem in your drawing.
◼ Can you label the petals on the flower?

CHAPTER 3 Sorting and using materials

Lesson	Objectives	Main activity	Group activities	Plenary	Outcomes
Lesson 1 Properties card game	• To know that different materials have different properties.	Sorting materials into two groups, according to given criteria and then to their own criteria.	• Sorting materials according to three given criteria. • Name materials to match properties on cards.	Review names and properties of materials.	• Can name the properties of some common materials.
Lesson 2 Many materials	• To be able to identify some common materials.	Match labels to samples of common materials.		Discuss the different forms that materials, especially plastics, can take.	• Can identify and name some common materials.
Enrichment Lesson 3 What's in the bag?	• To know that the senses can be used to explore materials. • To use the sense of touch to explore and identify materials.	Use a feely bag to describe or identify a hidden object.	• Continue main activity. • Make a feely picture.	Review 'touch' vocabulary.	• Know that the sense of touch can help to identify materials.
Enrichment Lesson 4 What sound does it make?	• To know that the senses can be used to explore materials. • To be able to distinguish different materials by sound.	Experiment with percussion sounds. Guess a hidden material used to make a sound. Compare the sounds of different shakers and beaters.		Discuss why different materials make different sounds.	• Know that the sense of hearing can help to identify materials.
Enrichment Lesson 5 Say what you see	• To know that the senses can be used to explore materials. • To be able to observe closely and describe materials.	Describe a material in visual terms; other children try to identify it.		Review vocabulary. Discuss the importance of detailed observation, using all the senses.	• Know that the sense of sight can help to identify materials.
Lesson 6 It could be made from...	• To know that different objects can be made from the same material.	Sort a collection of objects according to type, then according to material.	• Play 'Material dominoes' with objects. • Say what materials some objects might be made from.	Discuss the usefulness and limitations of certain materials in different contexts.	• Know that different things can be made from the same material.
Lesson 7 What is it made from?	• To know that an object can be made up of several materials.	Look at some everyday objects made from more than one material; identify what materials have been used and why.	• Identify the materials used to make some composite objects. • Suggest some unsuitable materials for these objects, and explain why.	Review the work done, focusing on the properties of the materials.	• Know that some objects are made up of more than one material. • Can identify some of these materials. • Can explain, in simple terms, why different materials are used for different parts of an object.
Lesson 8 Materials at school	• To know that a range of materials are used in our environment. • To know that materials can be used in a variety of ways.	Walk around the school, inside and outside; identify materials and relate their uses to their properties.	• Place labels on a photocopiable drawing of a school (inside). • Place labels on a photocopiable drawing of a school (outside).	Children report back on findings and compare materials used indoors to those used outdoors.	• Can recognise and name some familiar materials in their environment. • Know that some have been used in a variety of ways.
Lesson 9 Magnets	• To know that some materials are magnetic, but most are not.	Predict whether various materials will be attracted to a magnet, then test.	• Predict for a new set of objects, then test. • Make a fridge magnet.	Establish that all the materials attracted to magnets are metals.	• Can distinguish between magnetic and non-magnetic materials. • Can give examples of each.
Lesson 10 Non-magnetic materials	• To know that not all metals are magnetic.	Sort a collection of metal objects into 'magnetic' and 'not magnetic'.		Introduce the idea that only iron is magnetic.	• Know that all magnetic materials are metal, but that not all metals are magnetic.
Lesson 11 Magnet investigation	• To find out whether a magnet can work through things. • To carry out a very simple investigation.	Investigate whether a magnet works through card and other materials.		Discuss how and why the relative thickness of the barrier alters the relative effect of the magnet.	• Can carry out a very simple investigation. • Know that a magnet can work through other materials.

Lesson	Objectives	Main activity	Group activities	Plenary	Outcomes
Lesson 12 Paper test	• To know that some materials are chosen because of their suitability for a particular purpose. • To carry out a fair test with help.	Carry out a fair test to find out which type of paper is best for drawing.	• Find out which paper is best for absorbing water. • Find out which paper is best for wrapping a book.	Review results and how the tests were kept fair.	• Know that different materials are suitable for different purposes. • Can carry out a simple fair test with help.
Lesson 13 Teddy's umbrella	• To carry out a simple investigation with help. • To know that some materials are waterproof and others are not.	Carry out an investigation to find out which material is best for keeping the rain out.	• Test more materials and examine them closely. Sort them into sets: 'waterproof' and 'not waterproof'. • Make an umbrella collage.	Review the investigation and discuss the reasons for choices of waterproof materials in real life.	• Can carry out a simple investigation with help. • Understand the term 'waterproof'. • Can draw a simple conclusion: that some materials are waterproof.
Lesson 14 Changing shapes	• To know that some materials are changed in shape by forces.	Change the shape of play dough in a variety of ways. Consider the types of force used.	• Make patterned clay tiles; consider the forces used. • Make a collage using pieces of torn-up paper; consider the forces used.	Review the work done and vocabulary used; consider other uses of force.	• Know that they can change the shape of some materials by using a force.
Enrichment Lesson 15 Working with wood	• To know that some materials are changed in shape by forces.	Use a hammer and nails, a saw and sandpaper on wood.		Consider the types of force used. Recap on vocabulary.	• Know that they can change the shape of some materials by using a force. • Know that we use forces when we hammer and saw.
Enrichment Lesson 16 Forces in the kitchen	• To know that some materials are changed in shape by forces.	Make biscuit dough and shape it into biscuits.		Consider the types of force used. Recap on ideas from previous two lessons.	• Know that they can change the shape of some materials by using a force.

Assessment	Objectives	Activity 1	Activity 2
Lesson 17	• To assess whether the children know that different materials have different properties. • To assess what the children know about magnets.	State some simple properties of common materials and list some objects made from these materials.	Identify some things that are or are not attracted to a magnet.

SC1 SCIENTIFIC ENQUIRY

Fit for the purpose

LEARNING OBJECTIVES AND OUTCOMES
● To think about what might happen before deciding what to do.
● To recognise when a test or comparison is unfair.

ACTIVITY
Children predict and find out which paper is best for writing on, using a felt-tipped pen. They are asked for their ideas about how to make the test fair. They also predict and find out which paper is best for soaking up water and for wrapping a parcel. They then discuss how fair their test was.

LESSON LINKS
● This Sc1 activity forms an integral part of Lesson 12, Paper test.

Lesson 1 ▫ Properties card game

Objective
● To know that different materials have different properties.

Vocabulary
stretchy, bendy, clear, see-through, transparent, opaque, flexible, rigid, mould, hard, material, rough, smooth, waterproof

RESOURCES
Main activity: A collection of different materials: wood, rock, elastic, plastic (rigid, flexible, clear, coloured), glass (something like a paperweight that is not easily broken), fabric, Plasticine, paper, and so on; magnifiers.
Group activities: 1 Materials as for the main activity, A3-sized grids (see below), pencils. 2 Cards from photocopiable page 116 (also 'Properties card game' (red), available on the CD-ROM).

PREPARATION
Try to collect pieces or lumps of material that have not been made into a recognisable object; this will help the children to concentrate on the properties of the material rather than the properties of the object. Most fabrics these days are mixtures of several different fibres, but try to find a fabric made from a single type of fibre (such as wool or cotton). Make a set of 24 properties cards for each group from photocopiable page 116, mount them on thick card and laminate them for durability. Prepare copies of a suitable properties grid (see below).

BACKGROUND
Make sure the children realise that the term 'material' does not just mean 'fabric'. These days, many synthetic materials are very convincing and may be difficult for children to sort from natural materials. Some materials have several useful properties. Wood is used for its strength and its insulating properties, and because it is relatively easy to cut and shape. Metal is strong, can be shaped and moulded, and conducts electricity. See the Vocabulary list for the main properties that children would be expected to identify at this stage.

Children need to be given experience of the ways in which some materials change. For example, water can be changed into ice, chocolate can be melted and then allowed to harden again. Some materials, such as dough and clay, change profoundly when they are heated. Later, children will learn that some changes in materials are reversible and some are not.

Beware! 'Rough' and 'smooth' are often used as criteria for sorting, but these are usually properties of the objects rather than the material. A metal file is rough because it has been made so, not because metal is naturally rough. Natural rocks are rough, but a pebble has been worn until it is smooth.

Differentiation
Group activity 1
Some children may need adult support in this activity.
Group activity 2
For children who need support in this activity, use 'Properties card game' (green) from the CD-ROM, which contains only four words for the children to sort. To extend children, use 'Properties card game' (blue), which contains a wider range of words.

STARTER
Ask the class to look at and handle the collection of materials.

MAIN ACTIVITY
Working with the whole class, pass the materials around. Can the children name any of them? Ask: *What do they look like? What do they feel like?* See how many words the children can think of to describe them. Make a list on the board or flipchart. Introduce any appropriate words that the children have not suggested. Words such as 'flexible', 'transparent' and 'opaque' may be new to the children; each time you use such a word, add a definition to help the children's understanding. Encourage them to use a magnifier to examine the materials closely.

Hold up each material in turn and ask the children to suggest ways of sorting the materials into two sets according to their properties. To begin with, suggest criteria such as 'hard' or 'soft', 'flexible' or 'rigid', 'transparent' or 'opaque'. Then allow the children to sort with their own criteria; ask them to give reasons for these. Encourage them to use any new vocabulary introduced earlier, and to suggest labels for their sets using correct scientific language. Write labels for the sets according to the children's suggestions.

GROUP ACTIVITIES
1 Give each pair (or group of three) an A3-sized copy of a grid like the one below, and ask them to sort the materials into the appropriate columns. The children may need help with reading the words initially.

Flexible	Rigid	Opaque	Transparent	Hard	Soft

2 Give each group of four a set of 24 properties cards (see page 116). Go through the set, making sure that the children can read and understand each card. Place the cards face-down on the table. The children take turns to pick up a card and read it out. If they can name a material that matches the property on the card, they can keep the card. If not, they return it face-down to the bottom of the pile. Each material can only be used once. When the cards run out, the player with the most cards wins.

ASSESSMENT
Check that when the children are sorting the materials, they are able to identify some of their simple properties.

PLENARY
Return to the collection of materials and discuss the properties of each with the children. Ask them to name the materials. Encourage them to use the new vocabulary introduced during the lesson. Name a property (such as 'opaque'), and ask the children to choose a material with that property.

OUTCOME
● Can name the properties of some common materials.

LINKS
Maths: sorting into sets.

Lesson 2 ◼ Many materials

Objective
● To be able to identify some common materials.

RESOURCES
Samples of wood, glass, paper, metal, rock, plastics; labels with names of the materials.

MAIN ACTIVITY
Gather the children around you, look at the collection of materials and ask the children to name those they know. Make sure they name the material and not the object. Ask them to match labels to the materials they can identify. Tell them the names of any they are unable to identify, and attach the appropriate labels.

ASSESSMENT
During the plenary session, hold up the materials and ask the children to identify them.

Differentiation
Some children may need help with reading the labels and some may be able to identify more than one example of each material (such as foam plastic, polythene and rigid plastic; balsa wood and oak).

PLENARY
Discuss the fact that some materials can occur in different forms, especially made or manufactured materials. Talk about the variety of ways in which plastics are used: hard containers, bags, windows, CDs, clothing and so on.

OUTCOME
● Can identify and name some common materials.

Lesson 3 ◼ What's in the bag?

Objectives
● To know that the senses can be used to explore materials.
● To use the sense of touch to explore and identify materials.

Vocabulary
stretchy, bendy, flexible, rigid, mould, hard, material, rough, smooth, cold, warm, natural, made, manufactured

RESOURCES
Main activity: A collection of materials that feel different, such as a small wooden block, plastics (a piece of synthetic sponge, a section from a squeezy bottle, a piece of a carrier bag), metal, fabric, glass (a paperweight), paper, cork, wax; feely bags. Make sure that there are no sharp edges on which children could hurt themselves.
Group activities: 1 Enough sets of equipment, as listed for the main activity, for one set per group. **2** Large sheets of paper, a variety of collage materials of different textures (sawdust, bottle tops, cotton wool, fabric, sand and so on), adhesive, scissors.

BACKGROUND
It is important to use pieces or lumps of materials rather than objects at this stage, because children often find it difficult to distinguish between the object, the actual properties of the material, and its attributes. Young children only need to be able to name some simple properties of a small range of common materials, but it is important for us to be clear about the differences between the intrinsic properties of materials and their attributes (what properties can be given to them in the manufacturing process). For example, all plastics are waterproof and have a relatively low melting point. These are properties of the material. But plastics can be made rigid or flexible; transparent, translucent or opaque. These are attributes of the manufactured products. Wood is strong, it floats and it insulates; these are properties. It can be made rough or smooth, flat or curved, dyed or polished; these are attributes.

STARTER
Working with the whole class, look at a range of materials and talk about what they might feel like. Tell the children that they are going to use their

Differentiation
Group activity 1
Some children may need help to use the correct vocabulary. To extend children, challenge them to describe two fairly similar materials (such as paper and sheet plastic) and distinguish between them.
Group activity 2
All the children should be able to participate in this activity.

sense of touch to identify these materials. Encourage them to feel the materials and think of words to describe them. Introduce any new words you think relevant.

MAIN ACTIVITY
Use a feely bag or box in which to hide the materials, so that the children can only explore them by touch. It is important that they have seen and felt the materials before these are put in the feely bag. At first, put a single material in the bag and ask a child to try and describe it using the sense of touch alone. Ask: *What does it feel like?* Encourage them to use any words they can think of, but help them to focus on words that describe the properties of the materials (see Background). Ask the class to guess what material is in the bag. Take the material out to check the answer.

Next, put two materials in the bag. Name one of the materials and ask a child to find that one in the bag. You will not have the time (or stamina!) to let every child in the class have a turn in this way; but the activity can be continued by groups (see below) so that every child will eventually have a turn. As a general rule of hygiene, make sure that the children wash their hands after playing the game.

GROUP ACTIVITIES
1 Continue from the main activity, using one feely bag for each group. One child should describe what he or she can feel while the other children in the group try to guess what material it is. Encourage the children to use the vocabulary introduced in the main activity.
2 Working in groups of four, let the children make feely pictures. Using a large sheet of paper, they should 'take a pencil for a walk' to create a random pattern, then fill in each area with a different collage material (see Resources). Encourage the children to describe the materials they are using in terms of what they feel like. Alternatively, you could stick several large sheets of paper together and have six to eight children at a time making a class feely picture (to cover a display board).

ASSESSMENT
Do the children understand that their sense of touch is helping them to identify the materials? Are they able to use some of the vocabulary appropriately?

PLENARY
Have another look at the materials the children have been working with. Remind them that they have used their sense of touch to help them describe and identify the materials. Hold up some of the materials and ask: What 'touch' words can we use about this material?

OUTCOME
● Know that the sense of touch can help to identify materials.

LINKS
Unit 1a Lesson 3, The senses; Lesson 6, A sense of touch.

ENRICHMENT
Lesson 4 ▷ What sound does it make?

Objectives
● To know that the senses can be used to explore materials.
● To be able to distinguish different materials by sound.

RESOURCES
Samples of materials (Plasticine, wood, metal, plastic sheet, rigid plastic, paper, dough and so on); percussion instruments, beaters made from various materials, a large cloth or cardboard screen, empty plastic pots with lids.

MAIN ACTIVITY
Bang materials on the table, rub them together, crush them or drop them onto a hard floor. Let the children choose a material to drop or bang and listen to carefully. Hide materials behind a screen and ask the children to guess the materials from the sounds. Make shakers from small plastic pots, fill with different materials and compare the sounds. Use different beaters with percussion instruments and compare the effects.

ASSESSMENT
During the main activity, note those children who are able to identify the materials.

Differentiation
Be sensitive to the fact that some children may have difficulty in hearing some sounds.

PLENARY
Talk about why materials make different sounds. For example, hard materials tend to make louder or harsher sounds than softer materials.

OUTCOME
● Know that the sense of hearing can help to identify materials.

ENRICHMENT
Lesson 5 ▷ Say what you see

Objectives
● To know that the senses can be used to explore materials.
● To be able to observe closely and describe materials.

RESOURCES
A collection of different materials (as for Lesson 3).

MAIN ACTIVITY
Lay out the collection of materials where the children can see them. Take turns to describe a material, without touching or naming it. The others try to guess which material is being described. Let the children name some uses of the material as part of their description, for example 'Sometimes it is used for windows' (glass).

ASSESSMENT
During the main activity, note those children who can describe or identify materials.

Differentiation
Restrict the number of materials for children who need support. To extend children, introduce materials with similar visual properties where the differences may be more subtle.

PLENARY
List the vocabulary used to describe the materials. Talk about how observations need to be careful and detailed. Discuss how our observations can be further enhanced if we can use all of our senses.

OUTCOME
● Know that the sense of sight can help to identify materials.

Lesson 6 ▶ It could be made from...

Objective
● To know that different objects can be made from the same material.

Vocabulary
same, different, materials, wood, plastic, metal, paper, clay, objects, strong, pliable, shaped, joined

RESOURCES ◉
Main activity: A collection of similar objects made from different materials (two or three examples of each object), such as toy cars (wooden, plastic and metal), bricks (wooden and plastic), cups (paper, plastic and pottery), spoons (metal, plastic and wood) and bowls (paper, plastic, pottery and wood).
Group activities: 1 A collection as above. **2** Photocopiable page 117 (also 'It could be made from...' (red), available on the CD-ROM), pencils.
Plenary: Pictures of other objects made from the same materials as the objects in the collection.

BACKGROUND
As children become more familiar with different materials, they will appreciate that some have more than one useful property and are therefore suitable for a range of purposes. For example, metal can be shaped (when heated) into bowls, cups or jewellery; but it is also strong, and so can be used to make furniture, ships or bridges. Both of these properties make it ideal for making tools to work other materials. Wood is warm to the touch, is strong, can be shaped and joined, and is pleasing to look at, so it is ideal for use in building and furniture-making. Always encourage the children to think about why a particular material has been chosen to make an object.

STARTER
Gather the children around you and look at the collection of objects. Ask the children to name the objects and say what they are used for.

MAIN ACTIVITY
Sort the collection into sets according to the object: all the cups, all the spoons and so on. When the collection has been sorted, look at each set and ask the children to name the material from which each object has been made. Explain that pottery objects are made from clay. Now ask the children to re-sort the objects according to the material from which they are made. Discuss why different materials might be used to make each object. For example, plastic cutlery is very useful for parties, because it is safe and saves lots of washing-up; but it is not really strong enough for everyday use, so metal is better. Wooden bowls look nice and are good for keeping fruit in; but they would burn if put in the oven, so they are not suitable for cooking.

Differentiation ◉◉
Group activity 1
Some children may still need help with identifying the materials rather than the objects. Other children could be given objects where the material is not so obvious (such as painted wood or metal) and asked to name the materials.
Group activity 2
Support children by giving them 'It could be made from...' (green) from the CD-ROM. The resource contains fewer words for the children to choose from.

GROUP ACTIVITIES
1 Groups of three can play 'Material dominoes'. One child chooses an object from the collection and places it on the table. The next child chooses a different object made from the same material. The third child chooses a similar object made from a different material, and they go on alternating – for example: wooden fork, wooden bowl, metal bowl, metal knife, plastic knife, plastic cup.
2 Give each child a copy of photocopiable page 117. Ask them to write the names of the materials from which the object could be made in the space opposite each picture. They can use the words at the bottom of the page to help them.

ASSESSMENT
Observe the children playing the dominoes game, and use the photocopiable sheet to check their understanding.

PLENARY

Choose a few objects from the collection that are made of the same material. Review the properties of that material, and talk about which property has made it suitable for each object. Discuss the limitations of the material. For example, wooden or plastic bowls would burn or melt if heated; pottery plates are easily broken, but paper plates are weak and can only be used once. Use pictures to stimulate discussion about other uses of the materials in the collection: buildings, bridges, cars and so on.

OUTCOME

● Know that different things can be made from the same material.

Lesson 7 ● What is it made from?

Objective
● To know that an object can be made up of several materials.

Vocabulary
materials, object, made, manufactured, plastic, wood, metal, stone, leather, paper, strong, waterproof, bendy, pliable, flexible, rigid, same, different

RESOURCES ◉

Main activity: A collection of objects made up of two or three (fairly evident) materials, such as a shoe, a trainer, a Wellington boot, a pencil, a pencil case, an umbrella, a chair, scissors (with plastic handles), a plastic pencil sharpener, a torch.
Group activities: 1 Photocopiable page 118 (also 'What is it made from?' (red), available on the CD-ROM), pencils, the objects listed on page 118.
2 The objects listed on page 118.
ICT link: 'What is it made from?' interactive, from the CD-ROM.

BACKGROUND

Many objects are made from more than one material because no single material is the most suitable for every aspect or function of the object. The materials from which composite objects are made are chosen largely for their properties, but also for their price, availability and appeal. For example, wood makes a pencil strong and more comfortable to hold. The lead alone would break easily, be messy to use and be difficult to hold. (The 'lead' in a pencil is really graphite.) Scissors need metal blades to cut efficiently, but may have plastic handles for more comfortable and secure handling. It is not always easy to identify the individual materials that go to make up an object; in particular, plastics can be made to mimic a wide range of other materials. Plastics have also taken over many of the roles of more traditional materials such as wood. A wooden item has to be cut, shaped and finished individually, whereas many plastic objects can be produced from the same mould with little finishing required. It is therefore much less labour-intensive and much less time-consuming to make objects from plastic. Plastic is a manufactured material, but it is chemically derived from oil – a natural substance that has formed from the decomposed bodies of sea creatures that died several millennia ago.

STARTER

Working with the whole class, recap on some familiar materials and remind the children what they look and feel like. Choose a familiar object made from one material. Discuss the material, its properties, and why that particular material has been used for that particular object.

MAIN ACTIVITY

Introduce an object that has been made from two or three materials and ask the children to identify them. Can they say why the different materials have been chosen? You may need to help them identify the properties that have made these materials suitable. Invite the children to handle and explore several simple objects made from more than one material. Identify and discuss the materials that have been used. Encourage the children to describe these materials and to relate their uses to their properties. For example, the outside of a Wellington boot is made from plastic and plastic is waterproof – ideal for splashing through the puddles on a rainy day! The insole is usually cotton, which is warm and makes the boot more comfortable to wear.

If a writing pencil is one of the objects discussed, the children should be made aware that the 'lead' is actually a natural material called graphite (though it is usually called 'lead'). As well as making the pencil stronger and more comfortable to hold, the wood is easy to shape and cut to the correct length in the pencil factory. The children could compare a plain wooden pencil and a painted one. Why do you think the pencil has been painted? Does it make it easier to hold or to write with, or does it just make the pencil look more attractive?

GROUP ACTIVITIES
1 Ask the children to complete photocopiable page 118 by ticking the appropriate boxes. It would be helpful if you could also provide the corresponding objects for the children to handle. They could work individually, or in groups of about four with one child (or an adult helper) filling in a group sheet.
2 Working in groups of about four and using the same objects as in group activity **1**, ask the children to suggest materials that could NOT be used for each particular object, and explain why. For example, a paper shoe would get soggy when wet and fall to pieces – and it would not wear very well even if you could keep it dry. This activity could be purely oral, or the children could record in their own way.

ICT LINK
Children can use the 'What is it made from?' interactive, available on the CD-ROM, to match objects to materials. They must click on the correct squares to show which material an object is made from. If they are correct, a tick appears; if not, a cross appears.

ASSESSMENT
Can the children identify the materials in some objects made from more than one material? Can they say why some of these materials have been chosen?

PLENARY
Discuss some of the objects and identify the various materials from which they have been made. Talk about why particular materials have been used. Reinforce the properties of the materials – for example, that some are easily shaped, some are strong and some are soft and pliable. Encourage the children who have done group activity **2** to report back on some of their 'strange' objects.

OUTCOMES
● Know that some objects are made up of more than one material.
● Can identify some of these materials.
● Can explain, in simple terms, why different materials are used for different parts of an object.

Lesson 8 ▪ Materials at school

Objectives
● To know that a range of materials are used in our environment.
● To know that materials can be used in a variety of ways.

Vocabulary
metal, glass, plastic, brick, clay, wood, wax, paper, stone, concrete, tarmac, same, different

RESOURCES ◉
Main activity: The environment within and around the school.
Group activities: 1 Photocopiable page 119 (also 'Materials at school – 1' (red), available on the CD-ROM), scissors, adhesive. **2** Photocopiable page 120 (also 'Materials at school – 2' (red), available on the CD-ROM), scissors, adhesive.

BACKGROUND
Plastics, these days, can be made to mimic or replace most materials, and their use is constantly increasing. Children will be very familiar with plastic bags, toys and cups, but may find some other forms more difficult to distinguish from the material they are replacing (for example, a plastic table-top and a wooden one). Plastics are now widely used in buildings, replacing the traditional materials: roof tiles, pipes, windows, doors and even paint are now often plastic. For this reason, there may be some confusion if you ask children about the materials used to build a house. An old cottage may still have wooden window frames, a thatched roof and metal pipes, but a modern dwelling is likely to have a very high plastic content. The surface finish of some materials may also be confusing – for example, metals may be plastic-coated; high-gloss paint may hide wood or metal. Some materials, such as concrete and tarmac, are aggregates or composites. Concrete is often made to look like natural stone, as in paving slabs and garden ornaments.

STARTER
Tell the children that they are going on a 'materials walkabout'. Explain that they are looking for the materials from which things are made, and also looking for examples of different things made from the same material.

MAIN ACTIVITY
Before going out, mention some of the materials that the children might find and help them to identify examples around the classroom. Talk about the fact that they might see the same material used in a variety of ways. Name one or two of the objects they are likely to find outside (such as railings, benches or litter bins), and discuss the materials they are made from. Draw their attention to some of the properties of these materials. Discuss why they have been used in the manufacture of those particular objects.

Walk round the school, first inside and then outside. Help the children to focus on various objects and the materials from which they are made. Encourage them to link the properties of the materials with the objects, and to compare and contrast some materials. For example, railings, lamp posts and chair legs are made of metal for strength, but chair seats would be very uncomfortable if they too were made of metal. A metal door would be strong, but far too heavy to open and close. Talk about materials, such as concrete, that have been made from a mixture of other materials. Ask the children how many examples of the same material they can find being used to make different objects, such as wooden doors and chairs.

GROUP ACTIVITIES
1 Give each child a copy of photocopiable page 119. Ask them to cut out the labels and stick them in the appropriate boxes to label the picture.
2 Give each child a copy of photocopiable page 120. Ask them to cut out the labels and stick them in the appropriate boxes to label the picture.

ASSESSMENT
Use the photocopiable sheets to check whether the children are naming familiar materials correctly.

<table>
</table>

Differentiation
Group activities
Support children by using 'Materials at school - 1' (green) and 'Materials at school - 2' (green) from the CD-ROM. These resources include fewer and less complex objects and materials for the children to match together. Challenge children to write their own labels for the objects with 'Materials at school - 1' (blue) and to suggest alternative materials from which objects could be made with 'Materials at school - 2' (blue).

PLENARY
Encourage children to report back to the whole class about their findings. Talk about the materials that were found both inside and outside, and the properties that make them suitable for both localities. Ask: *Why do you think both doors and pencils are made of wood? Is it because wood is both strong and easy to cut and shape? Were any materials only indoors or outdoors? Why might this be? Would tarmac be a sensible type of flooring for the classroom? Was any particular material found more often than the others?* Reinforce the new vocabulary learned.

OUTCOMES
● Can recognise and name some familiar materials in their environment.
● Know that some have been used in a variety of ways.

LINKS
English: labelling.

Lesson 9 ▪ Magnets

Objective
● To know that some materials are magnetic, but most are not.

Vocabulary
magnet, magnetic, attract, attraction, repel, repulsion, pick up, stick to, metal, non-metal

RESOURCES
Main activity: Good magnets of different shapes and sizes; a collection of materials such as small pieces of wood, plastic (a piece of synthetic sponge, a section from a squeezy bottle, a piece from a carrier bag), metal (a paper clip, a nut, a washer), fabric, paper, cork, wax, string; set rings for sorting. The samples of materials should be small enough to be picked up by the magnet if they are magnetic. Remove any non-magnetic metal samples at this stage. Plain metal discs are useful for this activity, since the object cannot be confused with the material.
Group activities: 1 Photocopiable page 121 (also 'Magnets' (red), available on the CD-ROM), more samples of some different materials, magnets.
2 Magnetic tape, card, scissors, adhesive, felt-tipped pens or crayons, collage materials.

BACKGROUND
Most children will probably already have some experience with magnets. They may have a collection of fridge magnets at home. Some of them may have noticed the magnetic catches on cupboard doors.

Make sure that any magnets you use are reasonably strong. Bar magnets are available from most educational suppliers. Old audio speakers (often available from car boot sales) can be a source of really strong magnets that would otherwise be expensive to buy. Magnets should always be stored properly in order to help them remain magnetic for as long as possible. Store ceramic bar magnets in pairs in the box they were supplied in. Store other magnets complete with a keeper. Magnets will lose their strength if dropped continually, though plastic-coated ceramic magnets (which have iron particles baked into the clay) are a little more resilient.

Children should be warned about the dangers of putting strong magnets next to equipment such as tape recorders, computers or television sets, which may be damaged by the magnetic field. At this stage, it is not necessary to mention 'magnetic fields' to the children: this is far too abstract a concept. They may discover during their play that 'the red ends push away' or 'don't stick', but learning about north and south poles and like poles repelling comes later. It is important that, at first, the children encounter only metals that are magnetic. This allows them to develop the concept that only metal is magnetic. The next stage is for them to discover that not even all metals are attracted to a magnet: it is only those that contain iron. Other metals, such as aluminium, tin, copper or gold are not magnetic unless they

Differentiation

Group activity 1
Children who have not experienced magnets before will need time to play with the magnets and discover that they 'stick' to things. To challenge children, use 'Magnets' (blue) from the CD-ROM.
Group activity 2
All children can participate in this activity. Some may be able to design their own game using magnets.

are mixed with iron. For example, aluminium soft-drink cans are not magnetic, but steel ones (which contain iron) are. Never use loose iron filings with the children – they make a terrible mess, are almost impossible to clean off magnets, and are toxic if ingested in any quantity. There is also a danger of children rubbing them into their eyes.

STARTER
Show the class the range of magnets. Ask: *Do you know what these are? What do they do?* Find out what the children already know about magnets. Do they understand the terms 'repel' and 'attract'? Reinforce these, giving definitions.

MAIN ACTIVITY
Tell the children that some of the magnets in the collection are stronger than others. Ask: *What do we mean by a 'strong' magnet?* Demonstrate that a stronger magnet will pick up more or heavier objects than a weaker one. Talk about the importance of keeping the magnets well away from TVs, tape recorders or computers, because of the damage they can do.

Go through the names of the materials in the collection, and ask the children to predict which of these materials will be attracted to a magnet. *Why do you think that?* Make a 'yes' and 'no' list on the board. Ask the children to test their predictions by taking turns to try one of the materials and putting it into the correct set ring. Ask: *Do you know what all the materials in the 'yes' set are made from?* Reinforce the fact that they are all made of metal.

GROUP ACTIVITIES
1 Ask the children to look at a new set of objects and predict which ones will be attracted to a magnet. They can then sort the objects using a magnet and record their findings on a copy of photocopiable page 121.
2 The children can make a simple fridge magnet by sticking magnetic tape to the back of a small picture card. The picture could be drawn and coloured in, cut from a commercial card, or collaged with sequins and other attractive scraps.

ASSESSMENT
Use the photocopiable sheets to check that the children can sort magnetic from non-magnetic materials. Do they know that all the magnetic materials are metals?

PLENARY
Talk about the things that were attracted to the magnet, and the materials from which they were made. Make the generalisation that all the things attracted to the magnets were made of metal. Reinforce any new vocabulary.

OUTCOMES
● Can distinguish between magnetic and non-magnetic materials.
● Can give examples of each.

LINKS
Maths: sorting.

Lesson 10 ▸ Non-magnetic metals

Objective
● To know that not all metals are magnetic.

RESOURCES
A collection of coins, or a set of discs of different metals (named if possible). Check the 'copper' coins that you use: the composition of the metal used for these coins has changed. Newer coins contain more steel, and are therefore magnetic; older coins are not.

MAIN ACTIVITY
Sort the metals and coins into 'magnetic' and 'not magnetic'.

ASSESSMENT
Observe and question the children as they carry out the main activity. Can they tell you that all materials attracted to a magnet are metal, but not all metals are magnetic?

PLENARY
Discuss why not all metals are magnetic. Introduce the idea that some metals contain a special metal called iron, and that this is attracted to the magnet.

Differentiation
Challenge children by asking them to find out the names of some of the metals using a named set of samples.

OUTCOME
● Know that all magnetic materials are metal, but that not all metals are magnetic.

Lesson 11 ▸ Magnet investigation

Objectives
● To find out whether a magnet can work through things.
● To carry out a very simple investigation.

RESOURCES
Fairly strong magnets, paper clips, sheets of card.

MAIN ACTIVITY
Ask the children (working in pairs) to put a paper clip on top of a piece of card, then to hold a magnet underneath and see whether they can move the paper clip. How many sheets of card can they add before the paper clip fails to move? Ask: *Does the magnet work through a table or a chair seat?*

ASSESSMENT
Observe and note which children are able to carry out this investigation. During the plenary session, note which children could say why the magnet appeared to stop working. (Too many layers.)

PLENARY
Discuss why the magnet stopped working when there were too many layers, and why some worked through more layers than others. Remind the children that the card is not magnetic: the magnet is working through it.

Differentiation
Ask children who need support to draw a simple road map and take the 'car' (paper clip) along the road to the garage. Challenge children by asking them to test two or three magnets to see whether they all work through the same number of sheets.

OUTCOMES
● Can carry out a very simple investigation.
● Know that a magnet can work through other materials.

Lesson 12 ▫ Paper test

Objectives
● To know that some materials are chosen because of their suitability for a particular purpose.
● To carry out a fair test with help

Vocabulary
fair test, properties, materials, suitable, soft, rigid, absorbent, shiny

RESOURCES
Main activity: Exercise book paper, tissue paper, kitchen towel, one large-tipped felt pen (preferably chisel-tipped) for each group, one stencil for each group.
Group activities: 1 Sheets of the same three papers used in thee main activity, plastic trays, water. **2** Sheets of the three papers for each group, a small book (for wrapping), sticky tape.

PREPARATION
Cut the three types of papers (see Resources) into approximately 150mm squares. Make enough for each group of two or three children to have one square of each type of paper.

BACKGROUND
As children work through this unit on materials they will begin to realise that many materials such as papers, fabrics and plastics differ widely according to the purpose for which they are produced. Some of the differences are very obvious such as a thin, supple plastic bag for holding food compared to a rigid, solid, thick plastic dustbin for holding rubbish. Some differences are more subtle, such as the waterproof fabric of an umbrella and the shower-proof fabric of an anorak.

STARTER
Reinforce the idea that materials are chosen for their properties and how suitable they are for a particular purpose. Remind the children about the work they did in Lessons 6, 7 and 8. Ask them to think of as many uses for paper as they can and make a list on a whiteboard or flipchart. Talk about the differences between the papers used for each purpose suggested. *Are they soft, rigid, absorbent, shiny?* Discuss whether all the papers would be suitable for all the purposes suggested. *Ask: Why not?*

MAIN ACTIVITY
Show the children the three different papers and tell them that they are going to find out if all the papers are equally suitable for drawing on with felt-tipped pens. Explain that they are going to do a fair test to find out.

Pass round a sample of each type of paper for the children to look at and feel. Ask them to predict which one they think will be the best, and why. Explain to the children that the test needs to be made as fair as possible otherwise it is difficult to tell which paper is best. Show them the papers, felt pens and stencils and find out if they have got any ideas on how to make the test fair using this equipment. (Using the same-sized papers, the same felt-tipped pen, the same stencil so that the marks they make on each paper are the same. There may be some discussion as to whether the person who makes the marks should be the same.) Sort the children into groups of two or three and ask them to test each paper by drawing, with the pen, inside the stencil, in the centre of each paper.

GROUP ACTIVITIES
1 Give the same groups a square of each of the papers used in the main activity and a plastic tray with some water in it. Ask the children to predict first and then find out which of the papers is best for absorbing the water.
2 Still in their groups, children can try wrapping a small book with the same papers as before. *Are any of the papers suitable for this task? Why?*

ASSESSMENT
Note the level of discussion and understanding during the main activity,

group activity **1** and the plenary discussion.

Differentiation

Group activity 1
All children should be able to take part in this activity, though their level of discussion and understanding will differ.
Group activity 2
Some groups will need more help with their wrapping and more adult guidance in their discussion.

PLENARY

Talk to the class about what they thought would happen in their test, and what did happen. *Were you right? Why were the tissue paper and the kitchen towel less suitable for the task?* Talk about how the children kept the test fair. (Same-sized paper, same felt pen for each paper, same stencil and same marks.) Ask if the exercise paper was best for absorbing the water. *Why not?* Talk about the suitability of each paper for wrapping a parcel. Ask whether the tissue paper worked well. *Would it be suitable to send through the post? Why not?*

OUTCOMES
- Know that different materials are suitable for different purposes.
- Can carry out a simple fair test with help.

LINKS
Unit 1c Lesson 6, It could be made from...; Lesson 7, What is it made from?; Lesson 8, Materials at school.

Lesson 13 ▪ Teddy's umbrella

Objectives
- To carry out a simple investigation with help.
- To know that some materials are waterproof and others are not.

Vocabulary
fair test, investigate, predict, waterproof, magnify

RESOURCES 💿
Main activity: The poem 'Happiness' by AA Milne (from *When We Were Very Young*, Mammoth); an umbrella, sheet plastic (a piece of a carrier or plastic bag), paper, a metal lid (with no sharp edges) or small metal tray, a piece of cotton or woollen fabric, a see-through plastic container, elastic bands, a small watering can, a tray, water, a small plastic teddy bear, an ordinary teddy bear.
Group activities: 1 More samples of waterproof and non-waterproof materials, a magnifier, a water trough (or washing-up bowl), scissors, adhesive, art paper. **2** Photocopiable page 122 (also 'Teddy's umbrella' (red), available on the CD-ROM), material samples, scissors, adhesive.

PREPARATION
Cheap and cheerful containers can be made from cut-off plastic drinks bottles. Turn the top upside-down to make a funnel. Bind the edges with sticky tape to cover any sharp points.

BACKGROUND
Children at this stage will need lots of help with planning and carrying out an investigation. Nevertheless, they need to be encouraged to contribute their ideas about how an investigation could be done. They should also be encouraged to think about what the results might be. It may be a fairly wild guess – in some cases, based on a favourite colour or because a material feels nice. A scientific prediction is usually based on past experience or an observable pattern, and most young children have limited experience on which to draw at this stage. Always ask children to give you a reason for their prediction.

Children will be able to tell you whether a test is not fair long before they are able to plan a fair test. Some may spontaneously volunteer the information; but for most, careful questioning will be needed. *Was it fair that we started from different places? Does it matter if one piece is much bigger than the other? How much water should we put on each one?* Questions such as these will help children to start thinking about the need for tests to be fair if the results are to be valid. It is also important for them to think about what they have found out and draw some kind of conclusion.

Differentiation
Group activity 1
Some children may need to be told what to do, but they may be able to make suggestions or choose from the available equipment. Encourage all children to make predictions even if they are unable to give reasons for them - any prediction, even one without a stated reason, is testable. Some children will be able to predict and give valid reasons for their predictions without help and able to say when a test is not fair.
Group activity 2
All children should be able to participate in this activity.

Fabrics may be made from natural materials such as wool, cotton or silk, but many these days are synthetic or a mixture of different fibres. Unless you have the label to hand, it is often impossible to identify what the mixture is. However, the emphasis of this lesson is on carrying out an investigation and on the property of being waterproof, so identifying the exact type of each fabric is less important.

STARTER
The poem 'Happiness' by AA Milne would be a good stimulus at the start of this lesson. Working with the whole class, present an ordinary teddy bear. Say that Teddy needs a new roof on his house, a raincoat, a hat or an umbrella, and you need to find the best material from which to make it. Remind the children what they found out in Lesson 7 about waterproof materials. Look at an umbrella and ask: *How do we know it is waterproof?* (It stops the rain from coming through.)

MAIN ACTIVITY
Show the children a selection of materials and ask which they think would be best for making an umbrella. Encourage them to give reasons for their choices. Draw their attention to the holes between the threads in a woven fabric, and ask what they think might happen if you poured water over that material. Ask them for ideas about how they could find out which materials are waterproof. Have the container and other apparatus on the table, so that the children may pick up some clues. Suggest that the test needs to be the same for each material, and ask how that could be done. Look for suggestions such as using pieces of material of the same size and using the same amount of water. If these ideas are not forthcoming, questions such as: *Do you think it will be fair if we pour more water over that one?* may elicit answers.

One way of carrying out this investigation is to put the small plastic bear in the bottom of a clear container, then place the material to be tested over the top and hold it in place with an elastic band. (Explain that the real Teddy would be too big for the container.) Stand the container in a tray (or work outside if the weather permits) and pour water from a small watering can over the container and material. If the little bear stays dry, then the material is waterproof; if it gets wet, oh dear! The children may come up with ideas on how to carry out the test, or you may have to tell them. Encourage them to predict which materials will be waterproof and which will not. Sort the materials into two sets. Carry out the test on each set and re-sort as necessary. Try not to give the impression that the children were 'wrong' if their prediction proved to be false: emphasise the fact that what happened was different from what they expected.

GROUP ACTIVITIES
1 Pairs or groups of three can explore more waterproof and non-waterproof materials, using a water trough (they could use a baby bath or washing-up bowl if a water trough is not available). Let them look at the materials through a magnifier, examining the holes between the threads in woven fabrics. After testing, they can sort the materials and stick small pieces of them onto sheets marked 'waterproof' and 'not waterproof' as a record.
2 Give each child a copy of photocopiable page 122. Help them to choose a suitable waterproof material for the umbrella and stick it onto the picture as a collage.

ASSESSMENT
Note whether the children understand the term 'waterproof'. Can they identify waterproof materials at the end of their investigation? Which children can make a simple prediction and understand when a test is not fair?

PLENARY

Help the children to understand what they have found out. Remind them what they thought would happen. Talk about how they did the test and what happened. *How did we keep the test fair? Why was the result different from what you expected? Was it because the material you chose was not waterproof when you tested it? Which of the materials would be best for making a raincoat, hat or umbrella? Which other properties need to be considered as well as being waterproof? Metal is waterproof, but why wouldn't it make a good coat? What would it be useful for?* (Maybe a roof, a car or a mug to keep water in.)

OUTCOMES
- Can carry out a simple investigation with help.
- Understand the term 'waterproof'.
- Can draw a simple conclusion: that some materials are waterproof.

Lesson 14 ◗ Changing shapes

Objective
- To know that some materials are changed in shape by forces.

Vocabulary
squeeze, squash, push, pull, roll, press, hammer, saw, cut, tear

RESOURCES
Main activity: Play dough (see recipe at end of this lesson), rolling pins, cutters, safe knives.
Group activities: 1 Clay, rolling pins. **2** A selection of papers to be torn for collage work, adhesive, spreaders.

BACKGROUND
Most forces are basically a push or a pull. Children will be familiar with the fact that they can change the shape of a material or object by such actions as banging, pressing, squashing and rolling (which are all types of push). They will also know that stretching and tearing (which are types of pull) will cause materials to change their shape. They need to be made aware that the above are all types of forces, and that the use of a force is necessary to cause a change in shape. Always use the correct vocabulary with the children, and provide definitions. For example: Use a little more force to flatten your play dough - push it harder. Be careful of using words such as 'pressure' in the context of changing the shape of materials. It has a different, precise scientific meaning which the children will learn about later. They should simply be taught that they are using a force to change the shape of things.

For Lesson 15, the children should be taught how to use tools correctly, safely and sensibly. Small junior hacksaws are quite safe for them to use, provided that they have been shown how to hold the wood in a vice and the wood is soft and easy to cut. Beware of bags of offcuts of wood, which are often too hard, thick and splintery.

STARTER
Remind the children that they have been learning about materials. Say that pushes and pulls can change the shape of things. For example: flattening dough is a push; tearing paper is a pull.

MAIN ACTIVITY
Work with the whole class at the beginning of the activity. Show the children a piece of play dough and ask them how many ways they can think of to change its shape. Encourage them to use appropriate vocabulary such as 'roll', 'push', 'press', 'squash', 'pinch', 'pull', 'stretch' and 'cut'. Discuss the fact that we are using a force every time we change the shape of the play dough. Ask them as you change the shape of the play dough: *Is this a push or a pull?*

Differentiation
Group activity 1
Although this activity is accessible to all, some children may need extra help to relate what they are doing to the idea of using a force to change the shape of an object. You may need to explain that rolling clay with a rolling pin and pressing other pieces of clay into it are examples of pushes.
Group activity 2
This activity should be accessible to all the children.

Sit the children at their tables and give them each a ball of play dough. Ask them to reshape their dough in as many ways as they can: into pancakes, sausages, worms and so on. Encourage them to cut the play dough with safe knives and cutters, make pancakes with rolling pins, and press their fingers into it to make patterns. Can they say whether they are using a pull or a push force as they shape their play dough? Can they get it back into the ball shape they started with? Reinforce the vocabulary used earlier.

GROUP ACTIVITIES

1 The children could work either individually or in pairs. Ask them to roll out some clay to make a tile, and then to push smaller pieces of clay into the tile to make a pattern. They should make sure that the base tile is not too thin, or they will end up with something that is full of holes and looks more like lace than a tile when they push their pieces into it! Talk about the fact that they are changing the shape of both the actual tile and the little pieces of clay being pushed into it. If possible, the patterned tiles could be glazed and fired.

2 Individuals or groups could tear paper to make a collage. This could be an abstract design or a picture showing something being pushed or pulled (such as a tug-of-war). Remind the children that they are using a force to change the shape of their paper by tearing it, and are pushing the small pieces onto the glue. Ask: Do you need more force to tear several layers at once?

ASSESSMENT

Do the children understand that when they change the shape of a material, they are using a force? Are they able to name these forces as pushes and pulls? When asked to describe what they are doing, are they able to use appropriate vocabulary?

PLENARY

Ask the children to present some of the tiles they have made to the whole class. Ask them to describe the sort of force they used to make them. See how many of the words they practised earlier they can remember. Can they think of any other activity where forces are used to change the shape of things? For example, squeezing the sponge in the bath to get the water out, cutting up their dinner, folding a piece of paper? Look at the collaged pictures made by the children, and discuss how they used a (pulling) force to tear the paper.

OUTCOME

● Know that they can change the shape of some materials by using a force, such as a push or pull.

LINKS

Unit 1e Lesson 5, Cheesy twisters.

> **Play dough recipe**
> 2 cups plain flour
> 2 tsbp cooking oil
> 2 cups water
> 1 cup salt
> 2 tsp cream of tartar
> A few drops of food colouring
>
> Mix all the ingredients together in a large saucepan and cook over a medium heat, stirring all the time, until the mixture leaves the sides of the saucepan. When cool, turn onto a board and knead the dough until smooth.
>
> Play dough is a good material to use, as it is often softer than Plasticine and less messy than modelling clay. It will keep for a very long time in an airtight tin; in fact, it usually gets unacceptably grubby before it becomes hard and crumbly!

ENRICHMENT
Lesson 15 ▸ Working with wood

Objective
● To know that some materials are changed in shape by forces.

RESOURCES
Small, light hammers; blocks of wood (balsa is ideal), nails, sandpaper, a junior hacksaw, a workbench with a vice; coloured wools, ribbons and threads.

MAIN ACTIVITY
Working in groups, the children can use sandpaper to smooth and round the edges of a block of wood, hammer some nails into the wood and decorate the block by winding coloured wool, ribbon and thread around and between the nails. They can take turns to place another block of wood in a vice and saw it in half.

ASSESSMENT
Talk to the children while they are working to find out whether they understand that they are using a force to change the shape of the wood.

PLENARY
Relate the hammering, sawing and sandpapering of the wood to forces (pushes and pulls). Recap on vocabulary learned and practised.

Differentiation
Children can be taught to hammer and saw safely at this stage, especially using balsa wood; but some may need closer supervision.

OUTCOMES
● Know that they can change the shape of some materials by using a force.
● Know that we use forces when we hammer and saw.

ENRICHMENT
Lesson 16 ◗ Forces in the kitchen

Objective
● To know that some materials are changed in shape by forces.

RESOURCES
Biscuit ingredients, rolling pins, bowls, biscuit cutters, baking trays, an oven, the recipe below.

MAIN ACTIVITY
Working in groups of four, the children can make the biscuit dough, roll it out, cut biscuits and decorate them – using, practising and reinforcing all the forces vocabulary and ideas learned in Lesson 14.

ASSESSMENT
Talk to the children as they are rolling and shaping their biscuits to find out whether they understand that they are using a force to change the shape of the dough.

PLENARY
Discuss what the children have been doing and relate this to other work on changing shapes by using a force. Ask them to identify actions and forces that they used with the play dough and are using again here.

Differentiation
Some children will need extra support to link what they are doing to the ideas in Lesson 14.

OUTCOME
● Know that they can change the shape of some materials by using a force.

Biscuit recipe
150g plain flour
25g cornflour
125g butter
50g sugar

Mix the dry ingredients together in a bowl. Knead the butter into them until a soft dough is obtained. This is quite a sticky procedure, but each child in the group could have a turn. Divide the mixture into four, one piece for each child. Roll out and cut into shapes. Place on a greased baking sheet and bake at 180°C (350°F, Gas Mark 3) until light gold in colour.

Lesson 17 ◗ Assessment

Objectives
● To assess whether the children know that different materials have different properties.
● To assess what the chilren know about magnets.

RESOURCES
Assessment activities: 1 Photocopiable page 123 (also 'Assessment-1' (red), from the CD-ROM), writing materials. **2** Photocopiable page 124 (also 'Assessment-2' (red), available on the CD-ROM), pencils, colouring materials.
ICT link: 'Magnets' interactive, available on the CD-ROM.

STARTER
Ask the children: *Can anyone remember some of the properties of some of the materials we have looked at? What are the special words we have used?* (Strong, waterproof, transparent, hard, soft, flexible, rigid, magnetic and so on.)

ASSESSMENT ACTIVITY 1
Give each child a copy of page 123. Read through the text together and make sure they understand it. Ask the children to finish each sentence and then make a list of other things made from the same material.

ANSWERS

Accept answers that show understanding even if they do not make proper sentences.

1. '...we can see through it' or '...it is transparent'. The list could include: vase, bowl, tumbler, dish, bottle, fish tank, greenhouse, conservatory and so on.

2. '...it is strong or rigid' or '...it is not too heavy'. The list could include: chairs, tables, fences, gates, wooden spoon, chopping board and so on.

3. '...it is waterproof'. The list could include: bucket, spade, cups, saucers, bowls, lunchboxes, carrier bags and so on.

4. '...it is strong' or '...it can be sharpened to a point'. The list could include: tools, spoon, bucket, car, nails, screws, letterbox and so on.

LOOKING FOR LEVELS

Some children may only be able to identify a correct property for one or two materials, and to name one or two other objects made from the same material. They may provide their lists in pictorial form (and some may need to explain their pictures). Some children will identify at least one property for each material, and list more than three other objects.

ASSESSMENT ACTIVITY 2

Give each child a copy of page 124. Ask if there are any pictures they do not recognise. Name the objects shown. Read through the sheet with the children. Ask them to colour in things that will be attracted to a magnet, and to put a cross through things that will not be attracted. Ask them to answer the questions on the sheet.

ANSWERS

The things attracted to a magnet are: paper clip, drawing pin, nail, paper fastener, scissors. All the things attracted to a magnet are made from metal. In a house, there may be magnetic catches on some cupboard doors; most fridges have a magnetic catch, and may have fridge magnets on the door; a magnet could also be used for picking up dropped pins or retrieving other metal objects from awkward places.

LOOKING FOR LEVELS

Most children will identify at least four objects that are attracted to a magnet. All the children should know that things attracted to a magnet are made from metal. The children should identify one use of a magnet in a house. Some children may identify only two objects that are attracted to a magnet, and may be unable to identify a practical use for a magnet in the house. Some children will identify all the objects, and should be able to suggest two or three practical uses for a magnet.

ICT LINK

Children can use the 'Magnets' interactive from the CD-ROM, to sort magnetic and non-magnetic items by picking up the magnetic items with a 'virtual magnet' and placing them in a box.

PHOTOCOPIABLE

Properties card game

strong	hard
flexible	soft
stretchy	rigid

Photocopy this page four times to make a set of 24 cards. Cut them up, mount them on thick card and laminate them for durability.

■SCHOLASTIC

It could be made from...

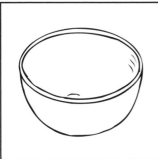	A bowl could be made from:
	A bucket could be made from:
	A mug could be made from:
	A knife, fork and spoon could be made from:
	A toy car could be made from:

■ Choose from these words:

wood   metal   glass   paper   fabric   stone   clay   plastic

Illustration © Kirsty Wilson

PHOTOCOPIABLE

What is it made from?

■ Put a tick against the materials each object is made from.

	plastic	wood	metal	cotton	glass	leather	fabric

Illustration © Kirsty Wilson

◣SCHOLASTIC

Materials at school – 1

■ Cut out the labels and stick one in each box to show what the things are made of.

| wood | wood | wood | wood | wood | plastic | plastic | plastic | plastic | plastic | metal | metal | paper | glass | wax |

Illustration © Kirsty Wilson

PHOTOCOPIABLE

Materials at school – 2

◼ Cut out the labels and stick them in the correct places on the picture.

glass

glass

metal

metal

metal

metal

plastic

wood

wood

brick/clay

brick/clay

brick/clay

brick/clay

Illustration © Kirsty Wilson

◣SCHOLASTIC

Magnets

These things are attracted to a magnet:

These things are not attracted to a magnet:

PHOTOCOPIABLE

Teddy's umbrella

◼ Cover Teddy's umbrella with waterproof material.

■SCHOLASTIC

Assessment – 1

1. Windows are made of glass because _____

_____

These things are also made of glass:

2. Doors are made of wood because _____

_____

These things are also made of wood:

3. Umbrellas are made of plastic because _____

_____

These things are also made of plastic:

4. Knives and forks are made of metal because _____

_____

These things are also made of metal:

PHOTOCOPIABLE

Assessment – 2

◼ Which of these things are attracted to a magnet?

◼ Colour in the ones that are. Cross out the ones that are not.

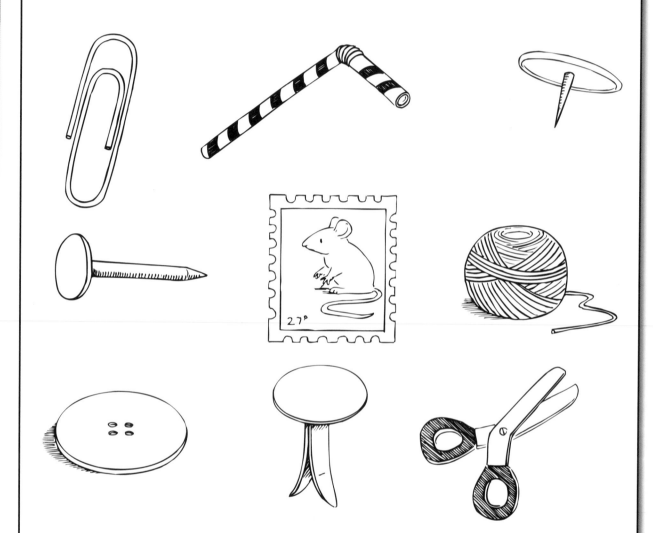

What are the things that are attracted to a magnet made from?

_____

Where might you find or use a magnet in a house?

_____

_____

Illustration © Kirsty Wilson

◾SCHOLASTIC

CHAPTER 4 Light and dark

Lesson	Objectives	Main activity	Group activities	Plenary	Outcomes
Lesson 1 In the dark	• To know that light is needed for us to see things. • To carry out a simple investigation.	Look at an object in a 'dark box': the more light is admitted, the more clearly the object can be seen.	• Put different-coloured objects in the box to see which shows up best. • Write about what they have found out.	Try seeing in a dark room. Review the 'dark box' investigation.	• Know that light is needed for us to see things. • Can carry out a simple investigation with help.
Lesson 2 Light Lotto	• To know that there are many sources of light.	Look at a collection of light sources. Look at light sources inside and outside the school. Discuss fire.	• Sort light sources on cards into 'families'. • Make a large class picture showing light sources.	Discuss the purposes of different light sources.	• Understand that light can come from many sources.
Lesson 3 How many lights are in your house?	• To know that light sources are used in different ways.	Discuss the use of light sources.	• Consider and record how many lights there are at home. • Write a story or poem about what it would be like without any light.	Discuss the uses of light and share the children's writing.	• Can recognise different uses of light sources.
Lesson 4 Brighter at night	• To know that light sources show up best at night.	Look at pictures of lights at night. Explore how lights show up better in the dark.	• Investigate how brightly torchlight shows up in the light and dark. • Make splatter paintings of fireworks.	Discuss why lights show up better at night.	• Can recognise that light sources show up best at night.
Lesson 5 Which is brightest?	• To know that light sources vary in brightness. • To carry out a simple investigation.	Test a number of different torches and rank them in order of brightness.		Review the investigation and results.	• Know that light sources vary in brightness. • Can carry out a simple investigation with help.
Lesson 6 Light safety	• To know how to keep safe with or near light sources.	Discuss the dangers associated with some light sources. Role play keeping safe at a birthday party.	• Draw up a set of rules for keeping safe at a birthday party. • Design a poster about the dangers of looking at the Sun.	Review the safe use of various light sources.	• Know some of the dangers associated with some light sources.
Lesson 7 Shining in the light	• To know that objects with shiny surfaces can only be seen in the presence of light.	Look at shiny and dull objects in a 'dark box'. Which are easiest to see in poor light?	• Use shiny materials to make a collage mobile. • Draw or paint a picture of someone wearing reflective clothing.	Relate the investigation to the uses of reflective clothing.	• Know that light is needed even to see shiny things. • Know that some shiny things, such as reflective armbands, can help us to be seen more easily when there is only a little light.
Enrichment Lesson 8 Bonfire safety	• To know about the dangers associated with bonfires and fireworks. • To know how to call the emergency services.	Think about keeping safe at a bonfire or firework party. Role play calling the emergency services, giving name and address.		Review the dangers of fire and fireworks.	• Know how to avoid accidents at a bonfire or fireworks party. • Know how to call the emergency services. • Know their own address.

Assessment	Objectives	Activity 1	Activity 2
Lesson 9	• To assess whether the children know that there are many sources of light.	Identify sources of light from pictures. Name more light sources.	Identify objects that can or cannot be seen in the dark.

SC1 SCIENTIFIC ENQUIRY

Shiny objects are not light sources

LEARNING OBJECTIVES AND OUTCOMES
● To think about what might happen before deciding what to do.
● To compare what happened with what they expected would happen and try to explain it.

ACTIVITY
Children predict which spoon may be more easily seen in the dark – a wooden spoon or a shiny metal one. They then test their idea using a dark box. They discuss their findings that light is needed even to see a shiny object in the dark and that shiny objects are not, therefore, light sources.

LESSON LINKS
Use this Sc1 activity as an integral part of Lesson 7, Shining in the light.

Lesson 1 ▪ In the dark

Objectives
● To know that light is needed for us to see things.
● To carry out a simple investigation.

Vocabulary
light, dark, see, eyes, dim, bright, shadow, cave, reflect

RESOURCES
Main activity: A cardboard box, masking tape, a craft knife, greaseproof paper, scissors, cloth, a small object (see Preparation); a copy of *A Dark, Dark Tale* by Ruth Brown (Andersen Press) or *The Park In the Dark* by Martin Waddell and Barbara Firth (Walker Books).
Group activities: 1 The 'dark box' (see Preparation); several similar small objects (such as counting bears) in different colours. **2** Writing materials, paper.

BACKGROUND
Objects can only be seen because light is reflected from them. Many young children believe that light comes out of their eyes, enabling them to see. Some children will never have experienced complete darkness, especially if they live in a town or city. Street lights mean that there is almost always some ambient light that allows things to be seen, if only very dimly. Draping some very heavy fabric over a table can make a dark place for the children to experience.

PREPARATION
Make a 'dark box' from a fairly large cardboard box (a photocopier paper box would do, but a slightly bigger and longer one would be better). Paint it black inside, and make two 'peep-holes' (the size of a pencil) in one end. Use some masking tape to cover one of the holes (you will need this in Lesson 7). Cut a long slit (about 2cm wide) in the top of the box to form a 'window' and cover this with greaseproof paper or some other translucent material. Cover the window with a piece of cloth or card that will exclude all light. Place a suitable small object near the back of the box. If you are working in bright light, you may find it helpful to have a cloth that is big enough to cover the child's head as he or she looks through the peep-hole (as you would with an old-fashioned camera).

STARTER
Read out a story such as *A Dark, Dark Tale* by Ruth Brown (Andersen Press) or *The Park In the Dark* by Martin Waddell and Barbara Firth (Walker Books).

MAIN ACTIVITY
Work with a group and talk about dark places the children may have been in. Some of them may have visited caves, have been out very late at night, or even have a dark corner somewhere in their home. What could you see in that place? Could you see anything at all? Were there lots of dark shadows? Could you see any colours? Ask the children for ideas about why they could not see very well. Remember that at this stage we are not looking for scientifically correct answers, but for the children to express their own ideas.

Invite a child to look in the 'dark box'. Make sure the cover is over the box, excluding all light. Can you see anything? Gently fold back the cover a little way. Can you see anything now? Fold the cover back a little more. What can you see now? Carry on, asking the child to describe what he or she can see at each stage, until the cover is completely removed. At first the children should see nothing at all; then they may see the object, but the colours will not be clear. They should see the object best when the cover has been completely removed.

GROUP ACTIVITIES
1 Let groups of three or four children investigate putting similar, different-coloured objects (such as counting bears) in the box to find out which colour shows up best. *How far does the cover have to be folded back before you can see what colour it is?* Pale colours, such as white or yellow, will show up before darker colours.
2 Ask the children to write individually about what they have found out. Encourage them to write down their ideas about how we can see things.

ASSESSMENT
Ask the children to describe what they could see in the 'dark box'. Can they explain the difference between what they could see when the box was covered and when it was uncovered? Do they know that we need light to be able to see anything?

PLENARY
If possible, close the classroom curtains and switch off the lights. *Can you still see things clearly?* Switch the lights back on and talk about the difference this makes to our ability to see things. *What has made the difference?* Help the children to understand that our eyes can only see things when there is light available. Ask them to describe what they could see in the 'dark box'. *Why couldn't you see anything at first?* Ask some of the children who carried out the investigation to describe what they did. *Which colour was the easiest to see? Was the test you carried out fair? Did you put all the objects in the same place? Did you measure anything?*

OUTCOMES
● Know that light is needed for us to see things.
● Can carry out a simple investigation with help.

LINKS
Unit 1A Lesson 3, The senses.
Literacy: writing a report.

Lesson 2 ▫ Light Lotto

Objective
● To know that there are many sources of light.

Vocabulary
light, bright, brightness, illuminated, dim, electric, battery, burn, neon lights, lamp, bonfire, camp-fire, fireworks

RESOURCES

Main activity: A collection of light sources (candles, torches, lanterns, table lamps and so on); pictures or posters of the Sun, bonfires, fireworks and neon advertising displays.
Group activities: 1 Cards from photocopiable page 140 (see Preparation).
2 Drawing, painting or collage materials, paper.

BACKGROUND

Many light sources contain glass, and children need to be aware that it is necessary to take care when near them. If you have an oil lamp in your collection, make sure that it is completely empty of any oil. Children can become quite intrigued by 'old-fashioned' forms of lighting. They have probably never known an environment without electricity, and find it difficult to imagine light not being available at the touch of a switch. Working by gaslight or candle-light was relatively difficult. This is one reason why people often used to get up at dawn and go to bed when it became dark.

The Sun is our main source of light. The Moon, although it gives us light at night, does not have any light of its own and only shines because it reflects light from the Sun. Stars (which are similar to our Sun) do shine with their own light, but they are so far away, and appear so small, that this has a fairly minimal effect.

PREPARATION

Use a copy of page 140 to make a set of cards that can be used to play a 'Happy Families' type of game. Colour the pictures, mount them on stiff card and cover them with sticky-backed plastic to make a permanent resource. The same cards could be used to play Snap or (if you make base boards) Lotto.

STARTER

Ask the children what gives us light during the day. Remind them that they should never look directly at the Sun, even through sunglasses as bright sunlight can damage their eyes.

MAIN ACTIVITY

Have the children sitting comfortably on the carpet. Ask them: *What happens when the Sun has set at night? Where do we get light from then? We might get light from the Moon if we are outside, but what about inside?* Look at some light sources from the collection. Look first at sources that are more familiar to the children, such as torches or table lamps. *When might we use such things?* We might need a torch to find our way along a dark path.

Group activity 1
For children in need of support, use 'Light Lotto' (green) from the CD-ROM. This version includes three instead of four light 'families'.

Group activity 2
All the children should be able to contribute to this activity.

Some children might go camping and use torches to find their way across the campsite at night. Table lamps are often used for decoration, or they might have one by their bed. *What do we have to do to make electric lights work?* Remind the children about switches, and look for the switch on a lamp that you have. Remind them also about the dangers of misusing electricity, and that they should always ask a grown-up to help them plug things in.

How did people light their homes before we had electricity? Look at any lanterns, oil lamps or candles you may have, and talk about how they work. The children may have had experience of a power cut; how did they cope with the lack of electricity? Did they use candles? You may have some specialist lights in your collection, such as a miner's hand-held lamp or helmet lamp. Walk around the school and look for lights inside the school. Note where they are placed. *Why has that light been put in that particular place?* Look for lights on stairs or in dark corridors. *Are all the lights the same shape?* Now look for lights outside the school. *Do you have security lights that come on as soon as it gets dark? Why do we need street lights? Why do we need traffic lights? Why are some road signs illuminated? How do they help to keep us safe?*

Back in the classroom, think about what else would give us light. Look at some of the pictures you have of bonfires or camp-fires. *How is this light different from the electric lights we are used to?* It is not as controllable or as bright; and although electric lights will get hot, they will not get as hot as a bonfire. *Could we carry a bonfire around with us, to light our way like a torch?* People used to carry small fires around in the form of candles or flaming torches. *What do we use candles for these days?* Most children will have had candles on their birthday cakes, and some may use them in religious festivals. Some people just like burning candles, particularly scented ones. Take this opportunity to remind the children about the dangers of playing with matches and fire, and the need to keep safe. They should never have a bonfire or use fireworks unless a grown-up is present.

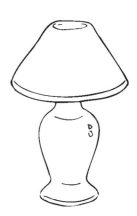

GROUP ACTIVITIES

1 Let the children play 'Happy Families' in groups of four, using the prepared cards. Each child is dealt a 'family name' card. This will tell them which type of light source they are collecting. They then take it in turns to take a card from the picture pile. If the card is in their 'family', they keep it; if not, they put it at the bottom of the pile. It would be helpful to have an adult working with the children the first time they play the game.

2 Involve the children in making a class picture showing various light sources. This could be either a daytime or a night-time picture. It could be a representation of a house (with the front wall removed to show the interior), garden, garage and street. The house could contain ceiling lights, wall lights, table lamps, a standard lamp, a fireplace and a TV. The garage could contain a car, a torch and a fluorescent light. In the garden, you could have a bonfire and a barbecue with the Sun shining (or the Moon and stars). Finish off the picture with a street light. Give the children pieces of paper approximately the size required for the item that they are drawing or collaging.

ASSESSMENT

Ask the children to name two or three different sources of light. Invite them to choose an item from the collection and describe where and how it would be used.

PLENARY
Ask the children to name some of the different types of light they saw on their walk and describe their purpose. Talk about the different ways in which we use lights: for working, reading and travelling; for decoration, information and safety.

OUTCOME
● Understand that light can come from many sources.

Lesson 3 ▪ How many lights are in your house?

Objective
● To know that light sources are used in different ways.

Vocabulary
navigate, sunset, streetlight, floodlight, fuel, reliable, gas, electric, oil, candle, illuminated

RESOURCES ⊙
Main activity: Flipchart, board or whiteboard.
Group activities: 1 Copies of photocopiable page 141 (also 'How many lights are in your house?' (red), available on the CD-ROM), writing materials. **2** Writing and drawing materials.
ICT link: 'How many lights are in your house?' interactive, available on the CD-ROM.

BACKGROUND
The Sun is there for everyone during daylight hours, as the light from the Sun is so strong that it can even penetrate through cloud. It gives us light to get on with all our work. Plants need sunlight to make food so that they can grow. The Moon sometimes gives light at night (it is not a true light source: it reflects the Sun's light), and this is very important in rural areas where there are no street lights. However, moonlight can be obscured by cloud and because of the phases of the Moon it is not always visible. The stars don't give a great deal of light, but they can sometimes be important for sailors who use  them to navigate. These natural sources of light are also very important for people who don't have access to artificial lighting.

Artificial lighting comes in many forms. Fire is probably the most basic but we have learned to use other fuels to produce light – mostly oil, gas or coal used to generate electricity. Nowadays light is used in different ways, and for different purposes: decorative as well as purely utilitarian.

STARTER
Working with the whole class, remind the children of the work that they did in Lesson 1 about different light sources.

MAIN ACTIVITY
Ask the children to name some light sources and, as they do, note them on the flipchart or whiteboard. Make sure that the list includes the Sun and stars. Group other sources according to the fuel they use. For example, gas (camping gas lamps, gas lights), wax (candles of various sorts), oil (oil lamps, Divali lamps, Aladdin's lamp), electricity (ceiling lights, desk or table lamps, torches, floodlights, advertising and so on). The Moon reflects light from the Sun, but is not a light source.

How do we use the different lights? (We use sunlight as much as we can. We have windows to let the sunlight into our buildings. Sometimes there are extra windows or skylights in the roof to give us even more light. We can't

Differentiation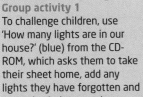
Group activity 1
To challenge children, use 'How many lights are in our house?' (blue) from the CD-ROM, which asks them to take their sheet home, add any lights they have forgotten and report back the next day.
Group activity 2
All the children can participate in this activity.

always see the stars so we can't rely on them.)

But do we only use light sources when it is dark? Point to the group on the board that includes candles. Ask: *How, and when, do we use candles?* (They have to be lit with a match. They are used on birthday cakes, in church or for other religious celebrations, in the garden, at barbecues or around the house to smell nice.) Tell the children that before we had gas or electricity, people often only had candles to light their homes and they often had to do their work by candlelight. Nowadays we use them for fun and celebrations. Remind the children of the dangers of playing with matches or lighted candles.

Now look at the oil lamp group. *Where might these be used?* (Historically, some rich people may have had oil lamps instead of candles. They are still used in some remote places where there is no electricity supply. Some farmers may still use oil lanterns, but these have mostly been replaced by electric torches.) Next, look at the light sources using gas as a fuel. Tell the children that before electricity was discovered, people used to have gaslights in their houses and the first street lights were also gas. A man, called a lamplighter, would go along every evening to light the lamps and then again in the morning to put them out. Ask: *Where do we use gas lights today?* (Sometimes when we go on a camping or caravanning holiday we use lights that run off a small cylinder of a special gas.)

Now look at the biggest group – light sources that use electricity. This will be the type of lighting that the children are most familiar with but try to help them appreciate how much, and in how many different ways, we use it.

Ceiling lights give a general light for everyone in the room, but a desk or table lamp gives a concentrated light over a smaller area. *When might that be useful?* (For someone reading or sewing or doing other delicate work.) Some people have a light just outside their front door. *Why is that useful? Why do we have street lights?* (So that people can see who is there or where they are going, to prevent accidents, to keep people safe.) Ask the children, next time they go on a journey, to check if all street lights are the same. Those on side roads are often a different design from those on main roads or motorways, and some roundabouts have very tall posts with a cluster of lights at the top. *Why do you think this is? Where else might you see clusters of lights on a tall frame or post?* (Some children may have been to a football match or other sports meeting and seen the floodlights.)

These are all 'useful' lights, but sometimes lights are used just for decoration. Can the children think of any examples? (Christmas decorations, coloured lights on shops or theatres.) Some of these lights are also there to tell us something important or to warn us of possible danger. They might be advertising food or drink, or what is happening inside the building. Ask the children if they can think of anywhere lights are used to warn us. (Illuminated road signs, traffic lights, road crossings, flashing lights on railway crossings, flashing blue lights on emergency vehicles or yellow ones on other road hazards.) *Why are flashing lights used?* (These are more likely to attract attention than a continuous light.)

GROUP ACTIVITIES

1 Give each child a copy of photocopiable page 141 and ask them to think very carefully about all the lights they have in their house; not just those hanging from the ceiling or on desks, but all the little warning lights on the television, video, washing machine, cooker and so on. Ask them to make a list of the lights found in each room.

2 Ask the children to use their imaginations to think and write about what it would be like if there were no light at all. *Would it be hot or cold without the Sun? What would happen to plants and animals? How would we find our way about?* The children could present their thoughts as prose or poetry.

ICT LINK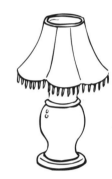

Challenge the children to identify the light sources on the 'How many lights are in your house?' interactive from the CD-ROM. Each time they click on an item that gives off light, the object will light up. If they can identify ten light sources, a 'Well done' sign will appear.

ASSESSMENT

Use the children's work from the group activities to assess their understanding.

PLENARY

Ask some of the children to share the lists of lights they have in their homes. *Do any of them have special lights anywhere, such as a bright light for Mum's sewing, or a night light?* Ask other children to read their stories or poems and share what they think it would be like without light.

OUTCOME

● Can recognise different uses of light sources.

Lesson 4 ◗ Brighter at night

Objective
● To know that light sources show up best at night.

Vocabulary
darkness, light, bright, dim, torchlight, glow

RESOURCES

Main activity: Pictures showing lights in the dark such as fireworks, traffic at night, a candle glowing in the dark, a torchlight procession.
Group activities: 1 A dark corner, a torch. **2** Black paper, bright or fluorescent paint, brushes, water, writing materials.

BACKGROUND

This activity is best done during the winter months when light levels are generally lower and the children will have some recent experience of darkness before bedtime. Darkness is the absence of light and many children will never have experienced total darkness. Sources such as street lights, advertising lights and televisions all provide some ambient lighting.

During the day, the Sun, the brightest light we know even when it is covered in cloud, makes other light sources seem comparatively dim. Therefore when the Sun is absent, other light sources appear brighter and show up better.

STARTER

Talk about when it is light (daytime) and when it is dark (night-time) and the difference between them. Make sure that the children understand that it is the absence of the Sun that causes night. Tell them that the Sun is so bright during the day that even though the stars are still there and shining, we cannot see them.

MAIN ACTIVITY

Show the children the pictures of night-time lights. *What is the same about all of them?* (They have all been taken at night.) *Why do events such as bonfire parties and torchlight processions always happen at night? What other lights can we see when it is dark?* (Street lights, car headlights, advertising signs and so on.) If you have a Belisha crossing near the school, take the children to look at it in the daylight. Notice that it is still flashing but is not very bright. Ask the children to look out for it at night and note the difference. It shows up much more brightly in the dark. Ask them to look out of their bedroom window when it is dark and look at all the lights they can see. *Are any of the lights you saw at night still there in the daytime? Are they as bright?*

GROUP ACTIVITIES

1 Go outside in small groups, in the daylight, and shine a torch onto the school wall. *How well does the torchlight show up?* Now go inside, find a dark corner and shine the torch on the wall. *Is it brighter or dimmer than it was outside? When do you think the torch might shine even more brightly?*
2 Let children make a splatter 'firework' picture on black paper using bright colours or fluorescent paint. Splatter pictures can either be made by flicking paint onto paper (if you feel very brave) or by dropping brush-loads of paint onto dampened paper. Try adding glitter for a really shiny effect. Mount as a class display and add a few sentences about why fireworks show up best at night.

ASSESSMENT

During the main activity and the plenary, note children's level of understanding and input. Some children may have a problem equating a dark corner with night-time. Assess the children's writing to find out how well they have understood.

PLENARY

Talk to the whole class about their work and ask them about some of the light sources they see at night. *What did they see from their bedroom window? Did they see any lights that were also there in the day?* (Crossing lights, traffic lights, advertising and so on). *Were they brighter by day or night?* Ask the children to explain why light sources show up best at night.

OUTCOME

● Can recognise that light sources show up best at night.

Lesson 5 ▫ Which is brightest?

Differentiation
Group activity 1
You may find that mixed-ability groups are an advantage in this activity.
Group activity 2
Some children might be able to write a sentence or two explaining why light sources show up better at night.

Objectives
● To know that light sources vary in brightness.
● To carry out a simple investigation.

RESOURCES
A collection of three or four different torches; a dark corner or a dark space under a table.

MAIN ACTIVITY
The children carry out a simple test to find out which torch is brightest: shining each torch in turn onto white paper with simple words written on it. Ask: *Which torch helps you read best? Can you rank the torches in order of brightness?* Discuss the need to shine the torches from the same distance to make it fair.

ASSESSMENT
Observe the children as they carry out their test. Note which children try to keep their test fair. During the plenary session, note which children can explain their findings.

PLENARY
Ask groups to report back what they have found. *Did the results change as time went on because of the batteries running down?*

Differentiation
Some children may need help to understand that shining the torches from different distances will not be fair.

OUTCOMES
● Know that light sources vary in brightness.
● Can carry out a simple investigation with help.

Lesson 6 ◗ Light safety

Objective
● To know how to keep safe with or near light sources.

Vocabulary
safe, burn, bright, dangerous, emergency services, light sources, heat

RESOURCES
Main activity: A collection of light sources (as for Lesson 2, Light Lotto); paper napkins, streamers, paper hats, paper cups and plates, a small table, an empty matchbox, candles, a 'pretend cake' (see Preparation).
Group activities: Paper, drawing and painting materials.

BACKGROUND
Small children do not appreciate that looking at a very strong light can damage their sight. The light-sensitive cells in the retina at the back of the eye can be damaged, and they cannot be repaired. Children should be told never to look at the Sun, even through sunglasses or other 'safe' materials such as smoked glass. Binoculars can be very useful for looking at the night sky, but must never be used for looking at the Sun: they will concentrate the Sun's rays directly into the eye, causing irreparable damage. You may have a child who gains access to a laser pointer and plays at making the red dot appear on the faces of classmates. This, too, is extremely dangerous and should be discouraged.

Many light sources produce heat, and it is often the heat that constitutes the greater danger as far as children are concerned. The Sun, candles, bonfires and fireworks are obvious sources of heat; but even a light bulb can get very hot after it has been on for a short time, and can remain hot for some time after being switched off. Mains electricity is always a hazard, and children should always be taught to treat with respect any equipment using this source of energy.

PREPARATION
Make a 'pretend cake' from a small, round biscuit tin. Decide how many candles you want to add to your 'cake' and punch the required number of holes in the top with a hammer and nail. Paint the tin white. Put a cake frill round the tin and poke plastic candle holders into the holes. Add the candles.

STARTER
Remind the class about some of the light sources they encountered in Lesson 2, showing them the same collection of objects.

MAIN ACTIVITY
Talk about the light sources that the children use. We all use the Sun during the day. Remind the children that they should never look directly at the Sun. *What lights do you use at home?* (Living room, bedroom, kitchen and so on.) These lights are usually quite safe as long as the children switch them on and off sensibly. *Do you ever use a torch?* These again are usually quite safe, but the children should be warned against shining any torch directly into another's eyes: a bright torch can cause temporary loss of vision. *Are there lights that tell you when equipment is switched on?* (The little red light on the television, kettle or washing machine.) Talk about how these lights help to keep us safe by warning us that the kettle is hot or that the washing machine is full of water.

Discuss light sources that the children may use only occasionally, such as candles or fireworks. These are fun lights, but they can be dangerous. Talk about how we can keep ourselves safe while still having fun. Show the children the pretend birthday cake with real candles, and ask them what things they think could be dangerous about the lighted candles. Do they realise that trailing hair could easily catch fire, or that an unfixed candle could fall over and set things on fire? *How would you keep the birthday party safe?*

Differentiation
Group activity 1
Some children might work together in a larger group to support each other in this activity, drawing up a set of rules between them.
Group activity 2
All the children should be able to participate in this activity, although some may need help to write words on their poster.

Set up a role-play situation with the birthday cake and candles on a small table. Have some paper napkins, 'matches' (an empty matchbox), streamers, paper hats and paper cups and plates on another table. Ask the children to choose the things that would be safe to put on the table with the lighted candles. Ask them to explain why the streamers, napkins or paper hats could be dangerous if they got too near the lighted candles. *Who should light the candles? Where and how should they sit or stand? Should they lean over the cake if they have long hair?* Remind the children that they should never play with matches or candles, and should always ask a grown-up to light candles.

GROUP ACTIVITIES
1 Ask individuals or pairs to draw up a set of rules for keeping safe at a birthday party.
2 Ask individuals to design a poster about the dangers of looking at the Sun and other bright lights.

ASSESSMENT
Watch the children as they set the party table. Are they able to explain why they have chosen the things they have? Assess the suitability of the rules and posters that they have made.

PLENARY
Remind the children of the need to use light sources sensibly. It is important to stress that light sources are useful and necessary, and we normally benefit from them; but they do hold dangers if we are careless in using them.

OUTCOME
● Know some of the dangers associated with some light sources.

Lesson 7 ▷ Shining in the light

Objective
● To know that objects with shiny surfaces can only be seen in the presence of light.

Vocabulary
reflect, reflective strips, shine, shiny, dull, light

RESOURCES
Main activity: A collection of shiny objects (such as a tablespoon, a teaspoon, plastic mirrors, scissors, saucepans and lids, silver foil, crumpled silver foil, holographic paper, coloured foil, reflective armbands), comparable dull objects (wooden spoon, paper and so on); the 'dark box' and cover from Lesson 1, a torch; pictures of a crossing patrol, or of emergency services people in uniforms with reflective strips.
Group activities: 1 Shiny and dull papers or materials, glitter, adhesive, spreaders, thick paper. **2** Reflective strips or silver foil paper.

BACKGROUND
Year 1 children will have explored shiny (reflective) things in Reception. Some children may still have misconceptions about how we see things, and think that shiny things shine with their own light. All objects reflect light, but dull objects scatter light in all directions. Shiny things reflect light more directly, which appears to make them shine. If the object is very smooth, like a mirror, it may allow us to see reflected images. If there is no light, then no light can be reflected and we cannot see the object at all.

STARTER
Gather the class together on the carpet. Ask the children to look at the collection of shiny objects and tell you what they have in common. The children should be able to tell you that they are all shiny.

MAIN ACTIVITY
Working with a group, choose one of the shiny objects and compare it with a similar dull object – for example, a metal tablespoon and a wooden spoon. Ask the children to describe some similarities and differences. Both spoons have a handle at one end and a bowl shape for picking things up at the other end. A metal spoon is smoother, shinier and thinner than a wooden spoon. The spoons are different colours. The metal spoon feels colder than the wooden one.

Invite the children to vote on which spoon they might see if it was really, really dark. Note on the board who voted for the metal spoon, who voted for the wooden spoon, and who thought they would see both or neither. Ask the children for their ideas about how they could find out. Remind them of the investigation they did with the 'dark box' in Lesson 1, and explain that they can use the same box to test these objects.

Put the two objects in the box and make sure it is well covered. Ask the children to take turns to look and see whether they can see anything through the peep-hole. Look at the predictions the children made and ask whether anyone wants to change their mind. Encourage them to think back to Lesson 1 and tell you why they cannot see anything. Remove the cover from the second peep-hole and ask them to look again. *Are you beginning to see the objects?* Shine a torch through the second peep-hole and ask them to look again. *What has made the difference? Can you see the objects better because of the light?* Ask the children whether they think there is anything in the collection that they would be able to see in the dark. *What about the reflective armbands?* Put these in the box and find out whether they can be seen in the dark, or whether you still need some light. These should shine quite brightly even at low light levels, but will still not be visible in complete darkness.

Discuss why people wear reflective armbands. *Where might the light come from to make them shine?* Talk about how street lights and car headlamps provide the light so that the armbands shine, helping to make them visible in near-darkness. Talk about people such as a crossing patrol,

Differentiation

Group activity 1
Some children may need help to pick out shiny materials.
Group activity 2
All the children should be able to participate in this activity.

firefighters, paramedics or police officers who wear reflective strips on their uniforms, so that they can be seen more easily at night. Refer to pictures if possible.

Reinforce the finding from Lesson 1 that we can only see things when some light is present, even if they are shiny. Leave the 'dark box' on display for the next day or two, so that the children can look again and carry out their own investigations.

GROUP ACTIVITIES

1 The children can work in groups of three or four, or as individuals, to make a shiny collage mobile (for example, showing icicles or raindrops). Give them a mixture of shiny and dull materials from which they have to choose the shiny ones. The mobiles can be hung where they will catch the light.
2 Ask the children to draw or paint a picture of a child, firefighter, crossing patrol, paramedic or police officer wearing reflective strips on his/her clothing. They can stick small strips of reflective material (or of silver foil) in appropriate places on the picture.

ASSESSMENT

Can the children say what we need in order to be able to see things, even if they are shiny? Can they describe how some shiny things help us to be seen more easily when there is not much light? Observe them choosing the materials for their collage: do they know which are the shiny materials?

PLENARY

Look at the mobiles the children have made, and talk about how shiny they are. Watch how they change if you move them in the light. Ask the children: *Could we see them if they were in the dark box?* Talk about why the emergency services have shiny (reflective) strips on their uniforms.

OUTCOMES

● Know that light is needed even to see shiny things.
● Know that some shiny things, such as reflective armbands, can help us to be seen more easily when there is only a little light.

LINKS

Unit 1D Lesson 1, In the dark.
Art: making mobiles.

ENRICHMENT
Lesson 8 ◻ Bonfire safety

Objectives
● To know about the dangers associated with bonfires and fireworks.
● To know how to call the emergency services.

RESOURCES
Pictures of bonfires, an old (unconnected) telephone.

MAIN ACTIVITY
Many cultures celebrate festivals with bonfires and fireworks. Discuss when the children would see these. *What do you like best about a bonfire and firework party? What are the rules for keeping safe? Should everyone, including grown-ups, take notice of these rules?* Talk about keeping well back from fire. Stress that the children should never handle fireworks, except a sparkler given by a responsible adult. No one should ever put fireworks in someone's pocket. Fireworks should always be kept in a metal box, away from matches. *What should you do if there is an accident?* The children should learn the procedure for calling the emergency services (when at home): dial 999 and give their name and address. They can practise by role-playing with a telephone.

ASSESSMENT
During the plenary session, ask the children to tell you some of the rules about bonfires and fireworks. Note which children know how to call the emergency services.

PLENARY
Remind the children of the dangers of playing with fire and fireworks: standing back from fires; never handling fireworks; never going back to a firework that hasn't gone off, and so on.

Differentiation
All the children need to be aware of these safety rules.

OUTCOMES
● Know how to avoid accidents at a bonfire or fireworks party.
● Know how to call the emergency services.
● Know their own address.

Lesson 9 ◻ Assessment

Objective
● To know that there are many sources of light.

RESOURCES ⊙
Assessment activities: 1 Photocopiable page 142 (also 'Assessment – 1' (red), available on the CD-ROM), pencils, colouring materials. **2** Photocopiable page 143 (also 'Assessment – 2' (red), available on the CD-ROM), pencils.
ICT link: 'Sources of light' interactive, available on the CD-ROM.

STARTER
You may wish to start the lesson by asking the children to remember some of the things they have learned in this unit. Before they do the assessment activities, remind them that we use our eyes to see, but that we also need a light source before we can see anything.

ASSESSMENT ACTIVITY 1
Give each child a copy of photocopiable page 142. Go through the pictures and make sure the children know what each object is. Read out the words. Ask the children to complete the sheet.

ANSWERS
The teddy bear, mirror, chair and spoon are not sources of light.

LOOKING FOR LEVELS
Most children should be able to identify four of the light sources correctly and add at least one suggestion. Some children may not be able to identify many of the light sources, and may include some non-light sources in their answer. Other children will identify all the light sources and add several more. They may even be able to complete the sentence at the bottom of the page.

ASSESSMENT ACTIVITY 2
Give each child a copy of photocopiable page 143. Read through the page with them and make sure they understand what to do. Ask them to complete the sheet.

ANSWERS
The lit torch and the lit lamp are the only things that would be seen in the dark. The other items, although shiny, are not light sources and can only be seen when reflecting light.

LOOKING FOR LEVELS
Most children should be able to identify both light sources. Some children may include the mirror as something that can be seen in the dark. Other children will be able to explain that the other objects, although shiny, are not light sources.

ICT LINK
You could also the 'Sources of light' interactive, available on the CD-ROM, to assess children's understanding of light sources.

Light Lotto

			Table lamps
			Torches
			Candles
			Fireworks

■SCHOLASTIC

Illustration © Kirsty Wilson

How many lights are in your house?

■ Record all the lights in your house in the spaces below.

Illustration © Kirsty Wilson

Assessment – 1

◀ Colour in all the things that are sources of light.

Write the names of some more sources of light: _____

_____

_____

📖 SCHOLASTIC

Assessment – 2

■ Draw a ✔ in the correct column to show if you can or cannot see an object in the dark.

	Can see	Can't see
Lit torch		
Metal spoon		
Mirror		
Lit lamp		
Silver paper		
Saucepan		

Illustration © Kirsty Wilson

CHAPTER 5 Pushes and pulls

Lesson	Objectives	Main activity	Group activities	Plenary	Outcomes
Lesson 1 Movement tally	• To know that there are different kinds of movement. • To collect data from observations and use a simple record sheet.	Carry out and identify different kinds of movement when playing. Keep a tally chart of movements.	• Create individual 'movement' pictures of themselves. • Make a block graph from the information on the tally chart.	Extract information from the block graphs. Name movements seen on a video of themselves.	• Can recognise and name different kinds of movement. • Can use a simple recording sheet to collect data.
Lesson 2 The way we move	• To know that forces help us to move our bodies. • To begin to identify the forces involved.	In a gymnastics lesson, identify some of the forces involved in travelling (as pushes or pulls).	• Groups devise a short sequence of movements using pushes and pulls.	Demonstrate some movements and sequences. Name the forces and body parts used.	• Know that forces help us to move our bodies. • Can name some of the forces involved.
Lesson 3 Pushes and pulls	• To know that forces, such as pushes and pulls, can move objects and change their direction. • To begin to understand cause and effect.	Use small apparatus to experience how forces cause things to move and change direction.	• Pairs pull on a skipping rope to feel the force. • Pairs throw soft balls at each other and discuss the forces being used.	Review the activities. Discuss the effects of increasing degrees of force.	• Can describe the pushes and pulls involved in moving an object or changing its direction. • Begin to understand cause and effect. • Can explain the potential dangers of some moving objects.
Lesson 4 Falling to Earth	• To experience the downward force of gravity. • To know that objects always fall down towards the Earth.	Drop a range of objects. Establish that they all fall down. Discuss whether any objects can 'fall' upwards.	• Make a marble run and observe how it works. • Pour water onto a water wheel and observe how it works.	Identify gravity as the force that makes everything fall downwards.	• Know that objects always fall downwards because of a force called gravity.
Enrichment Lesson 5 Cheesy twisters	• To know that forces such as pushes, pulls and twists can change the shape of objects.	Change the shape of play dough, describing the forces used (pulling, pushing, twisting).		Review the activity and vocabulary.	• Know that they can use forces (pushes, pulls and twists) to change the shape of objects.
Enrichment Lesson 6 Blowing in the wind	• To consider the wind as a force. • To know that wind is moving air. • To know that the wind can make things move.	Blow bubbles outside on a windy day and watch them being blown by the wind. Discuss the appearance of the bubbles.	• Make ribbon streamers and consider how they blow in the wind. • Make and fly carrier bag kites.	Review the observations made and the vocabulary used.	• Can describe how the wind makes things move. • Know that the wind is moving air. • Know that the wind can make things move.
Lesson 7 The dangers of moving objects	• To know that stopping a moving object can be dangerous. • To reinforce the understanding of cause and effect.	Roll a small loaded trolley down a ramp into a clay 'person' to highlight the dangers of moving objects.	• Roll balls into walls made from building blocks with different degrees of force. • Draw a picture of a fast-moving object and explain why it might be dangerous.	Discuss the dangers of getting in the way of fast moving objects.	• Understand that moving objects can be dangerous.
Lesson 8 Windy day walk	• To know that the wind is air that pushes on things in the environment and makes them move. • To know that the wind can exert a push on their bodies.	Go on a 'windy day walk' to observe how the wind blows trees, umbrellas and themselves.		Discuss how the wind's force is a push that can make things move.	• Can describe how the wind pushes on and moves things in the environment. • Can talk about the feel of the wind pushing on them.
Lesson 9 Floating and sinking	• To experience the upward push (force) of water. • To know that water pushes upwards on objects.	Push floating objects down in a tank of water and feel the water pushing up.	• Fill floating cups with water until they sink; discuss what is happening. • Write about what happened in the main activity and why.	Review the activities, using appropriate vocabulary to discuss the forces involved.	• Know that water pushes upwards on objects, and that this push is a force. • Know that a force is needed to push a floating object down into water and that when the force is removed, the object floats again.

Assessment	Objectives		Activity 1		Activity 2
Lesson 10	• To know that pushes and pulls are forces. • To know that forces can make things move.		Name forces by labelling pictures 'push' or 'pull'.		Paired practical activity with partner: move small apparatus and name forces used.

SC1 SCIENTIFIC ENQUIRY

Push, pull, start, stop...

LEARNING OBJECTIVES AND OUTCOMES
- To think about what might happen.
- To follow simple instructions to control risks to themselves and to others.
- To collect evidence by making observations.
- To explore using the senses...as appropriate, and make observations.
- To communicate what happened in a variety of ways (speech).
- To use first hand experience and simple information sources in order to answer questions.
- To make simple comparisons and identify simple patterns and associations.

ACTIVITY
Children use small apparatus to move objects and change their direction such as playing skittles, throwing balls or beanbags into hoops or batting balls to each other. They are asked to predict what will happen if they change the force of their throw or hit.

LESSON LINKS
Use this Sc1 activity as an integral part of Lesson 3, Pushes and pulls.

Lesson 1 ▸ Movement tally

Objectives
- To know that there are different kinds of movement.
- To collect data from observations and use a simple record sheet.

Vocabulary
move, movement, jump, skip, hop, run, roll, climb, walk, balance, crawl, travel, body, tally, graph

RESOURCES ◉
Main activity: Space for the children to move about in (for example, the playground, the park, an adventure playground), photocopiable page 157 (also 'Movement tally' (red), available on the CD-ROM), pencils, clipboards (one per group of six), a video camera (if possible).
Group activities: 1 Drawing materials, plain A4 paper, scissors (sharp enough to cut fabric), adhesive; collage, painting or printing materials.
2 Large squared paper, colouring materials.

BACKGROUND
'Forces and motion' is among the most difficult areas of the science curriculum for us to teach and for young children to grasp, because it is so abstract. At this stage, children should be given the opportunity to experience forces and identify them in simple terms. We cannot see a force, only its effect - for example, the resulting change in movement when a shopping trolley is pushed or when a wheeled toy is pulled. Forces are therefore often described in terms of the effect they have. Forces can start something moving (a push or pull), make it stop (a stone hitting the ground), make it slow down (friction from a rough surface or a car brake), make it go faster (a push or pull) or make it change direction (hitting a ball with a bat).

Identifying the various ways in which we move our bodies is a good way of introducing young children to forces. Friction helps us to walk; gravity brings us back to the ground when we jump. In this first lesson, children will identify the various ways in which they move their bodies; in the second lesson, they will begin to relate some of these movements to the forces involved.

STARTER
Sort the children into groups of six, each group with a clipboard, a copy of photocopiable page 157 and a pencil.

MAIN ACTIVITY

Tell the children that they are going to move about the playground in as many different ways as they can think of. Ask them: *How many ways of moving can you think of?* (Run, hop, skip, jump, walk on hands and feet, and so on.) *Think about which parts of your body you are using.* Tell them to find a new way of moving every time you call 'Change'.

Now say that four members of each group are going to move while the other two watch and record their movements on the tally chart. The four children moving should move as individuals. One of the 'talliers' calls out the different movements of the members of the group, and the other marks the tally chart accordingly. Give all the children a chance to move and to record the movements of their group. If possible, make a video of the children moving about.

GROUP ACTIVITIES

1 Ask the children to draw or collage a 'movement' picture of themselves. These pictures can be cut out and stuck to a background to make a class picture. The children can label their pictures with the type of movement each one shows. The pictures can be made more vivid by allowing the children to add fabric for their clothes, wool for their hair and so on.
2 Using the information from the tally chart, ask each group to make a block graph of their movements.

ICT LINK ☉

The children could use the graphing tool from the CD-ROM to create a graph.

ASSESSMENT

Observe the children as they move and record. Can they name the ways in which they are moving? Are they able to enter their data on the recording sheet? Note which children are able to transfer the information from their tally chart to a block graph.

PLENARY

Talk to the whole class about their work. How many kinds of movement did they identify? *Look at your graphs: which movement did you see the most often? Which did you see the least often?* If you have been able to video the session, show the video to the class and encourage the children to name all the different kinds of movement they can see. Remind them of the work they did (Unit 1A Lesson 18, Joints) when they were learning about themselves and the ways in which their bodies could move.

OUTCOMES
● Can recognise and name different kinds of movement.
● Can use a simple recording sheet to collect data.

LINKS
Unit 1A Lesson 18, Joints; Lesson 19, Animal movements.
Maths: making graphs and charts.

Lesson 2 ◘ The way we move

Objectives
● To know that forces help us to move our bodies.
● To begin to identify the forces involved.

RESOURCES
Main activity: The hall, large PE apparatus (benches, mats, wall bars, ladders, crossbars and so on).
Group activity: Space to move around in.

Vocabulary
move, travel, push, pull, twist, force

BACKGROUND

The forces involved when children are moving their bodies are usually muscular pushes and pulls, friction and gravity. At this early stage, it is usually sufficient for children to focus on the pushes and pulls and know that these are forces. To walk, you push against the ground with each foot in turn. To jump, you push with both feet; gravity pulls you back to the ground. It is the friction between a body part and a surface that allows us to move in a controlled way. Where there is less friction, movement is harder to control (for example, walking on a slippery surface or skating on ice). Children need to be helped to distinguish between a pull and a push as they move their bodies. Gymnastics sessions are a good way of doing this - for example, pulling themselves along a bench just using their arms, or pushing themselves up off the floor (in as many ways as possible) using different parts of the body.

STARTER

If your 'hall time' is limited, you may prefer to spread this lesson over two sessions. Talk to the class about what they learned in Lesson 1 (Movement tally). Ask: *Can you remember all the ways in which you were moving?*

MAIN ACTIVITY

Introduce the children to the idea that they were using forces to move their bodies in Lesson 1. Ask a child to run across the hall while the others watch. Ask: *What is Jane doing with her feet?* (Pushing against the floor.) Tell the children that a push is a force that can help them to move their bodies. Ask another child to move along a bench, lying flat and just using his or her arms. Ask the children what is happening. Encourage the children to use the words *pull, push, pulling, pushing* and *force*. Ask them to think about whether they would use a push or a pull force to move on the large apparatus. *What part of your body would you use?*

GROUP ACTIVITY

Ask groups of about four children to devise a short sequence of movements using pushes and pulls, then practise the sequence and be ready to show it to the whole class, describing each movement and saying whether the force being used is a push or a pull. This is a good opportunity to remind the children about safety: emphasise that the pushes and pulls in their sequence of movements should be gentle and safe, and that pushing or pulling other people too roughly can hurt them.

ASSESSMENT

Observe the children during the lesson. Ask them to name the forces (as 'push' or 'pull') and the body parts they are using.

PLENARY

At the end of the lesson, talk to the whole class and discuss what they have done. Ask some children to demonstrate some of the movements they have practised on the apparatus. *What part of the body did you use? Can you name the force that you were using?* Give the groups (or some of them) the opportunity to show their sequences of movements, naming the forces involved and the parts of the body they have used. More able groups should be able to talk about how the friction enables them to move.

Differentiation
Some children may be ready to consider the role of friction in movement - for example, the friction between our feet and the floor enables us to walk or run.

OUTCOMES
- Know that forces help us to move our bodies.
- Can name some of the forces involved.

LINKS
Unit 1A Lesson 1, Body parts; Lesson 18, Joints.

Lesson 3 ▪ Pushes and pulls

Objectives
● To know that forces, such as pushes and pulls, can move objects and change their direction.
● To begin to understand cause and effect.

Vocabulary
pull, push, change direction, start, stop, move, speed up, slow down, change shape, twist, roll, flatten, cut

RESOURCES
Main activity: A collection of small apparatus (large and small soft balls, bats, skittles, hoops, beanbags and so on).
Group activities: 1 Skipping ropes. **2** Balls or beanbags.

BACKGROUND
Children should be helped to develop the appropriate language to describe moving things. They need to realise that a throw is a type of push, as is hitting something with a bat or rolling it along the ground. Hitting a moving ball with a bat is a push force that changes the direction of the ball - in the case of young children, usually in a completely different direction from that intended! They should begin to appreciate that the amount of force (whether a push or pull) they apply will affect the way in which the object moves: a harder throw (push force) will make a ball or beanbag go faster and further. In Lesson 5, make sure they realise that a twist is a type of force (a push and a pull combined).

STARTER
Remind the class that they were using forces when they were moving their bodies. Tell them that they are going to find out more about forces in this lesson, using small apparatus. The children could work in pairs.

MAIN ACTIVITY
Go through the various available activities with the whole class - for example, throwing large and small balls to each other, batting balls to each other, throwing balls or beanbags into hoops, knocking skittles over by rolling balls at them. Ask some children to demonstrate each activity to the class. Remind them of the forces work that they did in the previous two lessons. *Can anyone remember the names of the forces we were using to move our bodies?* Remind them that these forces were called 'pushes' and 'pulls'.

Tell the children that they are going to work on the various activities, and that you would like them to notice the forces that they are using to move each piece of apparatus. Ask them to really think hard about what is happening - for example, when they are batting a ball to each other. Talk about the forces that are acting in this situation. Batting a ball is a push; hitting the ball back is another push that changes the direction of the ball. *What happens when you bounce a ball?* (You are pushing it against the floor.) *What happens when you bounce it harder?* (You are pushing it harder, so it bounces higher.) Allow the children time to work in pairs on each of the above activities before going on to the group activities below.

GROUP ACTIVITIES
1 Ask the children, in pairs, to pull gently on either end of a taut skipping rope so that they can feel the pull on the rope. They can take turns to pull a little harder, so that they can feel the force increasing. Ask them: *What is your friend doing when you are pulling? Are you both pulling in the same direction? What happens if you both stop pulling? What happens if one stops pulling before the other?* Remind the children that they are feeling a force, not playing tug-of-war, and that they must pull safely and gently. However, if you do have a safe, soft, grassy area, it could be fun to arrange teams of several children and have a tug-of-war.
2 Ask the children, in pairs, to throw a ball or beanbag gently at each other's bodies. Ask: *Can you feel it push on your body? Might it hurt if it was thrown really hard? Can you think of any other moving objects that might be dangerous?* (A moving swing, traffic, a cricket or golf ball.) *Why are they*

dangerous? (Because they can push on the body with a very strong force.) Discuss with the children the need for care and for playing safely.

ASSESSMENT
During the paired work, ask the children to explain what they are doing and to name the forces they have used on a specific piece of small apparatus.

PLENARY
Gather the children together and ask some of them to go through the activities again, describing what they are doing and naming the forces involved. *Are these the same forces that we use to move our bodies?* (Yes.) Talk about the fact that if you throw something harder, using a greater force, you cause it to go further and faster.

OUTCOMES
● Can describe the pushes and pulls involved in moving an object or changing its direction.
● Begin to understand cause and effect (for example, that the harder the push, the further and faster an object will move).
● Can explain the potential dangers from some moving objects.

Differentiation
Group activity 1
Some children using the skipping rope may be ready to recognise that if two people pull with equal force there is no movement, but as soon as one pulls harder than the other, they both move (one backwards and one forwards).
Group activity 2
All the children should be able to take part in this activity.

Lesson 4 ▪ Falling to Earth

Objectives
● To experience the downward force of gravity.
● To know that objects always fall down towards the Earth.

Vocabulary
fall, force, gravity, drop, Earth, pull, down

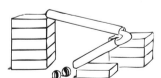

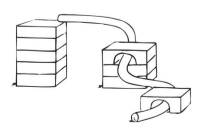

RESOURCES
Main activity: A collection of objects that are safe to drop, such as balls, cotton reels, paper and feathers.
Group activities: 1 The diagram of a marble run (available on the CD-ROM); marble run made from a construction kit or found materials, marbles. **2** A water tray, containers for pouring, a water wheel.

BACKGROUND
The concept of gravity is very difficult and abstract – but it is a force that has a major and constant effect on our lives. At this stage, children are not expected to understand gravity in Newtonian terms; but they need to experience the effect of gravity and know that all objects fall downwards and not upwards. Gravity is the attraction between any two objects that results from their having mass: the more massive the object, the greater the gravitational pull. Because it is the biggest object we have direct contact with, the Earth's gravitational pull is the one that dominates our lives. The force of gravity pulls all objects down towards the centre of the Earth. All objects, in the absence of air resistance or friction, accelerate downwards at the same rate. In practice, there is always air resistance; but if two objects such as a golf ball and a screwed-up ball of paper of the same size are dropped, they will fall at the same rate. If the piece of paper is flattened out, the increased air resistance will cause it to fall more slowly. This is how parachutes work.

STARTER
Ask the whole class to stand up, then to jump as high as they can. *What happens?* (They all come back down to Earth.) *Does anyone carry on going upwards?*

MAIN ACTIVITY
Show the children the collection of objects. Ask them what will happen if the objects are dropped. (They will fall to the floor.) *Do things always fall to the floor when they are dropped? What about a piece of paper and a feather?* Let some children come out and drop the various objects in the

collection while the others watch. *What happens? Can you think of anything that falls upwards?* Some children may suggest things such as gas-filled balloons and kites. Explain that the special gas in helium balloons makes them float, because it is lighter than air. Without that gas it would fall like an ordinary balloon. Also explain that the wind may carry a kite into the sky, but if the wind stops the kite falls. Say that the force that causes things to fall down towards the Earth is called 'gravity'.

GROUP ACTIVITIES

1 Show the children the diagram of a marble run from the CD-ROM. Make a marble run, using a construction kit or found materials (see illustration), and ask the children to roll marbles down it. *What happens? Do they all roll downwards? Can you change your marble run to make the marble go less fast?* (Make the slopes less steep.)
2 Ask the children to pour water from one container to another above a water tray. *What happens? Does it always pour downwards? Can you make it pour upwards? If you use the water to turn a water wheel, does the water go upwards then?* Let them try this and observe that the water falls, making the water wheel turn; the water does not flow upwards (though it may splash upwards before falling again).

ASSESSMENT
In the plenary session, establish whether the children realise that everything falls to the Earth. Do they know that this is caused by a force called gravity?

PLENARY
Talk to the children about what they have been doing. *Did everything you tried fall to the ground? Why? Could you make the water fall upwards? Why not? What is the force called that makes everything fall to the ground?* (Gravity.) It would be fun to finish the session by singing 'This is the way we jump (hop, skip) up and down... all fall down' to the tune of 'Here We Go Round the Mulberry Bush'.

OUTCOME
● Know that objects always fall downwards because of a force called gravity.

ENRICHMENT
Lesson 5 ▪ Cheesy twisters

RESOURCES
Ingredients for cheese straws (see recipe below), pastry boards, rolling pins, safe knives, pastry brushes, baking trays, safe access to an oven.

MAIN ACTIVITY
Working in groups of four, the children make some cheese pastry dough. As they are doing this, draw their attention to the forces they are using (for example, pushing the ingredients through their fingers to make a crumbling mixture, pushing the dough with their hands to knead it). They should roll out the pastry, cut it into strips and twist the pieces. Ask the children to name the forces they are using to change the shape of the dough. *What are you doing? What forces are you using?* Encourage the children to use words such as 'pulling', 'pushing' and 'twisting'. Bake the straws.

ASSESSMENT
While the children are working, note those who can tell you what forces they are using to shape the pastry.

PLENARY

Talk to the children about what they have been doing. Look at the finished straws. Have fun eating the straws! Ask some of the children to describe how they changed the shape of their pastry, and to say what forces they were using.

OUTCOME

● Know that they can use forces (pushes, pulls and twists) to change the shape of objects.

CHEESE STRAWS RECIPE

(Makes about 24 straws)
125g flour
50g butter or margarine
50g cheese, finely grated
1 egg, beaten
1 level tsp mustard powder
a pinch of salt

Put the flour, mustard powder and salt together in a bowl. Add the butter or margarine and rub (push and pull) together until the mixture resembles fine breadcrumbs. Add the cheese and mix thoroughly with a knife. Add the beaten egg and mix in well, keeping a little back to brush the finished straws with. Turn out onto a floured surface and knead (push and pull) lightly until just smooth. Take a quarter of the mixture each. Roll out (push and pull) to between 0.5cm and 1cm thickness. Cut (push) into long strips. Hold both ends of each strip and twist it into a spiral. Place on a greased baking tray and brush with the remaining egg. Bake in the oven at 180°C (350°F, Gas Mark 4) for 12-15 minutes until golden brown.

ENRICHMENT
Lesson 6 ▶ Blowing in the wind

Objectives
● To consider the wind as a force.
● To know that wind is moving air.
● To know that the wind can make things move.

Vocabulary
air, wind, blow, force, move, push, bubbles, burst, float, reflection, shiny, colourful, rainbow, transparent

RESOURCES

Starter: *Mrs Mopple's Washing Line* by Anita Hewett (Picture Puffin) or the poem 'The Wind' by Robert Louis Stevenson (in *A Child's Garden of Verses*, Puffin) - optional.
Main activity: The playground; bubble mixture pots (one per group of four), bubble wands (one or two per group). If you wish to make a record of this activity, you will need paper, paint and circular objects (empty cotton reels or card tube ends) for printing.
Group activities: 1 Ribbon, scissors. **2** Light plastic carrier bags, string.

BACKGROUND

Force is an abstract concept, and is therefore difficult for children to understand. The wind blowing on objects and moving them is a good example of a visible effect of a force. On a windy day, you can feel the push of the air as you battle against the wind. Washing blowing on a line, trees bending or flags flapping are common examples of the effects of the wind. In some regions, the power of the wind is harnessed to generate electricity and the large turbines can be seen on the skyline. People have used the force of the wind for centuries to push their sailing boats along and to turn their windmills. You may have a windmill near you that is open to visitors.

STARTER

Introduce the lesson by talking to the whole class about the wind. *Mrs*

Differentiation
Both group activities are accessible to all the children.

Mopple's Washing Line by Anita Hewett or the poem 'The Wind' by Robert Louis Stevenson (in *A Child's Garden of Verses*) would be a good initial stimulus for this lesson. Choose a day when there is some wind (but not too much), so that in the main activity (see below) the children can watch the bubbles blowing about for a reasonable length of time before they burst.

MAIN ACTIVITY

Ask the children where the air is. (All around us.) *Can you see it? How do we know it is there?* Some children may say that we need it to breathe, or that they can see it moving things. Ask the children what the wind is. (Moving air.) *Can you see it? Can you see what it does?* Talk to them about washing or flags flapping in the wind. *Can you feel it when the wind is blowing?*

Take the children out into the playground and organise them into groups of about four. Provide each group with bubble mixture pots and wands. Ask the children to take turns to blow bubbles and watch what happens to them in the wind. Encourage them to describe what is happening and what the bubbles look like. Use the vocabulary list for this lesson, defining words such as 'reflection' *(this means that you can see clear pictures of things in the bubbles)* and 'transparent' *(this means that you can see right through the bubbles)*. Ask questions such as: *What is happening to the bubbles? Why are they moving about? What is making them move? Can you see the wind? Can you feel it?*

If you wish, the children could make a circular print to represent their bubble and write a few words in it, such as: 'My bubbles blew away in the wind' or 'My bubble danced because the wind was blowing'. Some children could make more than one print and caption.

GROUP ACTIVITIES

1 Let each child make a streamer from ribbon, then go out, hold it up and watch it blow in the wind. Talk about what is happening. Discuss the fact that the wind is blowing (pushing) the streamer. Ask: *Is everyone's streamer blowing in the same direction? Why?*
2 Let each child make a carrier bag kite by tying a length of string to one handle of the carrier bag, then running in the wind to see how it flies. Make sure they understand that the force of the wind is making their bags lift. Beware! Make sure the children know that it is dangerous to put plastic bags over their heads.

ASSESSMENT

Note the children who are able to describe what is happening to their bubbles or streamer, and who understand that the wind is moving air. Also note those who understand that the wind is pushing on things and making them move.

PLENARY

Talk to the children about what they have been doing. Ask them what was happening to their bubbles and streamers. *What was moving them? What was the wind doing to move things?* (Pushing on them.) *What is the wind?* (Moving air.) Practise some of the vocabulary. *Does anyone know what some of the long words we have been using, such as 'transparent' and 'reflection', mean?*

OUTCOMES
● Can describe how the wind makes things move.
● Know that the wind is moving air.
● Know that the wind can make things move.

LINKS
Unit 1B Lesson 13, My weather chart.

Lesson 7 ▪ The dangers of moving objects

RESOURCES
Main activity: A ramp (a plank, a long plastic plant tray or a shelf), supports to raise one end of the ramp to approximately 300mm, a wheeled trolley that is large enough to carry a house brick (one could be made from a construction kit), a house brick (or similar heavy object), string or cord to secure the brick to the carrier, modelling clay, a clear area of skirting/wall.
Group activities: 1 Modelling clay, building blocks. **2** Drawing and writing materials.

PREPARATION
Make a figure out of modelling clay and set it up against an area of skirting/wall. Make a wheeled carrier large enough to carry a house brick and secure a brick to it with string or cord. Set up the ramp so that the lower end of it is pointing directly at the clay figure. Try the activity before doing it with the children to make sure that the brick and carrier hit the figure and damage it! Make sure that there is sufficient room round the activity so that should the brick fall from the ramp, no child is in the way.

BACKGROUND
Children need to understand that moving objects can inflict damage and that it can be dangerous to get in their way or try to stop them. They may well have some concept of the dangers of moving cars and other traffic but not have related this to the dangers associated with other moving objects (such as playground equipment), or even to the risks involved from getting in the way of or trying to stop other fast-moving human beings.

STARTER
Ask the class if they can tell you about any way in which moving objects can be dangerous. Talk about road safety and how dangerous moving traffic is. Discuss the fact that, though tough in some ways, the human body is very vulnerable when struck by, or when trying to stop, heavy or fast-moving objects. Tell the children that many footballing and rugby injuries occur when one player is trying to tackle or stop another from getting the ball and that there are very strict rules in both games about how to tackle another player in order to keep the injuries to a minimum.

Talk about the dangers of standing too near or trying to stop moving playground equipment such as swings and roundabouts. Remind the children about what they have learned about forces making things move and stopping them, and about cause and effect (refer to Lesson 3, Pushes and pulls).

MAIN ACTIVITY
Show the class the ramp, brick trolley and 'person' against the wall. Ask them what they think will happen to the clay person when the brick rolls fast down the ramp and hits it. Roll the brick down the ramp and then hold up and pass round the figure for the children to see the damage inflicted. Relate this to the damage that could be done to their bodies. Reinforce the idea that moving objects can be dangerous and that they should not try to stop them or get in their way. Talk about road safety and how important it is.

GROUP ACTIVITIES
1 Ideally in groups of two, ask the children to make a fist-sized ball of modelling clay and roll it at a wall made from building blocks. They should note what happens to the blocks. *Does rolling the ball harder and faster*

Differentiation

Group activity 1

All children should be able to take part in this activity, though the level of their understanding and discussion about what is happening will vary.

Group activity 2

Some children may need to tell you what their picture is about. Most children will be able to write a short explanatory sentence. Some children may be able to write about what is happening in their picture in terms of the forces involved.

make a difference? Talk about the fact that the wall is stopping the ball from moving and that this damages the wall.

2 Provide each child with writing and drawing materials. Ask them to draw a picture of a fast-moving object and write why it would be dangerous to try to stop it.

ASSESSMENT

As the children are doing group activity **1**, note the level of their understanding and discussion. During the plenary session, assess how well they have understood the consequences of trying to stop or get in the way of some moving objects. Use the children's pictures and writing to assess their understanding.

PLENARY

Ask the children to tell you what they have learned about what happens if you try to stop or get in the way of a heavy moving object. Talk about the forces involved. Invite some of the children to come to the front of the class and explain what is happening in their picture and to read out what they have written. Talk about cause and effect.

OUTCOME
● Understand that moving objects can be dangerous

LINKS
Unit 1E Lesson 3, Pushes and pulls.

Lesson 8 ▪ Windy day walk

Objectives
● To know that the wind is moving air that pushes on things in the environment and makes them move.
● To know that the wind can exert a push on their bodies.

RESOURCES

An area containing trees and bushes, and perhaps tall grass; a fairly exposed area; an old umbrella, a windy day.

MAIN ACTIVITY

Carry out a 'windy day walk' to observe how the wind blows through trees and bushes and moves them. Let the children stand in an open area to feel the push of the wind on their bodies. Open the umbrella and let the children take turns to feel the air pushing it.

ASSESSMENT

During the plenary, note those children who understand that the force of the wind is pushing on things and moving them.

PLENARY

Talk to the children about what was happening to the trees, bushes and grass. *What was pushing on you? Could you feel the wind on your bodies?* Talk about the wind being moving air that pushes on things and makes them move.

Differentiation
This activity is accessible to all the children.

OUTCOMES
● Can describe how the wind pushes on and moves things in the environment.
● Can talk about the feel of the wind pushing on them.

Lesson 9 ▪ Floating and sinking

Objectives
● To experience the upward push (force) of water.
● To know that water pushes upwards on objects.

Vocabulary
float, sink, push, force, underwater, surface

RESOURCES
Main activity: A water tray (deep enough to cover the largest object being used), and two or three objects of different sizes that float (a cork, a beach ball, a piece of balsa wood) per group; one of the following stories: *The Cow Who Fell in the Canal* by Phyllis Krasilovsky (Little Mammoth), the Bible story of Noah's Ark, *Norah's Ark* by Ann and Reg Cartwright (Red Fox), Chapter 6 of *The House at Pooh Corner* by AA Milne (Methuen).
Group activities: 1 Objects (such as plastic cups and containers) that float when they are empty, but sink when they are filled with water; tanks, water trays. **2** Paper, pencils, colouring materials.

BACKGROUND
The scientific explanation of what happens when objects float and sink is complex, and it is not expected that children will begin to understand it until Key Stage 3. At Key Stage 1, they should be given opportunities to explore floating and sinking - mostly in terms of predicting and testing whether a range of objects will float or sink. They can also experience and describe what is happening when they try to push objects that float down into water: they can feel the water pushing back, and understand that this is a force.

STARTER
Read one of the suggested stories about boats and floating to the children as a stimulus for this lesson (see Resources).

MAIN ACTIVITY
Working with the whole class, put a large ball into a tank of water and ask the children to tell you what it is doing. (Floating.) *What would you need to do if you wanted to make the ball sink?* (Push down on the ball.) *What would you need to do to keep the ball underwater? What would happen if you let go?* Divide the children in groups of four together with a set of equipment. Invite them to try out the various objects. While they are doing this, ask them questions such as: *What can you feel? What is happening to the ball? Why won't the object stay down in the water? What happens when you let go?* Ask the children to think very carefully as they try the different objects. *Do you have to push just as hard on each one to get it to go under the water? Do they all bob up again and float?*

GROUP ACTIVITIES
1 Ask the children to put some empty cups and containers on the water surface. Ask: *What will happen as they are filled with water?* Let the children try it. *Why do they float when they are empty and sink when they are full?* (The push down when they are empty is too small, but when they are full the push down is bigger than the push up from the water in the tank.)
2 Ask the children to write about what happened in the main activity when they tried to push the ball under the water. They should try to write down their ideas about why the ball popped up again.

ASSESSMENT
Note which children understand that the water is pushing up, and that this upward push is a force. Can some children say that when they are pushing down a cup or filling it with water, the downward push (force) is bigger than the upward force, and that is why the cup goes under the water?

PLENARY
Ask the children to describe what was happening in the main activity. Encourage them to use the words 'push', 'force', 'float' and 'sink' in their

Differentiation
Group activity 1
Some children may still be at the experiential stage and need help to describe what is happening in this activity. Some children may begin to understand and explain what is happening.
Group activity 2
Some children may prefer to present their work in the form of pictures.

explanations. Ask whether all the objects needed the same force to push them under the water. *Can anyone say why the objects bob up again when you stop pushing?* (Because the objects float and a force is needed to push them down - when that force is removed, they float again.) Ask: *Why do you think the empty containers floated and the full ones sank?* Help them understand that heavier things experience a greater downward force, and that the air in the empty containers made them lighter than the full ones.

OUTCOMES
● Know that water pushes upwards on objects, and that this push is a force.
● Know that a force is needed to push a floating object down into water and that when the force is removed, the object floats again.

Lesson 10 ▪ Assessment

Objectives
● To know that pushes and pulls are forces.
● To know that forces can make things move.

Vocabulary
float, sink, push, force, underwater, surface

RESOURCES 💿
Assessment activities: 1 Photocopiable page 158 (also 'Assessment' (red), available on the CD-ROM), scissors, adhesive, pencils. **2** Medium-sized or large balls, skipping ropes.
ICT link: 'Introducing forces' interactive, available on the CD-ROM.

STARTER
Start the lesson by telling the traditional story of 'The Enormous Turnip'. Remind the children that a pull is a force. Can they name any other forces?

ASSESSMENT ACTIVITY 1
Give each child a copy of photocopiable page 158. Ask them to cut out the labels at the foot of the page, look carefully at the pictures and stick the appropriate 'push' or 'pull' label under each one.

ANSWERS
Push: 1, 3, 4, 7, 8. Pull: 2, 5, 6, 9.

LOOKING FOR LEVELS
Most children will be able to label six of the pictures correctly, though some may complete only two or three pictures successfully. Some children may be able to label them all correctly if given help with reading the instructions.

ASSESSMENT ACTIVITY 2
Ask the children to work in pairs. Give each pair a medium-sized or large ball. Ask them to pass the ball back and forth to each other by throwing and catching it, bouncing it and then rolling it. After each exercise, ask: *What force are you using to move the ball?* Give each pair a skipping rope and ask them to play a gentle 'tug-of-war'. Ask: *What force are you using?*

ANSWERS
Throwing, bouncing, rolling are all pushes. Catching and tug-of-war are pulls.

LOOKING FOR LEVELS
Most children will identify throwing, bouncing and rolling as push forces and tug-of-war as a pull force. More able learners will also identify catching as a pull force. Less able learners may have difficulty in relating the movements to the forces involved because of the abstract nature of forces.

ICT LINK 💿
Encourage the children to play the activity 'Introducing forces' from the CD-ROM on a computer or interactive whiteboard.

Movement tally

■ Tick ✔ every time you see someone:

running	walking	jumping	hopping
total:	total:	total:	total:

skipping	waving	climbing	swinging
total:	total:	total:	total:

PHOTOCOPIABLE

Assessment

🖤 Cut out the labels and stick one to each picture to show if it is a 'push' or a 'pull'.

push	push	push
push	push	pull
pull	pull	pull

Illustration © Kirsty Wilson

📕 SCHOLASTIC

CHAPTER 6 Sound and hearing

Lesson	Objectives	Main activity	Group activities	Plenary	Outcomes
Lesson 1 Sounds around the school	• To know that there are many different sources of sound in the school.	Go on a 'sound walk' around the school. Think about the sources of the sounds heard.	• Make a zigzag book of sounds heard. • Mark the sounds heard at each location on a simple map of the school.	Review and compare the findings of different groups.	• Know that there are different sources of sound in the school. • Can offer some explanation for sounds they hear.
Enrichment Lesson 2 Sounds in the locality	• To know that there are many different sources of sound in the locality.	Go on a 'sound walk' in the local environment. Think about the sources of the sounds heard.		Review and compare the findings of different groups.	• Know that there are different sources of sound in the locality. • Can offer some explanation for sounds they hear.
Enrichment Lesson 3 Why does it make that sound?	• To identify some objects that make sounds.	Collect pictures of objects that make sounds. Consider the types of sound made and their purposes.		Discuss the purposes of sounds made by objects.	• Can identify some objects that make sounds. • Can explain the purposes of some of the sounds.
Enrichment Lesson 4 Make a shaker	• To make a simple musical instrument.	Make and play a simple shaker and an elastic band guitar.		Discuss why the shakers and guitars make different sounds.	• Can make a simple musical instrument.
Enrichment Lesson 5 Pleasant or unpleasant?	• To know that a 'noise' is often an unpleasant sound. • To know that loud noises can be harmful.	Discuss what sounds are pleasant or unpleasant. Discuss dangers of very loud sounds, and ways of protecting the ear.	• Make a set of rules for a quiet school. • Sort sounds into 'pleasant' and 'unpleasant'.	Review the ideas discussed.	• Know that not all sounds are pleasant. • Know that some loud noises can be harmful.
Lesson 6 The sound of voice	• To know how we make sounds with our voices. • To conduct a simple investigation.	Investigate how we can alter the vocal sounds we make by modifying the use of the mouth, tongue and nose.	• Use voices to make sound effects to accompany a story; record it on cassette. • Children stand behind a screen; the rest of the class try to guess who is speaking.	Discuss how the groups made the sound effects. Practise tongue-twisters and animal sounds.	• Know that they can change the sounds they make with their voice.
Lesson 7 How is it played?	• To know that there are different ways of making sounds.	Sort musical instruments and materials according to how a sound can be made with them.	• Sort pictures of instruments according to how they are played. • Use percussion, voices and materials to make sound effects for stories.	Perform stories with sound effects.	• Know that there are different ways of making sounds.
Lesson 8 Different sounds	• To know that we make use of sounds in a variety of ways.	Discuss everyday uses of sound.	• Complete a sheet about different types of sound. • Create musical sounds to reflect different moods.	Talk about the uses of sound. Listen to the children's musical sounds.	• Can describe different ways in which we use sound.
Lesson 9 DIY orchestra	• To know how to make a range of sounds using a collection of materials and objects.	Make musical instruments.	• Make up a simple tune using instruments. Record this or play it to the rest of the class. • Investigate sounds around the classroom.	Listen to the children's instruments, tunes and sounds.	• Can make a simple instrument to make sounds.
Lesson 10 Match the instruments	• To be able to relate home-made instruments to real instruments.	Match home-made instruments to real ones.		Play the home-made instruments.	• Can relate home-made instruments to real instruments.
Lesson 11 Blocking out sound	• To know that we hear with our ears, but that we can alter the amount of sound entering our ears. • To be able to carry out a simple investigation and record the results.	Discuss how to carry out a simple investigation to find the best material for making ear defenders.	• Investigate which material is best for stopping sound entering our ears.	Review the investigation and results.	• Know that we hear sounds with our ears, but that we can alter the amount of sound entering our ears. • Can carry out a simple investigation and make a simple record.

Lesson	Objectives	Main activity	Group activities	Plenary	Outcomes
Lesson 12 Locating sounds	• To investigate how we know from which direction sounds are coming.	Ask a blindfolded child to say which direction a sound is coming from. Repeat with the child using movable ear trumpets.		Discuss binaural hearing and its importance for various animals.	• Know how our ears help us to locate sounds. • Can carry out a simple investigation with help.
Lesson 13 Fair test	• To know that devices can be made to improve our hearing. • To plan and carry out a simple investigation with help.	Discuss methods of improving hearing, including ear trumpets and stethoscopes.	• Use a stethoscope to listen to each other's bodies. • Make a yoghurt-pot telephone.	Discuss ways to enhance hearing.	• Know that hearing can be enhanced. • Can plan and carry out a simple investigation with help.
Lesson 14 Hearing for safety	• To know that our hearing helps to keep us safe.	Discuss warning sounds including crossings, bells, sirens. Go outdoors to demonstrate the role of hearing in road safety.	• Find out about animals that use warning sounds. • Practise crossing the road in a role-play situation.	Review warning sounds, road safety and contacting the emergency services.	• Know that our sense of hearing helps to keep us safe.
Lesson 15 Warning sounds	• To know that sounds can act as warnings.	Think about sounds that give us a warning.		Discuss important sounds.	• Know that some sounds give us warnings.
Lesson 16 Loud or quiet?	• To know that loud sounds can be heard over a greater distance than quiet sounds. • To carry out a simple investigation.	Investigate how 'loud', 'quiet' sounds change with distance.	• Draw and write about sounds made to be heard at a distance. • Investigate the audibility of spoken messages at different distances.	Review the main activity.	• Know that loud sounds can be heard over a greater distance than quiet ones. • Can carry out a simple investigation.
Lesson 17 Can you hear it now?	• To know that sounds get fainter as they travel away from a source.	Walk away from a 'standard sound' and stop when it becomes inaudible. Try in reverse.	• Research how people send messages over a distance.	Discuss how and why the volume of a sound changes with distance.	• Know that sounds get fainter as they travel away from a source.
Lesson 18 Loud versus quiet	• To know that loud sounds travel further than quiet sounds. • To carry out a simple investigation.	Compare loud and quiet sounds.		Consider why loud sounds travel further than quiet sounds.	• Know that loud sounds also get fainter as they travel away from a source but travel further than quiet sounds. • Can carry out a simple investigation.
Lesson 19 Beads in a pot	• To know that sound is a form of energy. • To make and test a simple prediction.	Watch moving energy change to sound energy, and vice versa. Use a tuning fork to see sound and movement energy.	• Investigate if more movement makes more sound. Make a prediction on the sound made by beads in a pot. • Watch rice on a drum to show that sound can move things.	Report findings from the group activities.	• Can recognise that sound is a form of energy. • Can make and test a simple prediction.

Assessment	Objectives	Activity 1	Activity 2
Lesson 20	• To recognise that sounds are heard through our ears. • To describe how sounds are generated by specific objects. • To know that sounds get fainter as you move away from the source.	• Match musical instruments with words to say how sounds are made. • Explain in writing how we hear sounds.	Complete a sheet to show understanding of how sounds are fainter the further away you are from a sound source.

SC1 SCIENTIFIC ENQUIRY

Sounds are louder when near

LEARNING OBJECTIVES AND OUTCOMES
- To think about what might happen.
- To carry out a simple investigation.
- To compare what happened with what they expected.

ACTIVITY
From a collection of objects such as a ticking clock, a cassette recorder with short pieces of very loud and very quiet music, a bouncy ball, and so on, children are asked to predict which sound would be easy or difficult to hear across the hall or playground. They are then asked to sort the collection into two sets. Finally, they test their predictions and re-arrange the sets if necessary.

LESSON LINKS
Use this Sc1 activity as an integral part of Lesson 16, Loud or quiet?

Lesson 1 ▸ Sounds around the school

Objective
- To know that there are many different sources of sound in the school.

Vocabulary
loud, quiet, soft (of sound), ring (of sound), machine, engine, motor

RESOURCES
Main activity: Portable cassette recorders, or clipboards and pencils.
Group activities: 1 Stiff paper or thin card (approximately 15cm × 40cm).
2 Drawing and colouring materials, photocopies of a map of the school buildings.

BACKGROUND
It is important for children to develop their listening skills. Sounds can tell us much about our surroundings, and listening is an important observational skill. Children, as we know, often hear things without actually listening! The children in your class may have gone on a listening walk during their Reception year and identified some of the sounds in the environment; but this time, encourage them to think a little more about what is making each sound and what the sound can tell us. A portable cassette recorder will help the children to recall the sounds heard, and act as a stimulus for further discussion back in the classroom.

STARTER
This part of the lesson will need to be done with the whole class, since everyone will need to be quiet. Tell the children to sit, very quietly, with eyes closed, and listen.

MAIN ACTIVITY
With their eyes closed, encourage the children to listen carefully and to put their hands up when they hear a sound. Ask questions such as: *What is the sound? Who or what do you think is making it? What does it tell you?* For example: *I can hear footsteps. It sounds like the secretary, Mrs Calendar. She wears high heels. She might be going to her office.* Repeat the questioning for two or three sounds, so that the children get the idea of trying to explain the sound.

Divide the children into mixed-ability groups of four. Provide each group with a clipboard and pencil, or a portable cassette recorder. Explain that each group will have to report back on the sounds they heard to the whole class,

Differentiation
Group activity 1
Support children by allowing them to draw pictures of what they think is making the sounds. To challenge children, ask them to record the sounds in sequence and add a sentence of explanation to each picture.
Group activity 2
Most children will need some help with reading the map, but some children may be able to add names to the classrooms and label other rooms.

so they need to write down or record each sound to help them remember. Once you have organised the children into groups, set off on a walk around the interior of the school. If you have extra adult help, you could send some of the groups on an alternative route to avoid congestion. Encourage the children to listen to all the sounds they usually take for granted. *What sounds are coming from that classroom? What are people doing there? Are there any noises coming from the office or school kitchen? What is making the sound? Is it a telephone, someone using a keyboard, someone mixing food in a bowl? What do the sounds tell us?* (Someone is perhaps taking a message, writing a letter on the computer, or making a dessert.) Listen for sounds coming from the boiler room, the cupboard, the hall. *Can you hear any sounds from outside?*

When you get back to the classroom, give the children a short time to think about the sounds they have heard and get ready to report back in the plenary session.

GROUP ACTIVITIES
1 Let individuals make a zigzag book to record what sounds they heard during the walk.
2 Pairs could use a simple map of the school and mark on it the sounds heard in each location visited on the walk. Could another class follow the map and hear the same sounds?

ASSESSMENT
Listen to the children as they report back on the sounds they heard. Are they able to say what made each sound and give some explanation of what was happening?

PLENARY
Invite each group to report back to the rest of the class on the sounds they have heard. If they were using cassette recorders, they may be able to play some of the sounds again. Did every group hear exactly the same sounds, or did one group hear something different? Did every group have the same explanation for each sound?

OUTCOMES
● Know that there are different sources of sound in the school.
● Can offer some explanation for sounds they hear.

LINKS
Unit 1A Lesson 3, The senses.
Geography: simple maps and routes.

ENRICHMENT
Lesson 2 ◗ Sounds in the locality

Objective
● To know that there are many different sources of sound in the locality.

RESOURCES
Clipboards and pencils, or portable cassette recorders.

MAIN ACTIVITY
With the children, go on a walk around the school grounds or your local area. Give each group a clipboard and ask them to record the sounds they hear. Encourage them to listen out for traffic, animals and people. Ask questions such as: *Is it dustbin day? Can you hear aeroplanes or other machines? Can you hear the birds twittering in the trees?*

ASSESSMENT

In the plenary session, as the children report, note those who understand that they have recorded a range of different sounds.

PLENARY

Each group should report back as in Lesson 1.

OUTCOMES

- Know that there are different sources of sound in the locality.
- Can offer some explanation for sounds they hear.

ENRICHMENT

Lesson 3 ▫ Why does it make that sound?

Objective
● To identify some objects that make sounds.

RESOURCES

A collection of old catalogues or magazines, large sheets of paper, scissors, glue, spreaders.

MAIN ACTIVITY

Talk about things we use that make sounds: CD players, radios, TV sets, microwave ovens, toys, a dog's squeaky ball and so on. Ask the children to work in groups to cut out pictures of similar things from old catalogues or magazines and stick them down on display paper. Ask them to describe the sound each thing makes and explain the purpose of the sound.

ASSESSMENT

Listen while the children are describing the sound each thing makes. Can they explain the purpose of the sound?

PLENARY

Talk about why things make sounds. For example: *The microwave pings to let us know that it has finished cooking; the dog's ball squeaks to encourage the dog to play with it and have fun.*

Differentiation
Some children might find a list of sounds that they can choose from helpful (for example: 'ring', 'ping', 'bleep', 'squeak').

OUTCOMES

- Can identify some objects that make sounds.
- Can explain the purposes of some of the sounds.

ENRICHMENT

Lesson 4 ▫ Make a shaker

Objective
● To make a simple musical instrument.

RESOURCES

Plastic pots with lids, rice, buttons, foil, beads, lentils, cotton wool and so on; plastic lunchboxes or margarine pots, elastic bands in different sizes; paint, sticky paper for decoration.

MAIN ACTIVITY

The children make shakers: put items in pots and investigate the sounds made by different fillings; then choose one to cover and decorate. They investigate the sounds made by different-sized rubber bands on a container, then make a 'guitar' that will play at least three different notes. They invent and play a simple 'guitar' riff or sound pattern.

ASSESSMENT

During the plenary session, as the children demonstrate their sounds, note

Differentiation
Some children may be able to devise a way of writing down their sound pattern for others to copy.

those who understand that different shaker fillings or different-sized elastic bands make different sounds.

PLENARY
Demonstrate some sound patterns. Talk about why different shaker fillings or different-sized elastic bands make different sounds.

OUTCOME
● Can make a simple musical instrument.

ENRICHMENT
Lesson 5 ▶ Pleasant or unpleasant?

Objectives
● To know that a 'noise' is often an unpleasant sound.
● To know that loud noises can be harmful.

Vocabulary
noise, pleasant, unpleasant, damage, deafness, loud, ear defenders, volume (loudness)

RESOURCES 💿
Main activity: Pictures of things making a noise (for example, traffic, an aeroplane, a helicopter, birds, a baby laughing, workmen wearing ear defenders); ear defenders, a cassette recorder, a cassette of gentle music and another of loud noise (such as a pneumatic drill, traffic or an aeroplane), a personal stereo.
Group activities: 1 Drawing and writing materials. **2** Photocopiable page 184 (also 'Pleasant or unpleasant?' (red), available on the CD-ROM), colouring materials, blank A4 paper, scissors, adhesive.
ICT links: 'Pleasant or unpleasant?' interactive, available on the CD-ROM.

BACKGROUND
Describing sounds as pleasant or unpleasant ('noise') is very often a matter of taste. To some of us, current pop music may well be a horrible noise, while to others it is bliss! Most people would agree that loud noises made by some types of machinery (such as drills, diggers and aeroplanes) are unpleasant and to be avoided if possible. Young children will not appreciate that a persistent loud noise can, over time, damage their hearing. Many use personal stereo headsets; and while those designed specifically for children often have limited volume, others have no such limits and can damage the hearing if worn regularly and played at full volume.

STARTER
Play a short tape of gentle, quiet music to the class.

MAIN ACTIVITY
Ask the children whether they think the music was pleasant or unpleasant, nice or nasty. *Why do you think that? What does it remind you of?* Talk about other pleasant sounds that the children like. Do they like to hear

Differentiation

Group activity 1
Some children may benefit from working in a larger group with an adult. They can then draw up a set of rules agreed by them all.

Group activity 2
All the children should be able to take part in this activity. For children who need support, use 'Pleasant or unpleasant?' (green) from the CD-ROM, which omits the question about favourite sounds. To extend children, use 'Pleasant or unpleasant?' (blue), which asks children to state their favourite and least favourite sounds and to give reasons for their choices.

people laughing, birds singing, bacon sizzling? What unpleasant sounds do they really dislike? Listen to a tape of unpleasant sounds such as an aircraft, a pneumatic drill or a dog barking. *Why do you dislike these sounds?* (They are too loud, they hurt their ears, they remind them of something unpleasant.) Say that 'sounds' are everything we hear, but sometimes we call the sounds 'noises'. These are often sounds that are unpleasant. Show the children some pictures of things that make pleasant or unpleasant sounds; ask them how they would react to the sounds.

Look at a picture of workmen wearing ear defenders and/or examine a pair of ear defenders. Ask: *Why do workmen wear ear defenders when they are using some kinds of machinery?* Talk about how very loud noises can damage the hearing. Show the children a personal stereo. Do any of them have one? Talk about how it, too, can damage their hearing if they listen to it for a long time with the volume turned up very loud. Talk about what it means to be deaf, and how deaf people communicate words by signing.

Ask: *Where do we hear unpleasant sounds or noises in school? Do we scrape and clatter chairs when we put them under the table? Do we sometimes make too much noise in the corridors when we are moving about? Do people scream and shout in the playground? Do noises from outside stop us working properly? What could we do about these unpleasant noises?* Explain how soundproofing and double glazing can help to protect rooms from outside noise.

GROUP ACTIVITIES
1 Working in pairs, ask the children to make a set of rules for a quiet school. These might include: lifting chairs when putting them away; walking quietly in corridors and not shouting inside; no screaming (unless hurt). Your school may have particular noise 'trouble spots' that the children can identify and think about.
2 Give each child a copy of photocopiable page 184. Make sure that all the children understand what sound each picture represents. Ask them to colour pleasant sounds in one colour and unpleasant sounds in another, or to cut out the pictures and paste them into sets under appropriate headings on a sheet of A4 paper. Some children may have different opinions about what is a pleasant or horrible sound. Compare the children's favourite sounds and ask them to give reasons for their choices.

ICT LINK
The children can also use the 'Pleasant or unpleasant?' interactive from the CD-ROM, to sort different sounds into two sets: pleasant and unpleasant. A sound effect will be played, then children should drag and drop the picture under one of the headings to show whether or not they like the sound. This can be an open-ended activity to use as a discussion point.

ASSESSMENT
Use the photocopiable sheet to assess the children's understanding. If they have made an unusual choice, discuss with them their reasons for doing so. For example, some children may have put the barking dog in the 'unpleasant' category because they are frightened of dogs; other children may have a dog at home and count its bark as a pleasant sound.

PLENARY
Talk about the noises the children like or dislike. Remind them of the noises around the school, and discuss the rules they have suggested for making school a quieter place. Discuss the importance of protecting their hearing.

OUTCOMES
- Know that not all sounds are pleasant.
- Know that some loud noises can be harmful.

Lesson 6 ▪ The sound of voice

Objectives
● To know how we make sounds with our voices.
● To conduct a simple investigation.

Vocabulary
voice, vibrate, whisper, shout, sing, talk, speak, communicate, lips, tongue, teeth

RESOURCES
Group activities: 1 A cassette recorder, story books. **2** A screen to hide a child.

BACKGROUND
We make sounds with our voices by passing air over our vocal cords to make them vibrate. Changing the shape of these cords allows us to alter the pitch of the voice, but we need to alter the shape of the mouth and nasal cavity to change the kind of sound we make. A round, open shape produces an 'aahh' sound; drawing back the lips into a straighter line produces 'eeee' sounds; 't' and 'd' sounds employ the tongue and teeth; 'n' involves directing the sound through the nose rather than the mouth. We usually only make sounds when breathing out; by increasing or reducing the amount of air passing over the vocal cords, we can change the volume. Always encourage children to speak clearly and distinctly. Be sensitive to children with speech problems who may have difficulty in making some particular sounds. You may have children who are experiencing a temporary difficulty, such as the loss of their front teeth, and who may be willing to talk about why they now find certain sounds difficult.

STARTER
This is a fun activity, but rather noisy! Ask the whole class: *How do we communicate with each other?* We write letters, send emails, draw pictures - but mostly, we talk to each other. Ask: *How do we talk to each other?* (Face to face, on the telephone, perhaps through a cassette recording or on video.) Hopefully, the children will know that we use our voices when we talk.

MAIN ACTIVITY
Where do our voices come from? Encourage the children to put their fingers gently against their throats. *All together, say 'aahh'.* If the children do this quite loudly, they may be able to feel their throats vibrating as they make the sound. It is easier to feel a low vocal sound than a high one. Ask the children to close their mouths and make the sound again. *How has it changed?* 'Aahh' should have changed to 'mmm'. Talk about the parts of the mouth that we have used to make these two sounds. Very simply, the difference was made by having our lips open or closed. So our lips are very important in making different sounds.

Ask the children which other parts of their mouths they think are important. Many children will appreciate that they use their tongues, but may not realise the importance of the teeth in helping them to speak clearly. Choose three or four children and ask them to repeat a nursery rhyme such as 'Twinkle, Twinkle, Little Star' without moving their tongues. *How easy was it?* Could the other children understand what they were saying? Ask them to try again, but this time using their tongues. *Was that better?* Talk about where they put their tongues to make a 't' sound.

Experiment by changing the shape of the mouth to find out what other sounds can be made: clicks and clucks, whistles, hisses, kissing sounds, tuts and so on. Encourage the children to think about how the different parts of their mouths help them to make the sounds.

What happens to our voices if we hold our noses while we speak? Invite a different group of children to recite 'Twinkle, Twinkle, Little Star' while holding their noses. *Which sounds were particularly difficult to make?* Remind the children how difficult it is to make 'n' or 'm' sounds if they have a bad cold (because the nose is blocked).

Differentiation
All the children should be able to take part in these activities.

GROUP ACTIVITIES
1 Challenge groups of about four to use their voices to make sound effects to accompany a story, and record this on a cassette to play back to the rest of the class. One child could act as reader or narrator.
2 Invite several children to stand behind a screen. Each takes a turn to speak, and the rest of the children must try to guess who is speaking.

ASSESSMENT
Do the children understand that they make sounds with their voices? In the main activity, ask them to describe how the shape of the mouth alters the sound coming out.

PLENARY
Listen to the children's story tapes. Ask each group to describe how they made the sound effects. Practise making some specific sounds (such as 'p') then learn a suitable tongue-twister (such as 'Peter Piper picked a peck of pickled pepper'). Sing 'Old MacDonald Had a Farm' and make the appropriate noises.

OUTCOME
● Know that they can change the sounds they make with their voice.

Lesson 7 ◾ How is it played?

Objective
● To know that there are different ways of making sounds.

Vocabulary
shake, pluck, scrape, bang, blow, crackle, click

RESOURCES 💿
Main activity: A variety of musical instruments (try to include instruments that are played in different ways – by banging, blowing, shaking, plucking or scraping); cellophane, paper, wooden blocks, coconut shells, a bell or buzzer, sandpaper, a bowl, a jug of water, a party blower; a set of labels (see Preparation). If real instruments are not available, you could use pictures, but it is better to use the real thing if at all possible.
Group activities: 1 Photocopiable page 185 (also 'How is it played?' (red, available on the CD-ROM), scissors, glue, blank A4 paper (or colouring materials). **2** Musical instruments and other materials as used for the main activity, familiar stories.
Plenary: A short extract from a recording of *Peter and the Wolf* by Prokofiev (optional).

Differentiation

Group activity 1
For children who need support, use 'How is it played?' (green) from the CD-ROM, which contains a smaller range of instruments for the children to sort. To extend children, use 'How is it played?' (blue), which challenges them to name another instrument that you can blow, shake, pluck, bang or scrape.

Group activity 2
Most of the children will be able to do this activity using a simple, familiar story. Some children might make up their own story.

PREPARATION
Make a set of labels with the words 'shake', 'bang', 'pluck', 'scrape' and 'blow'.

BACKGROUND
Sound is made by something vibrating. Vibrations may be produced in a variety of ways; in musical instruments, they are usually made by banging (or tapping), shaking, plucking, blowing or scraping part of the instrument. The speed of the vibrations affects the pitch of the sound. A short string will vibrate faster than a longer one, and will produce a higher note. Slower vibrations produce a lower sound. Similarly, a longer column of air will produce a lower note than a short column. This can be demonstrated quite easily using a school recorder: covering more holes creates a longer column of air, and the pitch of the note becomes lower. Sounds can also be made in such ways as scrunching paper, rubbing sandpaper blocks together, scratching a slate, dropping a lump of play dough and pouring water.

STARTER
Gather the children together on the carpet and look quickly at all the instruments you have collected. Ask the children whether they know what kind of thing all these objects are. Can they name any of the instruments?

MAIN ACTIVITY
Ask the children to sit very still with their eyes closed. Clap your hands several times. *Can you tell me how I was making that sound?* Ask the children to close their eyes once more and this time, choose one of the instruments and play one or two notes. *Can you guess which instrument it was?* Now choose something like the cellophane and scrunch it up so that it crackles. *Can you guess what was making the sound this time?*

Invite the children to think again about the sounds they have just heard. *Can you all clap your hands? How did you make the sound?* Ask them to tap their legs and chests. *Did you make the same sound or is it different?* Ask them how you made the second sound. *Did I bang, blow, pluck or scrape the instrument? Are there any other instruments here that you would play in the same way?* Ask different children to identify these and play a few notes on each to demonstrate. *Are there any other instruments that would go in the same set?* Put that set of instruments to one side, then ask a child to choose another instrument from the collection and say how it would be played. Make another set that would be played in the same way. Continue in this way until you have sorted all the instruments.

Look at the 'bang', 'pluck', 'scrape' and 'blow' labels and help the children to read them. Ask them to put each set of instruments back on the table by the appropriate label. *Is there anything left that did not fit into the sets you have already sorted? What about sound 3 – how was that made?* Look at the sound-making materials left, and talk about how they can be used to make a sound. *What does the sound remind you of?* Crinkly paper might sound like a fire burning; water pouring from a jug could be a fountain or waterfall.

GROUP ACTIVITIES
1 Ask the children, working individually, to cut out the pictures of instruments from a copy of page 185 and paste them into sets on blank paper according to how they are played. Alternatively, they could colour the instruments according to which set they belong in (for example, things that are shaken in blue and so on).

2 Groups of five or six could use percussion instruments, sound-making materials and voices to make sound effects for a familiar story. One child could act as reader or narrator.

ASSESSMENT
At the start of the plenary session, give the children three or four different instruments from the collection and ask them to describe how each is played. Use the photocopiable sheet as an assessment tool.

PLENARY
Ask the groups to perform their stories with sound effects. You may choose to listen to a short excerpt from *Peter and the Wolf* and talk about the instruments used for the different characters. Sing 'Oh, We Can Play on the Big Bass Drum' and make the instrument sounds (or use appropriate instruments).

OUTCOME
● Know that there are different ways of making sounds.

LINKS
Literacy: retelling a familiar story.

Lesson 8 ▪ Different sounds

Objective
● To know that we make use of sounds in a variety of ways.

Vocabulary
sound, noise, call, voice, mood, instrument, feeling, pleasure, information, warning

RESOURCES
Main teaching activity: An old or toy telephone.
Group activities: 1 A copy of photocopiable page 186 (also 'Different sounds' (red), available on the CD-ROM) for each child, writing materials. **2** 'Mood cards' (see Preparation), a collection of musical instruments, a cassette recorder (optional).

PREPARATION
Prepare a set of 'mood cards' by writing the names of moods (angry, sad, happy, jolly, peaceful) for the children to interpret through musical sounds.

BACKGROUND
Sound plays an important part in our lives, and for most humans it is our main means of communication. We speak to each other directly, or by telephone, television or radio. We use bells or buzzers, and other sounds, to send messages or warnings. We enjoy music or drama. Retailers use sound to influence our shopping habits and increase their sales.

Unfortunately these days there is often so much sound around that we become accustomed to it and no longer listen to the individual sounds. The hum of the boiler or the motorway drone is no longer registered unless our attention is drawn to it. It is, however, important that we do learn to listen to the sounds around us. We can pick up clues and information about what is happening, some of which could be very important in helping to keep us safe. (Many modern lorries emit a warning sound if they are reversing, and pelican crossings bleep to let you know it is safe to cross the road.)

STARTER
Remind the children of what they learned in earlier lessons about sounds and noise. Ask the children to close their eyes. Can they still guess what is happening around them? *How do you know?* (They can hear sounds.)

MAIN ACTIVITY
Tell the children to open their eyes and ask: *What sounds can you hear?* (People talking, chairs and tables scraping on the floor, perhaps music in the distance, footsteps.) *What is happening? Most of us do lots of talking but why do we talk and what do we talk about?* Ask the children for some suggestions. (To greet people and pass on news, to ask for and give

Differentiation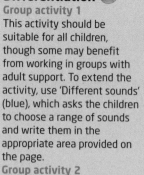
Group activity 1
This activity should be suitable for all children, though some may benefit from working in groups with adult support. To extend the activity, use 'Different sounds' (blue), which asks the children to choose a range of sounds and write them in the appropriate area provided on the page.
Group activity 2
All the children should enjoy participating in this activity.

information, to communicate when playing games or working together in lessons, we can shout to give warnings.) *What else can a voice tell you?* (The tone of voice can tell you whether a person is happy, sad or angry.) We can recognise people by their voices even if we can't see them. *These days we can make our voices travel over very long distances. How do we do that?* (Telephone, radio, television.)

Ask if any of the children talk to Grandma (or another relative or friend) on the phone. Ask the children what sort of things they talk about. Use an old or toy telephone to role-play a telephone conversation. Sometimes the telephone is very important in calling for help. Can the children remember how to make an emergency call? Ask one or two children to demonstrate how they would call the emergency services. Talk about how important it is only to do so when there is a real emergency, and the dangers of making false calls. *How do we know that someone wants to speak to us on the telephone?* (It rings or, if it is a mobile phone, it might play a little tune.) *What other sounds might we hear during the day that tell us something?* (Alarm clock, school bell, road crossing, microwave ping, doorbell.) Talk about each of these sounds and what they tell us.

Point out to the children that these are all useful sounds, but that sometimes we use sound to give us pleasure. *Can you tell me any sounds that you enjoy?* (There could be a wide range of answers to this question but, if no one else mentions it, suggest that music gives pleasure to lots of people.) Some people sing, whistle or play a musical instrument. Sometimes we just listen to music but at other times we dance or exercise to it. *Why do soldiers often march to music?* We often use music in celebrations or religious ceremonies. *Where else might you hear music?* (On the radio or television, on CD or tape, in shops, in lifts, at a football match.) *Does music sometimes make you feel happy or sad?*

GROUP ACTIVITIES
1 Give each child a copy of photocopiable page 186 and ask them to complete it.
2 Divide the children into groups of four and give each group a 'mood card' (see Preparation). Encourage the children to choose from the collection of musical instruments to create sounds to express the mood on their card. Give them a short time to work together and then ask each group to play their sounds, while the rest of the children try to guess what the mood is. If there is enough time, groups could exchange cards and create a new sound sequence.

ASSESSMENT
Use the children's completed sheets from group activity **1** to assess their understanding. Note those children who contribute to the plenary session and understand ways in which we use sound and that it plays an important part in keeping us safe.

PLENARY
Talk about how sound helps us to understand what is happening around us and how some sounds help to keep us safe. Collate the lists on a copy of the photocopiable sheet projected onto a whiteboard. Ask some groups to play their sounds from group activity **2** so that the rest of the children can try to guess the mood they are expressing.

OUTCOME
● Can describe different ways in which we use sound.

LINKS
Music: listening, creating and developing musical ideas.

Lesson 9 ▫ DIY orchestra

Objective
● To know how to make a range of sounds using a collection of materials and objects.

Vocabulary
percussion, shake, rattle, twang, bang, pluck, blow, scrape, stringed

RESOURCES
Main activity: Instruments from the music trolley; elastic bands, small pieces of wood and dowel and small empty boxes for guitars; drinking straws for flutes; catering-size tin cans, plastic sheeting and string for drums; long card tubes, beads, rice or dried peas for rainmakers; clay plant pots, beads, string and support for xylophones; combs, tissue paper, adhesive tape, string, scissors or other tools as appropriate.
Group activities: 1 Instruments made by the children, cassette recorders. **2** A range of beaters from the music trolley including rubber, wood and plastic. Use short lengths (20–30cm) of dowel if you have insufficient beaters.

BACKGROUND
The children made shakers or very simple elastic band guitars in Lesson 4. Make sure that they think of something different this time. A very wide range of instruments can be made by the children using almost anything you care to name. The list of resources provided above should not be restrictive: allow the children to use their imaginations and use anything you think safe and reasonable. Encourage them to make as wide a range of instruments as possible.

STARTER
Look at a selection of instruments from the music trolley and rehearse how the different sounds are made (pluck, bang, scrape, blow).

MAIN ACTIVITY
Working with the whole class, show the children the collection of materials and ask them to think about what kind of instruments they could make from some of them. Simple guitar-type instruments can be made from a box and elastic bands. Tissue boxes are often used but these tend to collapse if the bands are too tight. Margarine or ice-cream tubs work quite well: turn the box upside-down and try putting a small piece of wood (or a pencil) under the elastic bands. This acts like a bridge and by moving this 'bridge' different notes can be produced by plucking the band on either side. A large catering-sized coffee tin can be made into a drum by stretching a piece of plastic sheeting across the top. Claves or rhythm sticks are very simple to make from short lengths of dowel sandpapered until they are smooth.

Clay plant pots can be suspended from a pole to make a xylophone. Retort stands and bar clamps make good supports and you can use a wooden bead to stop the string slipping through the hole in the bottom of the pot. Cardboard tubes from kitchen rolls (or better still, those from rolls of fabric) can be made into rainmakers by adding rice or other seeds (which slide up and down as the tube is tipped) and sealing each end. Corrugated card stuck to a length of wood or pieces of sandpaper stuck to blocks make simple scrapers. Blowers can be made from plastic drinking straws, or combs and tissue paper.

Give the children time to experiment and make their instruments.

GROUP ACTIVITIES
1 Divide the children into groups of four to six, making sure that there is a good mix of instruments within the group. Ask them to make up a simple tune using their instruments. They could record their tunes on a cassette

recorder or play them to the rest of the class.

2 Give each child a beater of some kind. Ask them to explore the sounds that can be made by gently hitting the furniture and fittings in the classroom (tables, chair legs, radiators, cupboards, floors and so on). Warn the children not to 'beat' the computer, windows, or any other delicate objects! Encourage them to exchange beaters and try a different type. *What difference does this make to the sounds produced?*

ASSESSMENT

Observe the children as they make their instruments. Ask them to explain how they will work. *Will you need to bang, rattle, scrape, pluck or blow?*

PLENARY

Ask some of the children to show their instruments and say how they made them. Listen to the tunes composed by the groups. Ask some of the children to demonstrate any interesting sounds they discovered around the room.

OUTCOME

● Can make a simple instrument to make sounds.

LINKS

Technology: select tools, techniques and materials for projects.
Music: explore, choose and organise sounds.

Differentiation
All the children should be able to take part in these activities according to their abilities.

Lesson 10 ● Match the instruments

Objective
● To be able to relate home-made instruments to real instruments.

RESOURCES

The instruments made by the children in the previous lesson, pictures of musical instruments (or real ones, if available). Short video of an orchestra playing.

MAIN ACTIVITY

Spread out the pictures (or real instruments) on a table. Look at the items and talk about how each instrument is played. Ask the children to think about how their own instrument is played and to place it by the picture, or instrument, that best matches it. Discuss any instruments that are missing (either a real instrument that doesn't have a child's instrument to match it, or vice versa). After the children have matched their instruments to any available, play a few notes on the real thing to see if their instrument makes a similar sound or not. Watch the video and note how the instruments are played.

ASSESSMENT

Observe those children who can match their instruments to real ones and understand how they are played.

PLENARY

Sing the song 'Oh, We Can Play on the Big Bass Drum', but use the children's own instruments for the sounds.

OUTCOME

● Can relate home-made instruments to real instruments.

Differentiation
Some children may need to be reminded how the real instruments are played in order to match them with their own.

Lesson 11 ▪ Blocking out sound

Objectives
● To know that we hear with our ears, but that we can alter the amount of sound entering our ears.
● To be able to carry out a simple investigation and record the results.

Vocabulary
noise, silence, direction, protection, ear defenders, earmuffs, test, same, fair, predict, find out, decide

RESOURCES 💿

Main activity: Ear defenders (if possible); earmuffs (one set per pair), round plastic margarine pots (two per pair), newspaper, cotton wool, scraps of fabric, polystyrene packing, tissue paper; a chime bar, drum or similar way to make a standard sound.

Group activity: As for main activity; photocopiable page 187 (also 'Blocking out sound' (red), available on the CD-ROM).

BACKGROUND

The outer ear (the part we can see) collects sounds in the form of vibrations. These vibrations are transmitted by very small bones to the inner ear. From the inner ear, signals are sent to the brain, where they are interpreted as sounds. Wearing ear defenders or earmuffs can reduce the level of vibrations entering our ears, and so reduce the amount of sound that we hear. This can be useful for protecting our ears from prolonged loud noises, or for just blocking sounds if we need to sleep or to concentrate on something else.

Some children may suffer from a temporary condition known as 'glue ear'. This inhibits the vibration of the tiny bones in the middle ear, and thus causes a loss of hearing.

Animals often have a much better sense of hearing than humans. As well as being able to hear a wider range of sound frequencies (higher or lower sounds), they can often move their outer ears in order to pinpoint the direction from which a sound is coming.

In the following activities, the children carry out simple investigations to find out the effectiveness of different earmuffs or ear defenders and the difference it makes if you can 'waggle' your ears. Young children will still need considerable help to design an investigation, but they should be encouraged to think about how they can find out something and what might happen. Ask questions such as: *How do you think we could find out which are the best?*

STARTER

Gather the children around you and ask them to look at each other's ears. *Are they all the same?* Look at the earlobes. Some may be very small and 'fixed', while other children may have bigger, 'free' lobes. *What do we use our ears for?*

MAIN ACTIVITY

Make a sound using the chime bar and ask the children to put up their hands if they can hear it. Ask them to turn round so that they are sitting with their backs to you, and repeat the sound. *Who can hear it now?* Now get them to cover their ears with their hands. Repeat the sound, and ask again who can hear it. *If you could hear it, was it still as clear as before?*

Tell the children to turn round and face you again. Remind them what they learned in Lesson 5 about loud noises being harmful and why people wear ear defenders. Show them the collection of margarine pots and materials, and suggest that they make some ear defenders for themselves. Explain that they will need to find out what is the best material to pack them with. *What could we do? How could we find out?* If necessary, prompt them to say that they could put different materials in the pots and put them over their ears to see which blocks out the most sound. *Do we need to wear two pots? Why? Does it matter if we have one material in one pot and a different material in the other pot at the same time? Does it matter how much material we put in each pot?* Some children may be quite happy to use different materials and quantities at the same time, but others may be

Differentiation 💿
To support children in the group activity, use 'Blocking out sound' (green) from the CD-ROM. This version contains fewer items for the children to test and does not require them to write down reasons for their predictions. Some children, however, may be able to do this verbally. To extend children, use 'Blocking out sound' (blue), which asks them to suggest reasons for their findings.

starting to appreciate that some factors need to be kept the same if they are going to get any useful results. If they test different materials in two pots at the same time, they cannot be sure which material was best overall.

GROUP ACTIVITY

Working in pairs, the children should investigate the effect of using different materials to pack their earmuffs. They should listen to a standard sound, such as a chime bar or drum, while holding the earmuffs over their ears. Ask which material they think will be the best, and why they think that. They should listen to the sound without earmuffs to start with, and give that sound a score of 5. They can use a copy of page 187 to record the score for the sound as heard through different ear defenders, and to record and explain their prediction and conclusion.

ASSESSMENT

Observe the children as they carry out the investigation. Are they thinking about what they are doing? Are they trying to be systematic in testing the different materials? Are they recording as they go along? Use photocopiable page 187 to assess their ability to interpret their findings.

PLENARY

Ask the children to report back on what they have found out. *Which material was the best for blocking out sound?* Some groups may have different results. Discuss why this might be. *Did you all put the same amount of the material in the pots? Did you all stand the same distance away from the sound? Was the sound always at the same volume?* Stress that none of the results were 'wrong'; but because the investigation was carried out in a slightly different way, the results were different.

OUTCOMES

● Know that we hear sounds with our ears, but that we can alter the amount of sound entering our ears.
● Can carry out a simple investigation and make a simple record.

LINKS

Unit 1A Lesson 3, The senses.

Lesson 12 ▪ Locating sounds

Objective
● To investigate how we know from which direction sounds are coming.

RESOURCES

Simple 'ear trumpets' made from thin card (see diagram below).

MAIN ACTIVITY

Talk about animals that can move their ears in order to collect and locate sounds. Ask the children whether they can move their ears. *We have to move our heads, not just our ears. Is it better if we use both ears or cover one up?* Blindfold a child and make a noise in front, behind, to the side, above them. Can the child tell where the sound is coming from? Now let the child use ear trumpets and move them to 'collect' sound. *Does that make it easier to tell where the sound is coming from?*

ASSESSMENT
During the plenary session, note those children who can tell you why being able to move the ears is an advantage.

PLENARY
Talk about how our ears help us to locate sounds. Discuss how animals need to be able to locate sounds in order to escape predators or catch prey. Remind the children how it was easier to locate sounds using both ears than with one covered up.

OUTCOMES
- Know how our ears help us to locate sounds.
- Can carry out a simple investigation with help.

Differentiation
All the children should be able to do this activity. Some may be able to write about what they have discovered.

Lesson 13 ◗ Fair test

Objectives
- To know that devices can be made to improve our hearing.
- To plan and carry out a simple investigation with help.

Vocabulary
listen, stethoscope, hearing, enhance, vibration, ear trumpet, headphones, damage

RESOURCES ◉
Main teaching activity: A stethoscope, an ear trumpet made from card (see activity above), earphones; if possible, a picture of a water board official using a listening device to listen for leaks and a picture of an old-fashioned ear trumpet.

Group activities: 1 Stethoscopes, antiseptic wipes or disinfectant; short pieces of dowel (1.5–2cm diameter and 15cm long) or short pieces cut from a broom handle; card ear trumpets. **2** For each group: two or three different types of string, empty yoghurt pots, cocoa tins, syrup tins, plastic cups and so on; photocopiable page 188 (also 'Fair test' (red), available on the CD-ROM) if required.

PREPARATION
Make several cones from card to act as ear trumpets. Roll the card into a cone shape, fix with adhesive tape and cut off the extreme point.

BACKGROUND
Many children will have experienced temporary hearing impairment due to glue ear or a heavy cold. As we grow older hearing often becomes less acute. The children learned in earlier lessons that hearing can be seriously damaged by very loud noises and they need to be reminded of this. Individuals may naturally have different levels of hearing so be sensitive to any children who have difficulty.

Some occupations involve using devices to enhance hearing. A doctor may use a stethoscope to listen to a chest or a small listening trumpet to listen for foetal sounds in the womb. A water board official uses

Differentiation

Group activity 1
All the children can take part in this activity.

Group activity 2
Some children will just enjoy making a yoghurt-pot telephone but others may be able to compare two different strings or two different types of pot. Some children could find which they think is the best pot or tin and then go on to compare strings to make the best telephone they can.

a long listening device to hear the water running through pipes buried in the ground. Bomb disposal experts need a stethoscope to help them hear what is happening inside an explosive device. It may be safer to avoid discussing the use of a stethoscope to help crack a safe!

STARTER
Remind the children of what they learned about ear defenders previously. (They help to protect our ears from the damage that can be done by very loud noises.) Explain that in this lesson the children are going to learn about things that enhance our hearing and help us to hear very quiet sounds.

MAIN ACTIVITY
Whisper something to the children and ask: *Who could hear that?* Ask them to cup their ears with their hands and whisper again. *Did any of you find it easier to hear then?* Explain or remind the children that some animals can move their ears so that they can collect the sounds and hear better. (Cupping ears is a bit like this.) Humans can't usually move their ears. In the past, people used ear trumpets to collect more sound when they became hard of hearing. Show the children the card trumpet and explain that old-fashioned ear trumpets worked like this to collect more sound. Of course, people can always talk louder so that others can hear, but some sounds are very quiet and we may need help to hear them. Ask: *Who has been to the doctor? Did the doctor listen to your chest? What did he or she use?*

GROUP ACTIVITIES
1 Working in groups of three or four (according to the level of your resources), use a stethoscope to listen to each other's hearts or stomachs. If it is spring, and you have some fairly large trees in the vicinity, the children could go out and use a stethoscope to try and listen to the sap rising. Make sure that the stethoscope ear pieces are disinfected between users. Some children could use lengths of dowel to listen to water moving in radiators or to listen to someone tapping on the other end of a desk. Some groups could use a card ear trumpet to see if whispered messages are more easily heard using it. Groups could exchange their listening devices and try a different one, if there is time.

2 Investigate using plastic cups or tin cans with different strings to find out which is best for hearing messages. A yoghurt-pot telephone is simply made by making a small hole in the bottom of two yoghurt pots and threading a long length of string through each hole. To make one, tie a knot to secure the string inside each pot. Help the children to understand that the string needs to be pulled taut in order for the device to work.

   Some children could investigate the effect of different types of string or change the type of pot (syrup or cocoa tins work well, but beware of tins with sharp edges). Make sure that the children have two pots of the same type on the string at any one time and that they investigate either pots or strings, not both at the same time. Ask them to tell the rest of the class what they have found out. The children could record their findings on photocopiable page 188.

ASSESSMENT
Observe the children using the listening devices in group activity **1**. Who understands that these devices are enhancing their hearing? In group activity **2** observe the children as they plan and carry out their investigations. Note which children make sensible suggestions.

PLENARY
Talk about the different ways hearing has been enhanced. *How well did the different devices work?* Discuss people who have real hearing difficulties and the ways in which they can be helped. (Hearing aids, sign language, lip

reading and so on.) If possible, invite a visitor into the class to demonstrate and talk about sign language, or show how a hearing aid helps them to hear.

OUTCOMES
● Know that hearing can be enhanced.
● Can plan and carry out a simple investigation with help.

Lesson 14 ▪ Hearing for safety

Objective
● To know that our hearing helps to keep us safe.

Vocabulary
danger, warning, alarm, emergency, siren, bells, vehicles

RESOURCES
Main activity: A kitchen timer, an alarm clock (or a timer that rings), an old or toy telephone; pictures of traffic, an ambulance and a fire engine.
Group activities: 1 Reference books or CD-ROMs about animal sounds or animal warning signals. **2** A simple 'roadway' (use chalk or ropes) in the hall or playground, two or three ride-on wheeled toys, road safety posters (available from RoSPA).

BACKGROUND
Our sense of hearing is important for keeping us safe. We hear traffic approaching, alarm bells and sirens, and perhaps warning sounds from animals. Your local police force may be willing to come into school and bring model traffic lights, crossings and so on. You could perhaps arrange to have a fire drill as part of the lesson.

STARTER
Have all the children sitting together on the carpet. Set the timer or alarm clock to ring in a few seconds. Listen to it ring, then switch it off.

MAIN ACTIVITY
Ask the children: *When might we hear that sound? What is it telling us?* Perhaps that it is time to get up, or that the cake is ready to take out of the oven. *Do we have a school bell? What does it tell you?* These are sounds that remind us of something or give us a gentle warning: don't oversleep, don't let the cake burn and so on. *What other 'warning' sounds might we hear at school or at home?* (The cooker, the microwave and so on.)

Some sounds give us a stronger warning, and it is important that we listen to them and act. *What does it mean when you hear the fire bell? Do you all know the fire drill? Do you have a smoke alarm at home? Do you know what to do if you hear it?* Use an old or toy telephone to practise making a 999 call and giving the correct information. Emphasise that such calls should only be made in a genuine emergency. Talk about the sounds made by emergency vehicles. *Why do they need to make a special noise?*

Ordinary traffic can also be very dangerous, and we need to use our ears as well as our eyes. Take the children to the school gate or somewhere where they can observe traffic safely. Ask them to close their eyes and listen carefully. *Can you tell when something is coming? Can you tell whether it is a bus, a car or a lorry? Can you tell how fast it is going?*

GROUP ACTIVITIES
1 Ask pairs of children to use reference books or CD-ROMs to find out about animals that use warning sounds. *When might you hear a dog growling or a cat spitting? Have you ever heard a blackbird's alarm call? What sound does a rattlesnake make, and how?*
2 Let children practise crossing the road in a role-play situation, focusing on listening for traffic as well as looking. Go through the rules of road safety for pedestrians with the children. Organise the groups according to the available space and resources (for example, the number of wheeled toys).

Differentiation
Group activity 1
Children may need adult support to help them find information and read the reference materials.
Group activity 2
All the children should be able to take part in this activity.

Possible roles could include a crossing patrol person, a traffic police officer, shoppers, children playing, drivers and cyclists.

ASSESSMENT
During the plenary session, ask the children to describe some situations where our hearing is important in keeping us safe.

PLENARY
Talk about how important sounds are for keeping us safe. Go through the road safety rules again. Ask one or two children to show how they would make an emergency telephone call if they had seen a road accident.

OUTCOME
● Know that our sense of hearing helps to keep us safe.

LINKS
Unit 1A Lesson 3, The senses.
Unit 1C Lesson 4, What sound does it make?

Lesson 15 ◗ Warning sounds

Objective
● To know that sounds can act as warnings.

RESOURCES
A flipchart or whiteboard.

MAIN ACTIVITY
Ask the children to think about the sounds they hear during a day. How many sounds give a warning of some kind? It may just be a gentle reminder or it may be of real danger. Make a list on the flipchart or whiteboard of all these sounds, and talk about the importance of each one. *Are there any that should never be ignored?* (Ambulance, fire engine, police car, road crossing, a lorry reversing. Other sounds might include: alarm clock, microwave ping, doorbell, oven timer, shop bell, car or burglar alarm.) If possible, arrange a fire drill so that the children hear the alarm and can practise their response.

ASSESSMENT
Note the children's reaction to the fire alarm. Do they understand that it is a warning that must be acted upon? During the plenary session note those children who understand the importance of warning sounds.

PLENARY
Talk about the importance of listening for and heeding warning sounds. Return to the list you made on the flipchart and ask the children if they want to identify any sounds as 'important' sounds. Mark these in some way.

Differentiation
This activity is accessible to all the children.

OUTCOME
● Know that some sounds give us warnings.

Lesson 16 ◗ Loud or quiet?

Objectives
● To know that loud sounds can be heard over a greater distance than quiet sounds.
● To carry out a simple investigation.

RESOURCES
Main activity: A collection of objects that make loud and quiet noises, such as cymbals, a triangle, a drum, crackly paper, a ticking clock, a portable cassette player with short pieces of very quiet music and loud music, a sheet of paper (to tear), a bouncy ball and so on; three large boxes; the hall or playground.

Vocabulary
loud, quiet, silent, distance, near, far away

Group activities: 1 Paper, writing and drawing materials. **2** The hall or playground.

BACKGROUND
Light and sound are thought to be similar in that both travel in waves. However, while light travels in straight lines from a source, sound travels in all directions. We can't see round corners, but we can hear! Sound travels rather like the ripples from a stone dropped in a pond: as the ripples travel away from the source, they decrease until they are no longer discernible. A bigger stone (a louder sound) makes bigger ripples that spread further before they die away.

STARTER
Working with the whole class, ask the children to whisper very quietly (perhaps recite a familiar nursery rhyme). Then ask them to shout 'Hooray'. Which sound do they think they would hear if they were on the other side of the playground or hall?

MAIN ACTIVITY
Look at all the things you have gathered together and ask the children to think about what sort of sound each would make. *Would it be a loud sound or a quiet one? Which sounds would be easier to hear across the hall or playground?* Sort the things into two sets (boxes): 'easy to hear' and 'difficult to hear'.

Take the children and three large boxes into the hall or the playground. Ask the children to sit or stand in a very large circle (as big as possible), facing outwards. Stand in the middle of the circle and use the things you have collected to make different sounds. Choose items randomly from each of the two sets. If the children think it is a loud sound, they should raise two hands; if they think it is a quiet sound, they should raise one hand. If they don't hear it at all, they will obviously raise no hands. Take a majority vote on each item and re-sort the items into three sets: 'loud, 'quiet' and 'silent'. As the children vote on each sound, if the result is different from that predicted by them, place the object in front of its new box. When you have used all the items, ask the children to turn round and move in towards the boxes. Look at the three sets of 'sounds'. Note the objects that have been moved into a different set from the one predicted. Try some of the sounds that the children did not hear again. Ask: *Can you hear them now that you are closer?*

GROUP ACTIVITIES
1 Ask each child to draw a picture of something that makes a sound that has to be heard some distance away, such as a fire engine, ambulance, police car, church bells, school bell or playground whistle, then write a sentence about why we need to hear that sound from a distance.
2 Stand all the children in the group in a circle, with one child in the middle. The child in the middle gives a simple message or phrase to one child in the circle, who repeats it back; both children use a normal to loud voice. Do this several times. The child in the middle should then use a very soft voice or whisper. Can the other children still repeat the message as accurately? This game could be played several times, changing the child in the middle each time.

Differentiation
Group activity 1
Some children may not be able to write a sentence without help. Other children may be able to draw and write about several things.
Group activity 2
All the children should be able to take part in this activity. Be sensitive to any children whose hearing may be impaired.

ASSESSMENT
Make a quiet sound and a louder sound, then ask the children which one they think they would be able to hear from further away. Use the children's pictures and writing to assess their understanding.

CHAPTER 6

Differentiation
The children could work in mixed-ability pairs to make a list in the group activity. Some children may only be able to use very simple, pictorial reference books.

PLENARY

Look again at the things you used to make the sounds. Ask the children: *Why do you think we couldn't hear all the sounds when we were in the big circle?* Talk about the difference in volume between the sounds, and the difference this makes to the distance over which they can be heard. Did the children make reasonable predictions? Were there some sounds that they thought would be easy to hear, but that they didn't hear at all?

OUTCOMES

● Know that loud sounds can be heard over a greater distance than quiet ones.
● Can carry out a simple investigation.

Lesson 17 ■ Can you hear it now?

Objective
● To know that sounds get fainter as they travel away from a source.

Vocabulary
louder, quieter, distance, volume

RESOURCES

Main activity: The hall or playground, beanbags, a buzzer or cassette player (with a music cassette).
Group activity: Reference books about means of communication.

BACKGROUND

Sound waves travel in all directions from a source. They are often likened to the ripples on a pond. While this is a reasonable analogy, since sound waves travel in all directions the model should really be a sphere. As the ripples (waves) travel away from the source, they decrease until they can no longer be seen (or heard).

Some children's hearing may be less acute than others', for various reasons. It is important not to let any child feel inadequate. Stress that we are all different.

STARTER

Talk to the children about playing in the playground. *If your friend is on the other side of the playground, how do you attract his/her attention? Do you shout or whisper? Why do you need to shout?* Remind them of what they learned in Lesson 16 about sounds and distances. *If your friend were much further away, would they still be able to hear you?*

MAIN ACTIVITY

Take the children into the hall or playground. Stand them in a tight circle facing outwards, and give each child a beanbag. Turn on the buzzer. Tell the children to walk slowly away from the sound, then stop when they can no longer hear it and mark the spot with their beanbag. *Are all the beanbags the same distance away from the sound? Why might there be differences?* Remind the children that we all hear differently, and so it would be very strange if all the beanbags were the same distance from the sound.

Ask the children to leave their beanbags where they are and make a new circle, as large as possible. Now they should walk in towards the sound and stop when they begin to hear it. *Have you reached your beanbag, or are you in a different place? Why might the distance be different?* Some children may have gone further when walking away from the sound because they 'remembered' it even when they could no longer hear it.

GROUP ACTIVITY

Working in pairs or individually, the children can use reference materials to find out how people send messages if they are too far away to hear. They can make a list of different means of communication: Morse code, semaphore, telephone, text, letter, email and so on.

ASSESSMENT
Note which children can describe what happens as they move further away from a sound.

PLENARY
Talk about what the children noticed as they walked away from the sound. Was the sound just as loud the whole time? Did it suddenly stop, or did it gradually get quieter?

OUTCOME
● Know that sounds get fainter as they travel away from a source.

Lesson 18 ▪ Loud versus quiet

Objectives
● To know that loud sounds travel further than quiet sounds.
● To carry out a simple investigation.

RESOURCES
The hall or playground, a tape recorder and music, beanbags of two colours.

MAIN ACTIVITY
Repeat the activity from Lesson 17, but use a sound that can be increased or decreased in volume. Keep the volume very low at first and ask the children to drop one of their beanbags when they can no longer hear the sound. Repeat this with the volume as high as possible and compare the distances. The children could use beanbags of different colours for each volume.

ASSESSMENT
During the plenary session ask the children if they can say why they could hear one sound from a greater distance than the other.

PLENARY
Talk to the children about why they could hear the loud sound further away from the source than the quiet sound.

Differentiation
This activity is accessible to all.

OUTCOMES
● Know that loud sounds also get fainter as they travel away from a source but travel further than quiet sounds.
● Can carry out a simple investigation.

Lesson 19 ▪ Beads in a pot

Objectives
● To know that sound is a form of energy.
● To make and test a simple prediction.

RESOURCES ◉
Main activity: Cymbals, beater, a bowl of water, a tuning fork, a table-tennis ball on string (see Preparation).
Group activities: 1 A copy of photocopiable page 189 (also 'Beads in a pot' (red), available on the CD-ROM) for each child, pots with lids, beads. **2** Drum and beater, rice or confetti.

Vocabulary
vibrate, vibration, movement, energy

PREPARATION
Use adhesive tape or PVA glue to stick a length of string (about 30cm) to a table-tennis ball.

BACKGROUND
Energy is found in different forms. Sound energy is often transferred into kinetic or movement energy, and vice versa: moving cymbals collide to make sound; sound coming from an aeroplane can make the doors and windows in

Differentiation
Group activity 1
To support children in this activity, give them 'Beads in a pot' (green) from the CD-ROM, which does not require them to make a prediction before carrying out the investigation. As an extension, use 'Beads in a pot' (blue), which asks the children to provide a reason for their prediction.

a house vibrate. We are able to hear because sounds entering our ears make our eardrums vibrate. These vibrations are passed through the inner ear by tiny bones to the cochlea from where they are sent to the brain and interpreted as sounds.

STARTER
Working with the whole class, tell the children that sound is a form of energy. Show them a pair of cymbals and ask them what you need to do to make a sound with them. (Bring them together.) Bring the cymbals together, gently at first and then with more force. Explain to the children that you are changing movement energy into sound energy. If you use a lot of movement energy, you get more sound energy (a louder sound) than when you use just a little movement energy.

MAIN ACTIVITY
Hold up just one cymbal and hit it with a beater. *Does it make a difference how much movement energy you use?* Ask a child to gently touch a vibrating cymbal with their fingertip. *What can you feel?* Explain that the sound energy is changing to movement energy and causing the cymbal to vibrate. Show the children a tuning fork and explain how it works. (When struck, the fork vibrates to produce a sound.) Strike it several times so that the children can hear the sound. You may even be able to see the forks vibrate, depending on the note produced. Hold the table-tennis ball on its string and gently touch it with the vibrating tuning fork. The ball will bounce away from the tuning fork, magnifying the vibrations. *Why do you think the ball is bouncing like that?* Explain to the children that the sound energy is being changed into movement energy, which is making the ball move.

Gather the children around a table on which you have a bowl of water. This time gently touch the surface of the water with the vibrating tuning fork. You may get a slight splash, and then ripples moving out from the tuning fork. Again, sound energy is being changed into movement energy.

GROUP ACTIVITIES
1 Divide the children into groups of three or four. Give each group a small pot with a lid and enough beads or dried peas to fill the pot. Give each child a copy of photocopiable page 189 on which to record their prediction and findings. Tell the children that they are going to find out if they get a louder sound from their shaker by putting more beads in the pot, but first they must predict what they think will happen and write it on their sheet. Next they put a few beads in the pot, shake it, and decide whether the sound is loud or quiet. They then add more beads and test again. *Is the sound louder or quieter? What happens when you fill the pot with as many beads as you can?* (There should be very little noise because the beads do not have room to move in order to make a sound.)
2 Divide the children into pairs, or groups of three, and give each group a drum, a beater and a few grains of rice or a little confetti. Tell the children to put a few rice grains or pieces of confetti on the drum and beat it gently. *What happens to the rice or confetti? What happens if the drum is beaten harder?* (The rice or confetti will jump up and down as the drum skin vibrates. A louder sound will cause a bigger vibration, so the rice or confetti will bounce higher.) Ask the children to think about how the sound was made: the beater moved to hit the drum (movement energy), the drum made a sound (sound energy), which then made the drum vibrate (movement energy).

ASSESSMENT
Use the children's work from the group activities to assess their understanding.

PLENARY

Ask the children to demonstrate and explain what they have discovered. Help them to describe the forms of energy involved at each stage.

OUTCOMES

- Can recognise that sound is a form of energy.
- Can make and test a simple prediction.

Lesson 20 ▪ Assessment

Objectives
- To recognise that sounds are heard through our ears.
- To describe how sounds are generated by specific objects.
- To know that sounds get fainter as you move away from the source.

RESOURCES 💿

Assessment activities: 1 Photocopiable page 190 (also 'Assessment – 1' (red), available on the CD-ROM). **2** Photocopiable page 191 (also 'Assessment – 2' (red), available on the CD-ROM).

STARTER

Remind the children of the work they have done on sound in this unit. How many different ways of playing musical instruments and making sounds can they remember? Remind them that sounds are made by something moving or vibrating. Ask them if it is easier to hear loud or soft sounds. *Does it make a difference how near or far you are from the source of the sound?*

ASSESSMENT ACTIVITY 1

Give each child a copy of photocopiable page 190 and make sure they understand what they have to do. Ask them to complete the sheet, writing as much as they can to explain how we hear sounds.

ANSWERS

Violin – scrape (and pluck); tambourine - shake (and bang); drum – bang; recorder – blow; guitar – pluck.

LOOKING FOR LEVELS

Most children will be able to label each picture with one word (see Answers, above). Other children may answer 'pluck' and 'scrape' for the violin and 'shake' and 'bang' for the tambourine.

Most children will answer the question at the foot of the page ('How do we hear sounds?') by saying that vibrations travel to our ears and we hear the sounds. Some children may just answer 'with our ears'. Other children may be able to give a fuller explanation about how sounds are generated by moving or vibrating the air which then travels to our ears, making the eardrum vibrate so that we hear the sound.

ASSESSMENT ACTIVITY 2

Give each child a copy of photocopiable page 191 and explain what they have to do to complete the sheet.

ANSWERS

The figure nearest the sound source should be circled blue and the one furthest away should be red. Accept any explanation that indicates an understanding that sounds get fainter as they travel away from a source.

LOOKING FOR LEVELS

Most children will colour the figures correctly and be able to explain that sound gets fainter as it travels away from a source. They will know that the figure furthest away will hear a loud sound better than a faint one. Some children will colour the figures correctly but will not be able to give explanations.

PHOTOCOPIABLE

Pleasant or unpleasant?

Which is your favourite sound? Why? _____

_____

SCHOLASTIC

Illustration © Kirsty Wilson

How is it played?

◼ Sort these shapes into ones that you can bang, shake, pluck, blow or scrape.

Illustration © Kirsty Wilson

Different sounds

◢ We hear different kinds of sounds. Cut out the words at the bottom of the page and arrange them under the headings below.

These sounds give us pleasure:	These sounds give us information:	These sounds give us warnings:

police siren	school bell	pelican crossing
music	people talking	alarm clock
musical instruments	telephone ringing	sounds on the radio and television
level crossing alarm	fire alarm	

■SCHOLASTIC

Blocking out sound

I think the best material for blocking out sound will be _____

_____

because _____

_____

Stuffing in the earmuffs	Loudness: 1 (quiet) to 5 (loud)
none	5
fabric	
cotton wool	
newspaper	
tissue paper	

I found out that _____ blocked out the most sound.

Fair test

What are you trying to find out?

_____

_____

What do you think will happen?

_____

_____

What equipment did you use?

_____

_____

What do you need to keep the same to make your test fair?

_____

_____

What did you find out?

_____

_____

_____

_____

◢SCHOLASTIC

Beads in a pot

Will more beads make a louder sound?

My prediction.
I think...

Put four beads in a pot. What kind of sound does it make?

_____

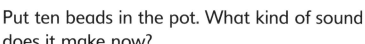

_____

Put ten beads in the pot. What kind of sound
does it make now?

_____

_____

Fill the pot with beads. What kind of sound does it make?

_____

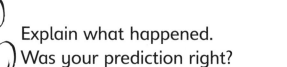

_____

Explain what happened.
Was your prediction right?

_____

_____

Illustration © Kirsty Wilson

PHOTOCOPIABLE

Assessment – 1

◼ Choose the correct words and write them underneath the pictures to show how the sounds are made:

| scrape | pluck | blow | bang | shake |

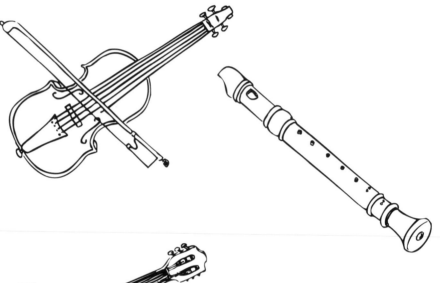

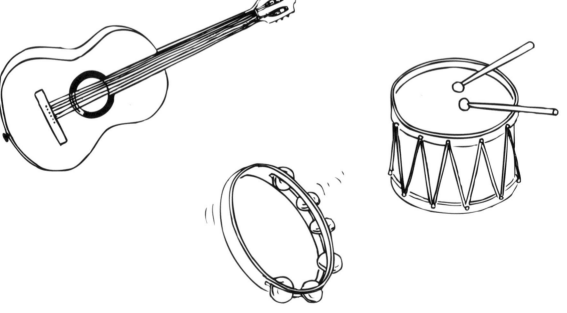

What do we use to hear sounds? _____

How do we hear sounds? _____

◣SCHOLASTIC

Assessment – 2

Which person will hear the loudest sound? Circle that person in blue.

Who will hear the faintest sound? Circle that person in red.

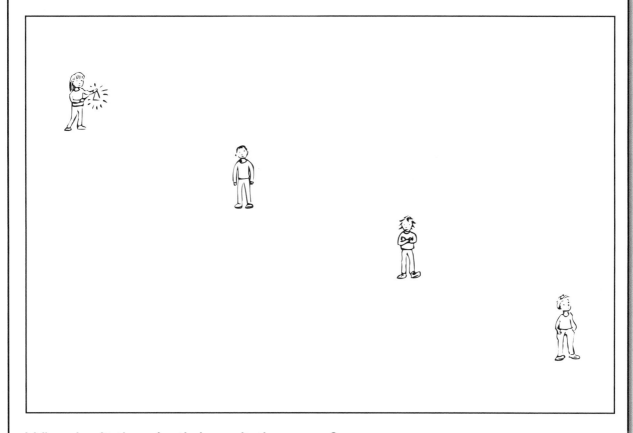

Why don't they both hear it the same?

_____

_____

If the sound were louder, would the figure furthest away hear it better than a fainter sound? Why?

_____

_____

_____

Illustration © Kirsty Wilson